# Cultural Heritage
## in Mali
## in the Neoliberal Era

**INTERPRETATIONS
OF CULTURE IN THE
NEW MILLENNIUM**

Norman E. Whitten Jr.,
General Editor

*A list of books in the series appears
at the end of the book.*

# Cultural Heritage
in Mali
in the Neoliberal Era

ROSA DE JORIO

*University of Illinois Press*
URBANA, CHICAGO, AND SPRINGFIELD

© 2016 by Rosa De Jorio
All rights reserved
Manufactured in the United States of America
1 2 3 4 5 C P 5 4 3 2 1
♾ This book is printed on acid-free paper.

Library of Congress Control Number: 2016938748
ISBN 978-0-252-04027-6 (hardcover)
ISBN 978-0-252-08172-9 (paperback)
ISBN 978-0-252-09853-6 (e-book)

# Contents

List of Illustrations   **vii**

Acronyms   **ix**

Acknowledgments   **xi**

Introduction: Malian Cultural Heritage and Governmentality   **1**

1. Commemorating the Nation's Heroes in Mali's Neoliberal Democracy   **25**
2. Remembering the Colonial Past   **53**
3. The Women's Museum Muso Kunda: Citizenship, Gender, and Social Memory   **76**
4. The Heritagization of Islamic and Secular Architecture: Djenné   **95**
5. The Fate of Timbuktu's Sufi Heritage: Controversies around Past Traces and Current Practices   **116**

Epilogue: Further Thoughts on Governmentality and Culture   **135**

Glossary   **147**

Notes   **149**

References   **171**

Index   **195**

# Illustrations

1. Political map of Mali  xvi
2. Modibo Keita Memorial, Bamako  34–35
3. Modibo Keita's statue, Modibo Keita Memorial, Bamako  39
4. Statue of Abdoul "Cabral" Karim Camara, Bamako  48
5. Statue of Louis Archinard, Ségou  54
6. Statue of Literacy, Koulouba, Bamako  60
7. Statue of Ciwaras, Koulouba, Bamako  60
8. The Square of Mali's Martyred Cities and Towns, Bamako  61
9. Statue of Gustave Borgnis-Desbordes, Bamako  63
10. Governors' Square, Koulouba, Bamako  64
11. Renovation and expansion of the women's museum Muso Kunda, Bamako  77
12. The women's museum Muso Kunda, Bamako  79
13. Great Mosque of Djenné  98
14. Musée de Djenné  109
15. Djingarey Ber Mosque, Timbuktu  119
16. Ruins of the mausoleum of Cheick Sidi Ahmed Ben Amar Arragadi, Timbuktu  126
17. The reconstructed mausoleum of a saint, Timbuktu  132

# Acronyms

| | |
|---|---|
| **ADEMA** | L'Alliance pour la démocratie au Mali (Alliance for Democracy in Mali) |
| **ADID** | Association pour le développement de l'Islam à Djenné (Association for the Development of Islam in Djenné) |
| **AKTC** | Aga Khan Trust for Culture |
| **AQIM** | al-Qaeda in the Islamic Maghreb |
| **CMLN** | Comité militaire de libération nationale (Military Committee for National Liberation) |
| **CNID** | Congrès national d'initiative démocratique (National Congress for Democratic Initiative) |
| **FAMA** | Le Front africain pour la mobilisation et l'alternance (African Front for Mobilization and Change) |
| **HCIM** | Haut conseil islamique du Mali (High Islamic Council of Mali) |
| **ICC** | International Criminal Court |
| **ICOMOS** | International Council on Monuments and Sites |
| **MC** | Mouvement citoyen (Citizens' Movement) |
| **MNLA** | Mouvement national de libération de l'Azawad (National Movement for the Liberation of Azawad) |
| **MUJAO** | Movement for Unity and Jihad in West Africa |

| | |
|---|---|
| **ORTM** | Office de Radiodiffusion-Télévision du Mali (Office of Radio and Television of Mali) |
| **PDES** | Parti pour le développement economique et social (Party for Economic and Social Development) |
| **PSP (new)** | Parti pour la solidarité et le progress (Party for Solidarity and Progress), a party that claims to be the heir of the old PSP party |
| **PSP (old)** | Parti soudanais progressiste (1946–58) (Sudanese Progressive Party) |
| **SADI** | Solidarité africaine pour la démocratie et l'indépendance (African Solidarity for Democracy and Independence) |
| **UDPM** | Union démocratique du peuple malien (Democratic Union of the Malian People) |
| **UDS** | Union démocratique segouvienne (Democratic Union of Seguvians) |
| **UM-RDA** | L'Union malienne du rassemblement démocratique africain/faso jigi (faso jigi) (Malian Union of the African Democratic Rally) |
| **UNEEM** | Union nationale des élèves et étudiants du Mali (National Union of Pupils and Students of Mali) |
| **UNESCO** | United Nations Educational, Scientific and Cultural Organization |
| **UNFM** | Union nationale des femmes du Mali (National Union of Malian Women) |
| **US-RDA** | Union soudanaise–Rassemblement démocratique africain (Sudanese Union–African Democratic Rally) |

# Acknowledgments

**THIS BOOK IS THE OUTCOME** of a long—and at times difficult as well as unpredictable—personal and intellectual journey. Mali's democratic and neoliberal turn and the accompanying transformations in the field of public culture and cultural heritage have sparked my imagination and propelled much of my research efforts over the past two decades. My own journey presented some unexpected detours and delays but ultimately came full circle.

There are many people and institutions to be thanked for their generous help in the data collection, analysis, and writing phases of this book. Fieldwork on cultural heritage in Mali as well as archival research was made possible by the following granting institutions: the Italian Institute for Africa and the Orient, the University of North Florida, the University of Florida, the Encyclopedia of Women and Islamic Cultures, and the Henry Luce Foundation.

In Mali I could always count on a number of scholars and researchers to offer me valuable help and counsel. In particular, I owe a great deal to Issaka Bagayogo of the Institut Supérieur de Formation et de Recherche Appliquée, my first-ever contact in Mali; Mamady Dembele of the Institut des Sciences Humaines du Mali for his intellectual generosity and support with my research; Modibo Diallo of the Modibo Keita Memorial, who always found time to discuss history and politics with me; Amadou Seydou Traoré for sharing his deep knowledge of Malian politics; Diarra Marie Goundiam of the women's museum Muso Kunda and Bah Diakité of the Ministry of Culture for kindly facilitating my research in their institutional settings and sharing their knowledge with me. I also thank Alpha Diallo, Anne Marie Traoré, Moussa Fofana, and Issa Fofana of Point Sud for their generous assistance and intellectual contributions to my fieldwork in Mali.

In the United States, several scholars read and provided useful insights on parts of this book. I especially thank Maria Grosz-Ngaté, Alioune Sow, Charlotte Joy, and Benjamin Soares for their insights and feedback. I am also grateful for the conversations on related topics I shared with Mary Jo Arnoldi and Joseph Hellweg. Early versions of chapter 5 were presented and benefited greatly from the feedback from numerous audiences; in particular, I thank the conference organizer, Nancy Um, for soliciting my contribution. Thanks, too, to Andrew Hernann, Leonardo Villalon, Fiona McLaughlin, Terje Østebø, Renata Serra, Aboulaye Kane, and Steven Brandt for their helpful comments on earlier versions of this chapter. I am thankful to Sane Chirphi Alpha (Timbuktu) and Mamadou Diamountani (Haut conseil islamique du Mali) for sharing their knowledge of Timbuktu, its mausoleums, and Mali's recent troubled history.

My deepest gratitude goes to Norman Whitten, series editor of the Interpretations of Culture in the New Millennium series, University of Illinois Press, for his continuing professional and personal guidance through the years despite my delays and setbacks. Special thanks go to Alma Gottlieb, who read and provided invaluable feedback on my original book proposal. I also recognize the two readers who anonymously reviewed this manuscript and recommended it for publication. Now that I know their names, I can express my gratitude publicly: thanks to Robert Launay and Paul Stoller, whose suggestions and deep insights improved my manuscript immensely and made it a much better final product.

I am extremely grateful for the help and intellectual generosity of two Malian colleagues in the United States, Amadou Beidy Sow (Indiana University) and Talatou A. Maiga (University of Utah). The book would not have been the same without their help. This book owes much to the phenomenal editing work (and organizational skills) of Marsha Brofka-Berends, whose patience and support were key to the completion of this book. I also thank Jennifer Kurtz for her kind and insightful editorial help with chapter 3 and Mary Lou Kowaleski for her careful copyediting work.

My deepest gratitude goes also to the late Bernardo Bernardi and Lilli Romanelli for their friendship and support during the completion of this work. Lastly, I dedicate this work to my parents, Rossana and Antonio De Jorio, for their love and support, my partner, Hans-Herbert Kögler, with whom I shared many engaging theoretical discussions, and our dear daughter, Victoria.

Some of the material contained here was used in previous articles but has been fully rewritten, updated, or modified for inclusion in this larger writing project and to reflect changes in my own thinking. Two of the chapters included here were previously published in English but have been substantially modified enough to warrant new titles. An earlier version of chapter 2 was originally published in *Africa Today* (no. 4, 2006) as "Politics of Remembering and Forgetting: The Struggle over Colonial Monuments in Mali" and is used here with permission of *Africa Today*. An earlier version of chapter 3 was originally published in *PoLAR: The Political and Legal Anthropology Review* (no. 2, 2002) as "Gendered Museum, Guided He(tour)topias: Women and Social Memory in Mali" and is used here with the permission of *PoLAR: Political and Legal Anthropology Review*.

# Cultural Heritage
in Mali
in the Neoliberal Era

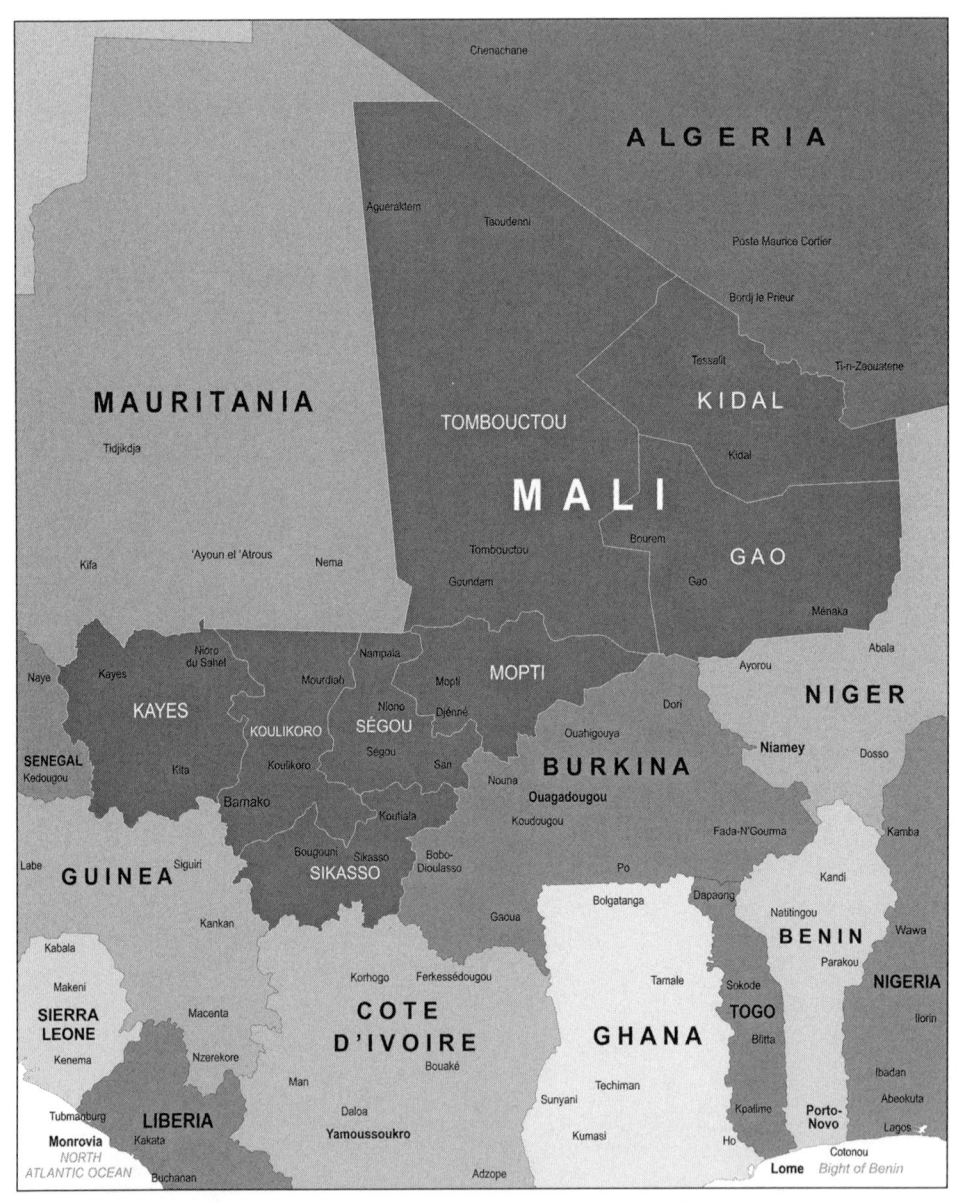

**FIGURE 1.** Political map of Mali. Courtesy of iStock/Bogdan Serban, copyright 2013.

# Introduction

## *Malian Cultural Heritage and Governmentality*

CULTURAL HERITAGE IN MALI has experienced profound transformations since the country's transition to democracy in 1991.[1] The democratic turn was accompanied by the intensification of neoliberal techniques of governance, including the growing pervasiveness of the market logic, savage privatization, rising socioeconomic inequality, and increasing regional imbalance. Mali also registered an explosion of multipartism (characterized by increased segmentation of the political field) and the proliferation of all kinds of organizations, including religious ones whose appearance and growing influence have led to the reconfiguration of boundaries between the secular and the sacred. The past two decades have also been marked by the rise of "political Islam" as well as the recent and devastating sociopolitical crisis from which the country is slowly, but unevenly, recovering.

In 2012 the unfolding of a military coup d'état in the south and the occupation of the north by a coalition of Tuareg and Islamist extremist groups led the media, aid practitioners, and scholars to reassess the actual workings of Mali's democracy.[2] Until recently, Mali had been held up as an example of an effective transition to democracy, political stability, and (at least from the viewpoint of the aid industry) a rather successful implementation of neoliberal changes (e.g., van de Walle 2012). This overall positive image survived despite reports of recurring Tuareg rebellions and growing insecurity in the north, intermittent opposition to the government, and mounting popular dissatisfaction with the limited results of twenty years of democracy (e.g., Soares 2005b; Villalon and Idrissa 2005). But no one—not even the most critical observers—could foresee the tragic events of March 2012 that led the country into a spiral of violence, widespread insecurity, and massive population displacement as thousands of people fled the occupied territories in the north to seek refuge in Mali's south or in neighboring countries.[3] Although a French-led military operation has since liberated the north from the Tuareg-Islamist occupation and new democratic elections were carried out in the summer of 2013 (leading to the installation of Ibrahim Boubacar Keita, popularly known as IBK, as Mali's new president), Mali's future is still uncertain in the postconflict era, which remains marred by accusations of government mismanagement of international funds, government reshuffling to maintain some international credibility, interference from international institutions, and lingering instability in the north.

I had already written several of the chapters prior to 2012, but the Tuareg-Islamist occupation of the north as well as events of the immediate postconflict period compelled me to rethink them and to further challenge the general overall positive assessment of Mali's democratic and neoliberal experiment. My research had already been critical of certain aspects of democracy, internal political struggles, and the devastating impact of neoliberal changes, particularly due to the increase in poverty most Malians experienced. But in the wake of the events of 2012, I needed to account for the unexpected devastation and the sudden exposure of even more dramatic contradictions than I (and others) had originally envisioned. A radical change of perspective was needed to accommodate such epochal changes, particularly for the study of Mali's cultural-heritage sector, whose development had been (mostly) positively received during at least the first ten years of Mali's democracy.[4]

In light of such considerable changes, my interest in heritage (having to do, minimally, with the commemoration of selected aspects of a community's past) as a privileged lens through which to analyze changes in Malian politics during the last two decades requires further clarification. I suggest here that a detailed study of cultural heritage and its transformations is key to understanding the 2012 impasse of the Malian democratic experiment and, more generally, to understanding critical aspects of modern power in postcolonial Mali. Since the immediate postindependence period, modern power in Mali has privileged (in a trend that has intensified and morphed according to the market logic of the neoliberal era) cultural heritage as a way to display and manifest itself on a regional and international scene.

Heritage is central to "a hegemonic, highly institutionalized project of commemoration that is productive of collective identities—most often in the function of nation-building" (De Cesari 2010: 625).[5] In particular, the evolution of the institution of the museum and its centrality to the working of the nation-state since the late nineteenth century reflect the central role that heritage played in the development of the nation-state: "a more general set of developments through which culture, in coming to be thought of as useful for governing, was fashioned as a vehicle for the exercise of new forms of power" (Bennett 1995: 19). Heritage and its historical transformations continue to be central to the articulation of postcolonial nation-states. Indeed, as Michael Rowlands and Ferdinand de Jong point out, "The state in Africa has a tendency to monumentalize itself. Such a policy is reinforced by UNESCO and other agencies that promote heritage technologies for the production of official pasts and futures" (2007: 15). This state tendency reflects the influence of colonization and the European nation-state model on the development of the nation-state in Africa (2007: 15). Furthermore, it manifests the increasing roles local, national, international, and transnational organizations play in the development of a "national" heritage. In the present global era, heritage mirrors major political transformations, particularly "modes of government that are being set up on a global scale . . . but also transnational alliances forged by activists and grassroots organizations" (Ferguson and Gupta 2002: 990).[6]

A key focus of this work is to understand how democracy and neoliberalism have affected state practices, particularly as seen through the prism of the heritage field. Have such radical changes, including the increased play of transnational networks and organizations (Appadurai 2002), ultimately resulted in the development of more independent heritage projects and contributed to the development of a public culture—that is, a culture that is public and, at least in part, independent of the state?[7] Or has the extension and proliferation of government in the era of globalization just replicated, reinforced, and extended autocratic state logics, state elitism, and the top-down logics and practices of the aid regime? Have more than twenty years of democracy in Mali yielded the development of a public culture that isn't entirely orchestrated by the state and its international partners? And when private heritage initiatives have been implemented, have they successfully provided new visibility to previously marginalized groups? Also, what is the relationship between state and private initiatives in the heritage field? Are so-called private initiatives (e.g., the women's museum) easily distinguishable from state initiatives—that is, are such distinctions even useful (unless further thematized)? Related to these questions but going beyond questions of agency (e.g., who is *representing* and who is *represented* in heritage initiatives) to also consider content (e.g., *what* is represented) is the issue of whether state-promoted heritage reflects or silences popular memories (e.g., Werbner 1998). Any meaningful work on heritage must consider the play of social memory in order to investigate not only what is remembered but also what is forgotten in heritage initiatives. Do heritage initiatives come to reflect citizens' memories of the past? Do they enable citizens to come to terms with past traumas and encourage reconciliation, or, rather, do they produce further rips in the social fabric? Furthermore, if heritage becomes fair game and is no longer the province of a centralized and autocratic state, what forms of patrimonialization are embraced by decentralized collectivities and groups (and what changes occur at the level of governmentality that they reflect and prompt)? By asking these questions (and others), this book analyzes instances of state- and quasi–state-promoted cultural heritage in Mali's neoliberal democracy and considers how heritage overlaps and intersects with social memory and public culture.

## Governmentality and Cultural Heritage

Building on seminal work by Michel Foucault (1991), some anthropologists of the state identify in governmentality a useful perspective to think about the diffuse and disseminated nature of power in contemporary societies (Ferguson and Gupta 2002; Gupta and Sharma 2006; Sharma and Gupta 2006; Ferguson 2006).[8] More specifically, governmentality reflects Foucault's attempt to understand the transformation of political power brought about by liberalism and its historical developments (e.g., Rose 1996; Rose, O'Malley, and Valverde 2006), and should be regarded as "the direction toward specific ends of conduct which has as its objects both individuals and populations and which combines techniques of domination and discipline with technologies of self-government" (Gupta and Sharma 2006: 277). In other words, governmentality has to do with the development of techniques and strategies for the management of people and things, including the development of subjectivities that sustain particular political projects (in this case, the neoliberal state). Both the regulation of people's conduct and the self-regulation of populations require the development of specialized bodies of knowledge, such as political economy, statistics, and archaeology, among others (e.g., Rose 1996; Rose, O'Malley, and Valverde 200).

African scholars have been cautious in applying a Foucauldian approach to the analysis of African power because of the unevenness of state presence in Africa (for instance, see Cooper's 1994 analysis of colonial Africa and Cole 2001) and have suggested looking at power in Africa as more arterial than capillary—a perspective that emphasizes the discontinuous presence of the state in Africa but also foregrounds greater agency on the part of African groups and actors. Others have rejected the Foucauldian perspective on the basis of the scarcely developed or failed neoliberal state in many parts of Africa (e.g., Joseph 2010). Still other scholars have found it useful to think of "governmentality as an approach (rather than) as a description of a specific form of neoliberal power relation" (Death 2011: 4; 2013). For instance, James Ferguson suggests that even the zones of exclusion that arise from globalization may be interpreted as "not a lamentably immature form of globalization, but a quite 'advanced' and sophisticated mutation of it" (2006: 41). Indeed, the uneven character of globalization (and transnational governmentality) is an important development of the present era (e.g., Sassen 2000) and one productively thematized by some authors on the basis of Foucault's conception of heterotopia, or "other spaces."[9] Examples of heterotopias have ranged from hyper-regulated enclaves, such as gated communities (Low 2008), to interstitial spaces of marginality from which alternative societal visions can be imagined and experienced, as in an Italian urban movement that seeks to develop productive partnerships with minority groups and displaced populations (Lang 2008; see also chapter 3, current volume). A number of scholars have thus productively engaged in empirically grounded analyses that have brought to the fore particular aspects of a regime of government, including its uneven spatial concentration.[10]

The idea of governmentality, which suggests the diffusion of modern power but also the articulation and intersection of multiple technologies of domination and self-regulation, is of particular relevance to the study of cultural heritage. Tony Bennett's classic work (1988, 1990, 1995, 2006) on the exhibitionary complex is a model here in that it "has become the basis of a more general framework that examines the museum within an array of related cultural institutions and as a means of governmentality through which values and notions of citizenship and publics are inculcated, imposed, and portrayed through exhibition design and behavioral habits as well as exhibition topics and themes" (Kratz and Karp 2006: 23). Within the history of the Western nation-state, the institution of the museum sought to tame the excesses of the popular classes by imposing new types of bodily discipline, by exposing their behavior to the public gaze, and by cultivating the virtues of containment and propriety in an attempt to make bourgeois lore into the communal norm. Kratz and Karp push this perspective further by focusing on museological processes as extending outside of the institution of the museum (2006: 2) and informing heritage practices and the articulation of power and knowledge in a variety of contexts. Thus, museums are not just contained within demarcated spaces but are transformed into "a portable social technology" via which statements about people's social identities, people's past, and projects of social change can be articulated and inscribed (2006: 4).

One example of the working of modern power can be found in the current obsession for documenting (and in the process, partly creating) Mali's cultural patrimony. Since Mali's democratic turn, one of the major activities pursued by the Ministry of Culture, often with support of other entities, such as the United Nations Educational, Scientific, and Cultural Organization (UNESCO), which is also involved in the production of a number of surveys and reports, has been the identification, classification, and reordering of knowledge pertaining to Mali's cultural heritage. This has resulted in the production of a number of bureaucratic reports—often structured in list form—documenting Mali's rich tangible and intangible cultural heritage.[11] These lists, other bureaucratic documents, and museum collections are various manifestations of "the symbolic power to order knowledge, to rank, classify, and arrange, and thus to give meaning to objects and things through the imposition of interpretative schémas, scholarship, and the authority of connoisseurship" (Hall 1999: 4). Western media are also intimately implicated in the textual and bureaucratic production of Mali's national heritage. Jean-Louis Triaud (2009) discusses the media's active role in the development of "knowledge" about the famed Timbuktu manuscripts, observing how the media contribute to both the circulation and the transformation (if not shared inflation) of information regarding those documents (e.g., the continuously growing number of manuscripts and claims about their supposed antiquity), thus creating a virtual sphere of information of another kind with clear political ramifications (see chapter 5 as well as Triaud 2009). In Mali, classificatory work is justified (following criteria and modalities UNESCO set up) as key to identify the cultural patrimony to be preserved and valorized, to provide decentralized communities with greater knowledge of their regional assets (as an articulation of the devolution of state functions to communities), and to promote economic development (i.e., tourism) at the regional level. Chiara De Cesari reads in such detailed classificatory work a sign of the widening state power, in that "it is precisely this type of capillary knowledge and 'meaningful presence' (Appadurai 1996: 189) as well as comprehensiveness of approach that is usually attributed to the phenomenology of the state" (2010: 628).

However, some specificities to the field of heritage must be foregrounded here. The museum does not only coerce or discipline citizens (although some of this is part of the museum experience). It primarily educates and inspires them through exposure to new cultural logics, visual arrangements, and (via the museum visit and tour) bodily experiences. Bennett regards museums as "people movers" (reflecting the more productive aspect of power), and indeed they "draw on the broader logic of culture understood as a historically distinctive, and complexly articulated, set of means for shaping and transforming people through their own self-activity" (2006: 52). Similarly, in their seminal article "Museums Are Good to Think," Arjun Appadurai and Carol

A. Breckenridge (2004) stress the educational role of heritage in postcolonial India, especially given that "complex societies such as India . . . have not surrendered learning principally to the formal institutions of schooling" (404). Ciraj Rassool similarly foregrounds the increasing relevance of heritage and public culture in forging national identities and citizenship in postapartheid South Africa, a function formerly exercised by the school (2000: 1). In the post-1991 Malian state—particularly as part of the government's effort to compensate for its inability to resolve the school crisis—national heritage (and its international sponsors) serve to cultivate democratic values, remind citizens of their historical roots, and provide them with the cultural references they need to navigate the complexities of globalization and counter cultural homogenization (P. B. Couloubaly 1993, 2001, 2004).

A useful adaptation of governmentality to postcolonial contexts is evident in the role quasi-state organizations (including entities of the aid regime) play in the articulation of modern power in Africa. Thus, I do not situate governmentality in a strictly national context, as envisioned by Bennett, but, rather, in a transnational one (following here work by Ferguson and Gupta 2002; Collier and Ong 2005; Sharma and Gupta 2006; De Cesari 2010). Bennett maintains that the exhibitionary complex is primarily a national enterprise, in that "public museums are largely, and probably entirely, the administrative creations of national, municipal, or local governments or private organizations" (2006: 47). But approaches such as Bennett's need to be reconsidered in light of "the transnational quality of today's governance" (De Cesari 2010: 626). Even the private heritage sector in Mali is not an independent sector for the most part and is heavily funded by foreign entities, nongovernment organizations (NGOs), and activists' networks (e.g., A. C. Touré 2006; Bergamaschi 2011; van de Walle 2012).[12]

Governmentality—particularly in its transnational form—enables scholars to think about power and its articulations outside the "container" of the state (and indeed question the boundedness of the national territory in the first place) and to consider the work of other entities that play statelike functions (such as NGOs, foreign states, and supranational bodies, such as UNESCO), whether in support or in opposition to actual state policies.[13] In the neoliberal era (that is, since the mid-1980s), the implementation of structural adjustment programs (SAPs) has radically curtailed state size and state operations by reducing state expenditures, downsizing state employment, liberalizing the state economy, and devaluing local currencies.[14] Although they supposedly address the increase in poverty (for most of the population) brought about by the implementation of structural adjustment programs, recent aid reforms still maintain their overall commitment to neoliberal principles (Bergamaschi

2011).¹⁵ The retreat of the state has simultaneously freed space for entities of varying scale and reach to assume some of the functions typically attributed to the nation-state.¹⁶

Writing about heritage work in Palestine (an analysis that applies to Mali, too), De Cesari uses "fields of government" to express some of the complexities of contemporary power and, in particular, "its multisitedness" (2010: 627). Indeed, power resides and is carried out in a multiplicity of institutional settings, including aid agencies, foreign entities, supranational entities, and grassroots organizations. Aradhana Sharma and Akhil Gupta point out that "conflicts, 'corruptions,' and inconsistencies are central to institutional organization and the reproduction of states" even within the context of the daily operations of the state (2006: 16). Nicolas van de Walle reports that the aid regime in place in Mali remains characterized by disorganized and contradictory intervention by international and transnational aid organizations. He notes: "A plethora of poorly coordinated donor-driven decision- and policy-making mechanisms dominate and in some cases have largely replaced domestic government institutions" (2012: 2). By no means does my analysis suggest that state and quasi-state organizations work in unison; indeed, transnational governmentality is characterized by disjunctures and frictions among participating entities and actors (see Mbembe 2003 and O'Dell 2013). Some statelike organizations (e.g., UNESCO; see chapter 4, current volume) have significantly extended the reach of modern power away from the traditional centers of power, such as the cities (in particular, the capital, Bamako), to the regional or local centers of power. Such organizations are increasingly playing a central role in the development of cultural heritage in Mali today. Others, such as terrorist groups and some Tuareg organizations, situate themselves in opposition to the state, as shown by the highly symbolic destruction of UNESCO World Heritage Sites under the Tuareg-Islamist occupation, although the state (with various state agencies and the executive branch playing significantly different roles) remains central to many of their political projects (discussed at length in chapter 5; also see Mbembe 2003 and O'Dell 2013). The study of governmentality—its forms, dispersion, and tensions—is key to the understanding of heritage and its transformations in present-day Mali.

## Heritage and Public Culture

To thematize further the more productive side of power, I draw on the work of a number of other scholars—in particular, Appadurai's research on public culture (1988, 1996, 2003, 2008; Appadurai and Breckenridge 2004).¹⁷ I start by clarifying the definition of "public culture" and why I decided to include this term, which overlaps in part with "national culture" and "national heritage" but is broader than those more commonly used terms. Public culture acknowledges that heritage (of which the museum is a paradigmatic expression) is a contested field, an arena for the confrontation of different actors and groups and (at least, in principle) not just the expression of state elites: "By public culture we mean a new cosmopolitan arena that is a 'zone of contestation' and different classes and groups formulate, represent, and debate what culture is (and should be). Public culture is articulated and revealed in an interactive set of cosmopolitan experiences and structures, of which museums and exhibitions are a crucial part" (Appadurai and Breckenridge 2004: 407). The concept of public culture points to the contested character of cultural flows and their uneven trajectories, foregrounding the fluidity and heterogeneity of cultural constructs.

This perspective indicates "that there is indeed a differentiation within the public sphere (though that we ever really achieved an inclusive public culture is questioned) but that this is a welcoming opening up, an ability of previously marginal or excluded voices to be heard" (Macdonald 2003: 5). The logics and practices that inhabit public culture in postcolonial contexts are far from homogeneous.[18] A similar consideration informs Brian Larkin's (1997) work on parallel modernities, in which he reconstructs the influence of Indian films on Nigerian popular culture and charts people's diverse engagements in the production of new cultural forms. His research "gives insight into the local reworking and indigenising of transnational media flows that take place within and between Third World countries, disrupting the dichotomies between West and non-West, coloniser and colonised, modernity and tradition, foregrounding instead the ability of media to create parallel modernities" (407). Larkin points to the exchange of cultural flows between postcolonial nations and the development of parallel modernities, thus questioning the tendency of postcolonial literature to focus exclusively on exchanges between colonial and postcolonial nations.

The emergence of a diversified public culture is one of the most significant changes in Mali's democratic and neoliberal era. The state is no longer the only major actor involved in heritage work, as it used to be during the First and Second Republics, when Mali was a one-party state (1960–91). State-like activities are increasingly conducted by a plethora of entities and actors: Some reinforce state power, others work in partnership with the state (but develop partly independent projects), and others undermine and sometimes even, as in the case of terrorist organizations, challenge state heritage projects. Studies of "heritage" need to take into account a variety of "local," national, international, and transnational groups and actors and their overlapping and divergent rationalities and practices. In Mali, these include political parties with competing views of Mali's past; transnational organizations for the preservation and valorization of Mali's cultural heritage, such as Djenné Patrimoine; supranational organizations, such as UNESCO, which often reinforce state power (see Rowlands and de Jong 2007; De Cesari 2012); religious organizations (see chapter 5); and regular citizens, who have become more and more involved in the ideation of heritage projects, given current donor emphasis on the liberalization of the heritage sector. Public culture aims to acknowledge (however imperfectly) the complexity of the heritage field in Mali's neoliberal era. This point is further articulated by Corinne A. Kratz and Ivan Karp, whose findings are based on a consideration of the role of heritage in postapartheid South Africa but are similarly applicable to Mali: "Museum and heritage resources have been vital in shaping, interpreting, and contributing to transformations in public culture in South Africa over the past fifteen years, caught up in intricate interplays between forceful national (and regional) imperatives, local interests, and globalizing processes" (2006: 18).

Nothing drew my attention to the relevance of heritage for the development of a public culture better than the complaints of a Bamako-based *grin* (a group of friends who meet regularly to discuss topics of common interest) of professionals I had interviewed twice, four years apart. In 2001 several of these professionals had been overly critical of Alpha Oumar Konaré's presidency (1992–2002) and the hegemony of the president's majority party, the Alliance pour la démocratie au Mali (Alliance for Democracy in Mali) (ADEMA), and strongly criticized his top-down initiatives in the field of cultural heritage. In 2005 these professionals articulated a rather different narrative. Faced with the overly conciliatory tones of Amadou Toumani Touré's presidency (2002–12), they looked with nostalgia at the public debates—many of which surrounded state-promoted heritage initiatives—and even confrontations of Konaré's period and felt both less informed and more constrained by the new disciplinary regime of reconciliation.

Although heritage is thus implied in my use of the term "public culture," its continued use as a stand-alone term is justifiable. Public culture does not always deal with heritage when it is understood (as here) to embody those aspects of the past or those aspects presenting a veneer of pastness that a society deems worth remembering and transferring to future generations (Davison 2008). Furthermore, heritage appears more connected to the inner workings of the state and state-like entities, whereas public culture suggests the creation of publics that present a certain degree of autonomy from the state and variously replicate, resist, or challenge state initiatives (and underlying cultural logics) in the field of cultural heritage. Finally, more recent literature (including Appadurai 2008) takes a more skeptical view of the actual possibilities opened by transnational governmentality in the development of a less state-dependent public culture, but the potential disjuncture is worth retaining as a sometimes actualized possibility (see Appadurai 2002).

## Social Memory and the Anthropology of Africa

In anthropology the study of social memory goes back to the seminal work of one of Emile Durkheim's students, the French ethnologist Maurice Halbwachs (1877–1945), who studied memory as a social phenomenon and wrote that "no memory is possible outside frameworks used by people living in society to determine and retrieve their recollections" (1992: 43).[19] Memory is forged in the course of people's interactions within their social groups (e.g., families, social classes, religious groups) and is key to the development of a shared identity (Russell 2006). For Halbwachs, collective memory refers to people's lived experiences; as such, memory is richer and more evocative than history, which is seen as more abstract, schematic, and objective.

Halbwachs's work has since framed many debates within memory studies. For instance, Pierre Nora's (1989) fundamental distinction between the *lieux de mémoire* (sites of memory) and the *milieux de mémoire* (environments of memory) further develops Halbwachs's distinction between history and memory. Nora sees history as a defining trait of Western societies, which, having lost their grounding in shared traditions, develop heterogeneous sites of memory (including such varied forms as monuments, school textbooks, and national rituals) in an effort to counter the inescapable forward movements of history and hold onto a shared—but fragile—national past.

Contemporary anthropological studies (in particular, Cole 2001) question several aspects of Halbwachs's theory. For instance, Halbwachs's understanding of memory as a shared group property is too vague and general by today's anthropological understandings of culture; indeed, "Halbwachs never really addressed the question of divergent memories or countermemories within a group" (Cole 2001: 23). Memory frictions and the conflicts between state memory and popular memories lie at the center of contemporary anthropological investigation (e.g., Werbner 1998; Shaw 2007; De Cesari 2010). Scholars also question several of Halbwachs's distinctions, such as the one between individual and group memories. Drawing on the work of Frederic Barlett, psychological anthropologists suggest continuities between individual and public memories, reminding us of the socially mediated nature of all processes of remembering (see Cole 2001; Wertsch 2008; and Wertsch and

Billingsley 2011). In this perspective, "rather than searching for an essentialist memory 'of the group,' we propose that remembering is distributed and shared among individuals 'in the group'" (Wertsch and Billingsley 2011: 30). This is not to suggest that memory is *equally* distributed among members of a group. Memory, as any other social phenomenon, is strongly dependent on people's situated positions within their social fields and thus deeply affected by power relations.[20]

Other scholars reject what Jennifer Cole (2001) calls "an interest-based model" of memory and highlight that memory is neither infinitely pliable nor dependent only on present considerations and needs. Rosalind Shaw insightfully develops this point by exploring the complex ways in which memory of the past and transformational events in the present interface, leading her to recognize "persistence, recurrence, and reproduction as integral parts of transformation and innovation rather than as their antitheses" (2002: 10).

Contemporary anthropologists have further built on British anthropologist Paul Connerton's work on social memory because of his interest in exploring the multiple ways in which collective memory is conveyed and sustained (1989: 1). He rejects the reduction of memory to texts and centers his analysis on how "practices of a non-inscribed kind [rituals and embodiments] are transmitted, in and as tradition" (1989: 4). He is particularly interested in the analysis of ritual ceremonies and bodily practices (including changes in fashion) via which public memory is cultivated and transferred.

Drawing on Pierre Bourdieu's notion of habitus, Connerton regards memory as passed on primarily via "commemorative ceremonies; but commemorative ceremonies prove to be commemorative only in so far as they are performative; performativity cannot be thought without a concept of habit; and habit cannot be thought without a notion of bodily automatisms" (1989: 5). Paul Stoller insightfully builds on Connerton's work to explore spirit possessions in Niger as an embodied phenomenon. For Stoller, "the sentient body is culturally consumed by a world filled with forces, smells, textures, sights, sounds, and tastes, all of which trigger social memory" (1995: 7). Rituals of possession and the powerful bodily experiences that accompany them are ways via which people come to terms with past and present violence (e.g., of the colonial period, of capitalism) and reassert some degree of agency in the process. Shaw reexamines some of Connerton's too-sharp oppositions, such as between inscribed recollections (texts) and noninscribed recollections (performances, embodiments), in light of Anthony Giddens's distinction between discursive and practical consciousness and concludes that "we can thus distinguish between, on the one hand, the reflexive sensibilities of discursive memory in explicit, intentional narrative accounts of the past and, on the other hand, the more tacit apprehensions of practical memory, 'forgotten as history' (Bourdieu 1990: 56) precisely because they are embedded in habits, social practices, ritual processes, and embodied experiences" (2002: 7). Rejecting easy dichotomies and, rather, stressing the continuities and intersections between these two forms of historical consciousness (that is, discursive and practical), Shaw uses this theoretical apparatus to analyze memories of the slave trade "forgotten as history but remembered as spirits, as a menacing landscape, as images of divination, as marriage, as witchcraft, and as postcolonial politicians" in Sierra Leone (2002: 9).

Other anthropologists focus on social memory as a site of tensions or conflict between different social groups (see seminal work by Werbner 1998). For instance, in her more recent work (2007), Shaw examines the ways in which Sierra Leone's dramatic civil war (1991–2002) is being remembered. In the war's aftermath, the state organized the Truth and Reconciliation Commission (TRC), with its underlying logic of truth telling, as a way to facilitate healing and appease social tensions.[23] Focusing on some of the conflicts surrounding the proper way to remember the civil war, Shaw discusses how several Sierra Leoneans refused to participate in TRC public hearings. For these segments of the citizenry, forgetting is a much more efficacious strategy to achieve healing, to put behind the atrocities experienced during the civil war, and to prevent the rekindling of old conflicts.[21]

Anthropological approaches consider multiple memories and their diverse forms in an effort to represent the views of diverse constituencies (who often have unequal access to the mechanisms of modern power) and not just those of the state. The anthropological lens also regards the disputed character of memory as key to identity formation and the articulation of political claims for both individuals and groups.[22] Memory also reflects different forms of consciousness—some of which are more discursive, whereas others are more practical. In this book, examples of discursive memory include not only politicians' speeches and media reports but also public debates and private conversations (e.g., chapter 2). The more practical side of memory is exemplified by state rituals of commemoration and by counter-rituals via which the political opposition expresses its political dissent. Remembering is a highly disputed activity—and one with profound political ramifications, as the case studies collected here thematize.

## Heritage and Memory

My perspective on memory also takes into account the work of anthropologists who share similar topics of investigation and endeavor to chart both the intersections and the disjunctures between heritage projects and social memories. De Cesari rightly sees the interest in heritage as "a dimension of the fin-de-siècle memory boom" (2012: 400).[24] Nonetheless, heritage and memory are often perceived as deeply divergent projects, as Michael Rowlands and Beverley Butler observe: "Heritage and memory became opposed in anthropology, as the expression of tensions between local and personal collective memories and globalizing and statebuilding acts of memorialization. Popular memory is seen as genuine, while heritage is mere state spectacle or for tourists" (2007: 1). Heritage and memory are often seen as distinct cultural products, with memory more closely reflecting people's genuine attachments and concerns and heritage more markedly tied to political and economic logics.

Rowlands and de Jong further question the opposition between cultural heritage and popular memory. They explore "what kind of memorializing tactics and strategies attach themselves to the technologies of heritage" and stress that "modern heritage and modern memory share a common origin in conflict and loss" (2007: 13, 17).[25] Heritage initiatives can, on occasion, prompt the circulation of memory flows and unleash public discussions of the past, or they can empower communities choosing to engage with the metalanguage of heritage work while seeking local and transnational recognition (see Schulz 2007 and de Jong 2007).

The unresolved relationship between heritage and memory (and the potential for their more meaningful intersections) is a productive disjuncture that can expose instances in which state-promoted heritage projects may not work and are indeed actively resisted by local actors who refuse to identify with the forms of commemoration (and their management) promoted by the state (see Low 2004). For instance, the creation of a memorial to commemorate Mali's first president, Modibo Keita (1960–68), could have brought together different national constituencies, such as the survivors and political heirs of Keita's socialist regime and members of the post-1991 heterogeneous political leadership, around a common project—that is, the clarification and discursive rearticulation of national history under conditions of democracy. By including their voices and memories in the process of heritagization (the process by which a cultural heritage or cultural patrimony is formed) of Keita, the Modibo Keita Memorial could also have yielded some closure for the many Malians who do not have positive memories of Keita's presidency and remember the violence and lack of freedom during that period. As a state-led heritage initiative, the Modibo Keita Memorial did not prompt identification with the commemorative forms chosen by the state and failed to address and heal memories of past suffering. It actually created new fractures in the social fabric. In this case, as in many other heritage initiatives, conflict and disjuncture lie at the center of heritage issues—phenomena that this work analyzes and theorizes.

## Cultural Heritage during the One-Party State Era

During the first thirty years of Mali's independence, from 1960 to 1991, the production of cultural heritage was carefully orchestrated and controlled by the one-party state. The creation of a national culture was designed to help Malians overcome regional and ethnic divisions and constitute a shared cultural heritage with which most citizens could identify while grounding them in "local traditions." This is not to suggest that the national project was an inclusive endeavor: the patrimonialization of regional and ethnic cultures resulted in the establishment of "the Mande ethnic political hegemony" (Rowlands 2007: 127; see also Schulz 2001), that is, the privileging of the cultural practices of the Mande people (Bamana, Jula, and Malinké) over those of others (e.g., the Tuareg and Moor).

The precolonial past provided an inexhaustible well from which the state could draw in the process of national construction. Mary Jo Arnoldi points out that during the first eight years of Malian independence, "the government, under the leadership of Modibo Keita, strongly emphasized precolonial history and traditional culture, especially of the ancient empires of Ghana, Mali, and Songhai" (2006: 56).[26] The state's project also integrated contemporary themes, particularly at the level of theatrical performances, such as plays thematizing the Malian youth's loss of identity and the damaging impact of Western capitalism (Arnoldi 2006). Similar to other African political elites, Malians were "carv[ing] out a national patrimony which would then serve to legitimize the new state by rooting it in a past constructed as unimpaired and spiritually distinct from Western role models" (Schramm 2004: 161).[27] The focus on the national past—made possible by the development in Mali of fields such as archaeology and the social sciences—was to create a sense of the nation's historical depth so that the "nation-states could imagine themselves as natural entities, existing since time immemorial" (Errington 1998: 37; see also Mann 2007). The choice of Mali as the country's postindependence name to replace its colonial name, Soudan (French Sudan), was intended to suggest continuity with the period of the great African empires that had blossomed in that region during precolonial times and from which the colonial period was a temporary departure.[28]

During Mali's first two regimes, from 1960 to 1991, a series of carefully planned festivals sought to embody and foster the twin ideas of national identity and national development. During Keita's presidency, the festivals, called the Semaine nationale de la jeunesse (National Youth Week), took place annually between 1962 and 1968 (Y. Touré 1996; Arnoldi 2006; Djebbari 2013). They involved local and regional youth competitions that culminated in a weeklong festival in Bamako, where the selected regional troupes participated in various artistic and athletic competitions. Under Keita, the First Republic used the Semaine to disseminate national values and convey political messages to the general population in an attempt to mobilize citizens around the objectives of Malian socialism, national economic development, and national unity: "the week-long (final) festival . . . included politically oriented seminars and obligatory public-works activities" (Arnoldi 2006: 57). Following the 1968 military coup, the annual Semaine came to a halt; it was resumed in 1970 with a slightly modified title, the Biennale artistique, culturelle, et sportive (Biennial of Arts, Culture, and Sports), and a new biannual frequency. The new regime under Moussa Traoré made some minor cosmetic changes to the festival (e.g., it removed references to the First Republic and softened some of the socialist tones of the nationalist rhetoric) but left it essentially unchanged (Arnoldi 2006). Both performances and media coverage were heavily scrutinized to detect and promptly eliminate critical references to the military regime, although some irony occasionally escaped notice.

The festivals became the most important national forum for the performance and valorization of Malian culture. Competitions involving theater and musical groups at various levels of the administrative pyramid (i.e., local, regional, and national) represented a very successful state-led endeavor for reviving or innovating local traditions, promoting the exchange of cultural traditions (for example, so that regional dances, such as the famous Ségouvian *bara* [a regional dance], would be adopted by other communities around the country), and facilitating encounters and exchanges among the youth of different regions.

Traoré's military dictatorship lasted from 1968 to 1991, and during its final years, state investment in the domain of culture was dramatically reduced. In 1988 the Biennale was discontinued—partly as a result of the acceleration of structural adjustment programs that dramatically reduced the state budget for culture and partly because of increased political instability that included mounting public dissatisfaction with Traoré's rule and the resurgence of Tuareg rebellions in the north.

Following the 1991 coup d'état and the 1992 democratic election of Alpha Oumar Konaré to the presidency, the domain of national culture once again became a government priority but was now located in a sociopolitical environment characterized by greater freedom of expression, as demonstrated by the exponential growth of newspapers, radio stations, various kinds of secular and religious organizations, and diverse political parties (which totaled more than a hundred in 2012).[29] In conjunction with a variety of international partners, the state organized a number of new initiatives in the field of culture to mark the new beginning but also to establish a distance from cultural activities so tightly associated with the one-party state.[30] It is in this context that the unprecedented investment in material culture, such as monuments, a memorial, and a museum,[31] and in the preservation of Islamic architecture, particularly those architectural sites that were included on the list of UNESCO World Heritage Sites, must be located and is analyzed in the pages to follow. Furthermore, the state, international partners, and (increasingly) private actors and groups invested significantly in the organization of cultural initiatives to promote African arts, such as literature and photography, and regional festivals, including the famous Festival au désert (Festival in the Desert) and the Festival sur le Niger (Festival on the Niger) (see Doquet 2008 and Sy 2012). The Malian state reorganized the Biennale in 2001 but progressively made several modifications that reflected the broader changes in the heritage sector during the democratic era.[32] The Biennale now included private artistic groups, for example, and welcomed the participation of one artistic group representing Malians in the diaspora (Djebbari 2013).[33] The new incarnation of the Biennale also demonstrated the state's commitment to decentralizing state institutions: the final competitions rotated among Mali's regional capitals and did not all take place only in Bamako, as they had in the past (Arnoldi 2006).

The Biennale (particularly those of 2008 and 2010) also served as a vehicle by which the Malian state attempted to better integrate the northern regions in the national imaginary with some puzzling outcomes. Elina Djebbari's work suggests that artistic competitions (especially in those two years) were severely affected by political considerations that led the northern regions to be favored in national competitions and ultimately caused resentment among southern artistic groups: "Although the professionalism of Bamako has long served as a model for other regions, juries have made Bamako the poor relative of the last competitions. Neither Kayes in 2008 nor Sikasso in 2010 have allowed Bamako to win a prize in the 'ballet' category (their flagship event) and get on the podium" (2013: 295). Political considerations affected prize allocation, thus further alienating important (in this case, southern) Malian publics from the Biennales.

The Biennales organized during the democratic period came to reflect the new national asset, characterized by the decentralization of state institutions, greater inclusion of previously marginalized groups, and the involvement of private organizations (symbolically representing the freeing of culture). But the careful political engineering behind the organization of the Biennales ultimately backfired and led to some discontent. The Biennales and the political motives behind them appeared as outdated remnants of the one-party era—as celebrations no longer appealing to the sensibilities and interests of contemporary Malians, who mostly avoided such gatherings.

Interviews I conducted with representatives of the Ministry of Culture in June 2014 suggested that the current government is not interested in reorganizing the Biennale (which was last held in 2010), given its cost and general lack of public interest in the event. These state representatives also indicated to me their belief that without a strong central power to enforce participation, popular attendance would remain weak. In its latest programmatic document, the Ministry of Culture continues and indeed intensifies the previous two administrations' practice of privileging the organization of regional festivals and national performances with more tightly circumscribed themes (e.g., La Semaine nationale du patrimoine culturel).[34] Pressured by Western donors, the state is increasingly seeking to facilitate the development of a private heritage sector by providing human resources, equipment, and help with identifying sources of funding.

Taking into account recent developments in the study of heritage as well as Mali's postcolonial history (particularly as it pertains to national culture), this book is an examination of cultural heritage in Mali during the democratic neoliberal era. I analyze specific heritage initiatives that are (according to the discussion on governmentality outlined above) mostly state-led but also include an attention to more independent heritage projects that often developed in the interstices of state initiatives.

## Methodology

This book is based on two years and three months of fieldwork in Mali conducted over an extended period of time (1991, 1993–94, 1999, 2001, 2003, 2004–5, and 2014). I gathered data in French and Bamana through onsite participant-observation, open-ended interviews, and archival as well online research. Even when I am not physically in Mali, I stay informed on opinions, events, and other developments in Mali by reading Malian newspapers regularly, daily email, news updates, and communicating regularly with Malians in the diaspora and in Mali.

Over the years I interviewed and conversed with a multiplicity of people, including government officials, heritage elites, politicians, members of the press, representatives of women's organizations, Malian scholars, religious leaders, teachers, students, and members of Mali's lower and middle classes. Because my research encompasses multiple locations, I am able to examine the intersections and frictions among local, national, and transnational entities and actors as they emerge from the analysis of specific heritage-field initiatives that are mostly state-led or involve some state participation. In addition to the views of actors and groups in the Malian cities of Bamako, Ségou, Djenné, and Timbuktu, my research also takes into account the perspective of some Malian groups and actors in the diaspora, in recognition of their continuing participation in various aspects of national life (e.g., heritage politics) as well as their social networks (Bernal 2005, 2014). My work thus aims to provide "a prismatic view—one in which perspectives are located in a diverse range of positions, places, and institutions and at different organizational levels, from macro to mezzo to micro" (Kratz and Karp 2006: 17).

As a result, my work emphasizes the perspectives of the Malian administration and of Malians working in the heritage sector, but it also makes a concerted effort to reflect the views of heterogeneous groups and actors. For instance, my discussion of the exhibits at Muso Kunda (chapter 3) includes an analysis of a school visit there by a group of high school and university students, their readings of the exhibits, and their interactions with museum representatives. In my examination of the commemoration of the colonial past (chapter 2), I reflect on the counterinitiatives of the political opposition, as well as on conversations and public debates on the colonial past fueled by state heritage initiatives among the population.

The first three chapters of this book are based on extensive fieldwork and participant observation in Bamako and Ségou, complemented by interviews and the analysis of primary sources. The last two chapters are grounded in face-to-face interviews in Bamako and in phone interviews with members of the Timbuktu and Djenné heritage elites, detailed reading of primary sources, and participation in virtual cultural spaces. For instance, chapter 4, which focuses on Djenné, is based on the close analysis of an online journal published by the cultural organization Djenné Patrimoine (an example of a transnational organization with international and national membership), which has contributed to the diversification of the heritage sector in Djenné; that chapter also draws on studies of bureaucratic documents (an emerging domain of inquiry in anthropology; see Hull 2012), close readings of blogs, and interviews in Bamako with some of Mali's heritage elite, including representatives of the Aga Khan Trust for Culture (AKTC), architects, and representatives of Djenné-based cultural institutions. Chapter 5, on Timbuktu, draws on the analysis of newspaper articles and bureaucratic documents, as well as participation in online social media (e.g., Facebook and discussion forums) and in-person interviews with members of the Timbuktu heritage elite during my fieldwork in June 2014 in Bamako and Ségou and via telephone a few months later.

Finally, the inclusion of media sources (particularly newspaper articles) provides important insights on how state narratives and practices are espoused—or rejected—by broader segments of Mali's population. The media, as Appadurai and Breckenridge observe, provide "the master narratives within which" representations of the past are reinterpreted by wider publics (2004: 412). Media sources provide information on "the complex ways in which 'national' or 'state' and 'popular' memories may be entwined with one another" (Cole 2003: 96). This is particularly appropriate in the post-1991 period, given the proliferation of radio broadcasts, journals, and magazines (see Schulz 2001 and 2007). Newspapers are not solely the province of the literate minority, who make up only 33.6 percent of the population (UNICEF 2013).[35] During most of the 1960s, party members of the Union soudanaise–Rassemblement démocratique africain (Sudanese Union–African Democratic Rally) (US-RDA), the then-ruling party, had a political duty to read and translate articles from the national newspaper (*L'Essor*) to the nonliterate majority (see Aoua Keita's 1975 autobiography). The flow of information and rich conversations across educational divides (via the institution of the grin, for example) remains an important characteristic of Malian society. The inclusion of interviews, political speeches, and media coverage in my research enables me to identify some of the master narratives within which recoveries of the past are made as well as some of the power dynamics entailed in such recoveries.

## Outline of the Book

The chapters of this volume examine specific cultural heritage initiatives through 2014. Chapter 1 presents an overview of some of the most relevant state initiatives in the field of cultural heritage from 1992 to 2012, focusing on which aspects of the past are remembered (and which are forgotten) and how the past has been commemorated in Mali's democratic and neoliberal era. This chapter discusses some of the dominant narratives via which the recovery of the past is carried out and emphasizes some of the continuities and differences in state narratives. For example, these include the narratives promoted by Alpha Oumar Konaré's presidency, which cultivated rational-critical perspectives, and those promoted by Amadou Toumani Touré's presidency, which (as its predecessor had done) still encouraged distance from the past but emphasized narratives of reconciliation to the detriment of much-awaited historical clarification, particularly regarding episodes of state violence during Moussa Traoré's dictatorship. Chapter 1 also documents the growing (but uneven) play of the political opposition in heritage matters—one of the major changes in the field of cultural heritage in the post-1992 period. It identifies some continuity in the narratives and practices of the opposition under Konaré's and Touré's presidencies, particularly its adoption of a survivor narrative. The opposition often manifested its dissent by criticizing state-led heritage initiatives and either proposing changes to them or organizing alternative commemorations. In their public statements, opposition representatives stressed the personal sacrifices they had made to free the country from oppressive rules to demand greater voice and weight in national matters.[36] This chapter follows some of the transformations in both the state's and the opposition's representations of the legacy of Mali's first president, Modibo Keita, as well as similar contestations of the legacy of Abdoul "Cabral" Karim Camara, a student leader who opposed the dictatorship of Moussa Traoré.

Chapter 2 examines the state memorialization of the colonial past via narratives, practices, and visual culture. It centers on the analysis of the ways in which the colonial past is represented in the Koulouba monument complex, an assemblage of monuments representing some of the major phases of Mali's history (but with a greater concentration of monuments on the colonial and postcolonial periods). The state experimented with a number of different techniques to represent colonization, including narratives that emphasize resistance to French colonization, those that evoke nostalgia for the colonial past, and those that prioritize hybridization, a perspective that boldly apprehends colonization as part of Mali's history and rejects the constraining dichotomies of colonizer and colonized and of tradition and modernity. This chapter also considers what went on behind the scenes as Konaré's presidency was arranging the transfer from Ségou to Bamako of the statue of Louis Archinard (originally erected in 1933 to commemorate Archinard's role in the conquest of French West Africa) in 2000. The attempted move, of which the Ségou-based population and most local political representatives were not informed, became at once a symbol of the autocratic nature of state power (and the continuity of state practices since the colonial era) and a vehicle for the expression of political dissent by the vociferous opposition, which was already dissatisfied with the political hegemony of the majority party, ADEMA. The attempted removal of the Archinard statue also helped unleash repressed memories of the French colonial period and sparked public discussions about continuities in the manifestation of state power since colonial times (and even before then). Amid such confrontations, a few Ségou-based groups became increasingly invested in the revaluation of the city's patrimony and began developing alternative heritage projects via which they could assert greater control over representations of their past (often couched in the idiom of family heritage).

Chapter 3 analyzes one of the first private initiatives in the field of heritage in the post-1992 period, the development of the women's museum Muso Kunda in Korofinna, Bamako. Conceived and realized by Adame Ba Konaré, wife of the then-president and herself a distinguished historian, with the help of experts from Mali's state heritage sector, the museum (which, after a period of uncertainty, was closed for renovations in 2011 and remains closed as of late 2015) reflects efforts by the democratic leadership to give women more visibility, to stress their historical and social contributions, and to promote greater women's participation in every sector, including the economic and political fields.[37] The museum displays multiple pasts simultaneously and experiments with new collections that reflect the search of Mali's cosmopolitan elites for a path to emancipation unique to Malian women. The museum's exhibits and narratives oscillate between a reaffirmation of women's specific contributions to Mali's society (and in particular their role as mothers and wives) and an emancipatory agenda that ritually reconfirms distance between Malian women and the confrontational tones attributed to Western feminism, a narrative already present in the speeches of women leaders since independence. This chapter also considers the visitor's experience of the museum (an often underdeveloped approach in museum studies; see Kratz and Karp 2006: 19) by analyzing museum tours undertaken by two of the museum's main target audiences (foreign tourists and Malian youth) and highlighting some of the unexpected interactions and conversations around issues of gender that developed between visitors and museum representatives.

Chapter 4 discusses the challenges encountered by the state and quasi-state organizations in transforming some of the Djenné-based sacred sites into public heritage sites, particularly in a context where local groups and hierarchies were already heavily invested in the management of the city's heritage, especially the preservation of the Great Mosque of Djenné. This chapter analyzes the centrality of Sudanese architecture in colonial and postcolonial representations of Mali, including the construction of models of the mosque in the context of worldwide expositions featuring Mali's artistic and artisanal products. It highlights some of the additional challenges (and possibilities) opened up by the inscription of the towns of Djenné on the UNESCO World Heritage Sites list and Djennenkés' critical perspectives on the criteria and objectives overseeing the management of UNESCO World Heritage Sites (including the arbitrary fixing of Djenné at the end of the nineteenth century and the beginning of the twentieth century as the model for the restoration of buildings). Through an analysis grounded in a postcolonial revision of Bennett's exhibitionary complex, this chapter also addresses state and quasi-state attempts to diversify the selection of the cultural patrimony to be restored.

It also examines the reinvention of the youth house of the Saho (described as an example of "pre-Islamic tradition" in the earlier literature),[38] which is being reconceived in bureaucratic reports and the media as an example of Mali's secular patrimony. Such transformations in state narratives of the Saho represent an effort to mitigate opposition by vocal religious leaders—whose perspective is shaped not merely by religious concerns but also by an array of other considerations (including economic and political ones).

Providing historical background in which to situate the events of 2012, chapter 5 deals with the destruction of the Sufi saints' mausoleums (a World Heritage Site) during the six-month occupation of Mali's northern regions by Tuareg-Islamist forces. Prior to the occupation, the government, foreign entities, and religious NGOs had deeply invested in the field of culture as a strategy to strengthen the influence of moderate Islam in Mali and to counter the Islamist groups' proselytizing in the north. This chapter investigates the symbolic implications the mausoleums' destruction held for different constituencies (e.g., some Islamist groups, UNESCO representatives, the local heritage elite, some of Mali's religious leaders) and charts some of the unintended consequences of the incursions by state and quasi-state organizations into the religious sphere—actions that ultimately have produced a conservative shift in the Muslim community. This chapter lends support to efforts promoted by some representatives of Mali's Ministry of Culture to sustain and diversify Mali's cultural patrimony by not limiting heritage work to the protection of Sufi shrines and suggests the importance of considering some of the debates—including those in the religious sphere—surrounding the protection and restoration of Sufi heritage sites in Mali today.

The epilogue contains further reflections on the intersection of heritage work and modern power, covering some of the post-2012 developments in Mali's heritage sector as well. It discusses key developments in the heritage field, including the emergence of new political and religious actors, the internal diversification of the state (as reflected also in the types of initiatives different state entities promote), and the forms of privatization promoted by the state in cooperation with international organizations. The chapter ultimately questions the opposition between private and public initiatives, suggesting overlaps and similar omissions, and expands on the significance of cultural heritage and its diversification in contemporary Mali.

# 1. Commemorating the Nation's Heroes in Mali's Neoliberal Democracy

THIS CHAPTER CENTERS on the conversations and controversies surrounding the heritagization (the process by which a cultural heritage or cultural patrimony is formed) of Mali's national heroes (via the construction of monuments and a memorial, and the development of new state commemorations) during the first two decades of Mali's multiparty democracy, from 1992 to 2012. In politicians' speeches, interviews with politicians and representatives of the heritage sector, and media reports, I distinguish two dominant narratives: the modernist discourse promoted by government officials, which emphasizes rationality and distance vis-à-vis the past (to facilitate collective healing from the violence of the one-party state and cultivate democratic values); and the "survivor" narrative of the political opposition, which emphasizes more emotional and visceral perspectives vis-à-vis the past (often grounded in direct participation in the historical events being represented). Although they indicate general structural continuities, such narratives are far from fixed: "Written texts are finite, while narrative memory, in principle, is not. Breaks, endings, decisive moments of closure depend upon the other institutions in which the stories are inserted" (Lambek and Antze 1996: xix; see also Wertsch 2008; Wertsch and Billingsley 2011). The memory narratives considered here rely on the political and institutional contexts of the heritagization of the postcolonial past during Mali's democratic and neoliberal era.

The democratic turn of 1991 was accompanied by a radical rethinking of Mali's cultural heritage, a key accompaniment to major political and social changes. This process entailed, among others, a search for more satisfactory ways to represent and commemorate the past. As Paul Connerton has remarked, "All beginnings contain an element of recollection. This is particularly the case when a social group makes a concerted effort to begin with a wholly new start" (1989: 6). The process of recollection is not entirely new and, indeed, is grounded on a certain "system of expectations" that comes to frame the so-called new beginnings (1989: 6).

Mali's democratic government sought to promote a program of renewal and expansion of its cultural heritage, hoping also to spearhead some radical changes to the population's shared system of expectations (e.g., by rejecting the subjection of culture to the interests of the powerful and their glorification). Countering the long-standing neglect of Mali's modern history and its main protagonists—as well as a tendency to glorify the precolonial past[1]—the democratic state, particularly under Alpha Oumar Konaré, endeavored to come to terms with Mali's postcolonial period (among other aspects of Mali's history) and especially the First Republic of Modibo Keita (1960–68) by encouraging a critical reading of the past but also extracting aspects of it that were deemed compatible with a neoliberal democracy. Accordingly, the democratic government either toned town or removed from state narratives many of the socialist tones of Mali's first republic, in keeping with the ongoing dismantling of the welfare state and the intensification of neoliberal changes.

Mali's transformation from a one-party state to a multiparty democracy had major ramifications for the renewal of the national heritage. In particular, the state was no longer the sole player in orchestrating heritage initiatives and now had to confront the emergence of new publics and their memories, as well as counterheritage projects.[2] What to remember or commemorate—and how—became the subject of endless confrontations between rapidly changing political parties and their allies. The construction of monuments and related public commemorations became hotly disputed sites for the expression of competing political ambitions and partly diverging political projects, often couched in survivor narratives (see Comaroff and Comaroff 2004). Kratz and Karp point out that "museums and heritage sites . . . [are] also perceived as a means of claiming or appropriating a role in broader public spheres and of legitimating identity, history, and presence, a perception that shaped this change and growth" (2006: 11). The increased diversification of the political field and the presence of greater expressive freedom have made the commemoration of the past a more open and disputed process. As in postapartheid South Africa, in Mali "almost every space of heritage production has seen complexity, controversy, and contestation" (Rassool 2000: 1).

This chapter is organized in three major sections. The first section provides a historical background against which to locate the democratic government's work in the field of cultural heritage and public culture. The second section presents an overview of some of the heritage work carried out under Konaré's administration (1992–2002).³ It documents state efforts to build a democratic culture as well as to cultivate rational-critical perspectives vis-à-vis the national past. The chapter follows continuities and changes in the commemoration of Mali's First Republic (and its controversial president, Modibo Keita), using those themes to orient the reader through the complexities and transformations of Mali's heritage. This section shows the centrality of party politics for the development of heritage and public culture during Konaré's administration. The third and last section describes heritage work under Amadou Toumani Touré (2002–12), analyzing some continuities but also noticeable shifts, particularly in Touré's adoption of the transnational trope of reconciliation and the proliferation of public rituals of appeasement and consensus building. This section also examines aspects of the shrinking opposition's countermemory project and the rekindling of struggles around Keita's legacy—as well as the emergence of new ones around the legacy of Abdoul "Cabral" Karim Camara, one of heroes of the opposition to Moussa Traoré's dictatorship.⁴ As a whole, this chapter presents a historical and cultural framework useful for contextualizing the case studies developed in following chapters.

## A Violent Past

The hero narrative and related heritage initiatives (e.g., the construction of statues and a mausoleum to commemorate the nation's heroes) articulated by the post-1991 state are intimately tied up with processes of national renewal. The politics of comprehensive remembering spearheaded by the state sought to come to terms with a divided national past, to initiate a process of collective healing, and to unite a fragmented citizenry around a renewed political project.

Mali's postcolonial past was much more violent than is often recognized.⁵ The first thirty years of Malian history were characterized by the hegemony of the one-party systems. During that period, all initiatives in the political field had to emanate from the party hierarchy, and any open opposition to the central government was actively discouraged and violently repressed (Simonis 1995). Between 1958 and 1960, toward the end of French colonization, the US-RDA party violently quelled the Ségou-based opposition party L'Union démocratique ségouvienne (Democratic Union of Seguvians) (UDS), which had a strong ethnic Bamana constituency.⁶ The affair culminated with the leveling of the village of Sakoi-Fulala and part of the village of Sakoiba (two places where UDS supporters resided) and the detention or public execution of some UDS party members (Simonis 1995; De Jorio 1997; Philippe 2013). This episode of Ségou's history remains very vivid in the memories of those who witnessed it, although it is rarely openly discussed.

Also around the time of independence, the representatives of independent women's groups were forced to dismantle their organizations. Some of these leaders became active within the Social Commission of the US-RDA party—the only legitimate institutional outlet for the expression of women's interests under the one-party regime. "Unruly" women leaders were temporarily relocated to Mali's north to avoid any potential interference from them in party decisions. This was the case, for instance, of Sira Diop, the president of the umbrella organization L'Union des femmes du Soudan (Women's Union of French Soudan), who became the second president of the national women's association, L'Union nationale des femmes du Mali (National Union of Malian Women) (UNFM), under Moussa Traoré (1977–80) (Ba Konaré 1993: 375).[7]

Under President Keita's First Republic (1960–68), a demonstration by a group of politicians and merchants against the issuance of the Malian franc and Mali's exit from the French monetary zone resulted in the 1962 arrest of the opposition movement's leadership: Fily Dabo Sissoko, Hamadoun Dicko, and Kassoum Touré (Imperato 1996: xxvii), as well as several other demonstrators.[8] The three were quickly tried and sentenced to life in prison. Two years later they died under circumstances that were never explained. In northern Mali the Tuareg revolts of the early 1960s, triggered by the extractive practices of the Malian state as well as the lack of any sustained state investment in the region, were also brutally repressed by the Malian army (Klute 1995: 58). The last year or so of Keita's presidency (a period known as the Active Revolution) was characterized by the popular militia's oppression of and brutality toward all strata of the population in a last desperate attempt by the country's leaders to save the First Republic and its socialist project. The US-RDA leadership claimed that the activities of the popular militia would preserve the republic by eliminating the corruption and growing instability resulting from the infiltration of conservative capitalist forces that supposedly were trying to take over the country politically.

In 1968 General Traoré came to power via what was then a widely supported coup d'état that ended the eight years of Keita's socialist regime and led to the imprisonment and death of several of Keita's political allies (Sanankoua 1990). From 1968 to 1979, the country was ruled by Le Comité militaire de libération nationale (Military Committee for National Liberation) (CMLN), with Traoré soon emerging as its leader. Despite the population's initial hopes for greater freedom,[9] Traoré's military regime was marred by political instability, corruption, and violence. Open expression of political dissent was harshly repressed, and extensive censorship of the media was put in place (interview with Rose Bastide Bamako, July 1994). For instance, in September 1970 "seven intellectuals [were] given 18 months in jail for offending the head of state" (Imperato 1996: xxix). Coup attempts organized either by military personnel close to former president Keita or by Traoré's rivals abounded as well. In a 1994 interview for the magazine *Jeune Afrique*, Amadou Toumani Touré (popularly known as ATT) reminded the Western press that "Moussa Traoré had escaped a dozen coup attempts" (1994: 12). Between 1968 and 1978, Traoré one by one eliminated all the men with whom he had originally organized the military coup, and "in February 1978, the most notorious members of the military government [Kissima Doukara, Karim Dembelé, and Tiécoro Bagayoko] were arrested and charged with corruption" (François 1982: 23). Under Traoré's orders they were killed while in detention a few years later.

During his time in power, Traoré attempted to counter the growing unpopularity of his regime and allegedly tried to prepare the country for a return to civilian rule (but at a much slower pace than his public declarations would indicate). In 1974 Malians were asked to vote on a new constitution; when they returned to the polls five years later to vote for a new president, Traoré was the only candidate on the list. In 1979 Traoré officially created L'Union démocratique du peuple malien (Democratic Union of the Malian People) (UDPM), the one party that was to rule the country between 1979 and 1991, and he dismantled the CMLN. In a short-lived attempt to clean up his regime's reputation and secure the support of the educated urban elites (*les intellectuels*), Traoré even appointed Konaré as the Minister of Youth, Culture, and Arts in 1978. Konaré held this position for two years before resigning over his dissatisfaction with the modest changes that had characterized the return to civilian rule.

Student demonstrations also began shortly after Traoré's military coup and continued at intervals throughout the entire dictatorship despite state repression (see Imperato 1996: xxviii). Student demonstrations intensified in the late 1970s in the wake of implementation of school reforms that "toughened the qualifications for entry into higher education and reformed the primary school syllabus" (François 1982: 22). Traoré's military regime made some concessions, such as an increase in scholarships for students and the "easing of examination requirements for degrees and certificates" (Imperato 1996: xxxiii), but overall state repression increased. In 1980, a particularly violent year, student protests organized under Camara, leader of L'Union nationale des élèves et étudiants du Mali (National Union of Pupils and Students of Mali) (UNEEM), resulted in increases in "arrests, imprisonments, forced recruitment into the army, the taking of hostages, rapes . . . torture and murder" (François 1982: 24). Camara was arrested, tortured, and killed while in detention. Schools were closed, and students lost two entire years of schooling.

Increasingly, opposition forces rallied around the figure of Keita, whose liberation student demonstrators increasingly demanded. Keita's unexplained death in 1977 further energized student opposition and, more broadly, marked the beginning of his rehabilitation in the national imagination.[10] Keita's funeral and the accompanying state repression marked a particularly traumatic collective experience and further undermined Traoré's legitimacy. The funeral was widely attended by students as well as broader audiences. Traoré's forces arrested several of the funeral participants and conducted additional purges among the ranks of his allies. A number of recently published memoirs that detail the horrors of political detention under Traoré "center on the traumatic encounter with the military regime and are structured around similar episodes of political activism, arbitrary arrest, interrogation, and incarceration, articulating in dramatic fashion the experience of Malian political opponents of Traoré's government" (A. Sow 2010: 72). Despite demonstrations and attempted coups, Traoré's rule endured because of the effectiveness of the state brutality, the weakness of the opposition, and international support for his regime.

In the last months of the dictatorship, a new Tuareg revolt ensued because of the continuing political and economic marginality experienced by most Tuaregs. At first it was, like earlier revolts, brutally repressed by the army. Under considerable international pressure, however, Traoré signed the Tamanrasset Accords in 1991, which granted greater autonomy to the northern regions. In a desperate and useless attempt to preserve his power, he then relocated the army to the south and concentrated troops in the capital of Bamako, where the pro-democracy movement was gaining momentum (Klute 1995: 58). In March 1991 Traoré's dictatorship was ended by popular demonstrations that cost the lives of at least two hundred participants. Villalon and Idrissa note that "of all the West African countries that undertook democratic elections in the 1990s, Mali had the bloodiest beginning of that process" (2005: 53). Faced with the prospect of a civil war, segments of the military led by Touré brought Traoré's dictatorship to an end.

Eighteen months after the coup d'état, Touré led an interim government of military officials and civilians that paved the way to Mali's first multiparty elections. In April 1992 Konaré was elected as Mali's first democratically chosen president. This election opened a relatively stable period in Malian politics, during which Mali was praised by the international community as a model of democracy in Africa and became a recipient of significant international aid.[11] Following Mali's turn to democracy, Mali's political leadership sought to symbolically redress the violence and political repression of the twenty-three years of Mali's military regime. The process of national renewal intended to help the country "escape the grim spiral of poverty, despair, exclusion, and fatality" (Konaré 1992) and replace it with a memory of empowerment and hope. In the process, some of Mali's postcolonial heroes were revisited and publicly commemorated.

## Mali's Neoliberal Democracy

The Konaré government's project of political and social reform marked a significant break from the policies of the one-party states that preceded it. Scholars and development experts generally agree that "Mali's decade under President Alpha Oumar Konaré (1992–2002) provided a model of political stability in the region" (Villalon and Idrissa 2005:49). Konaré's declared goals for the democratic state included "the re-enforcement of the fundamental democratic values, national cohesion, restoration of the credibility of the state, encouragement of a citizenry founded on the active participation of the population in the management of the country, and renewed trust in the institutions" (qtd. in Diarrah 2000: 370). Some of the major realizations of those goals included the consolidation of political and civil freedoms, as well as the decentralization of state institutions (Amselle 2006), in an effort to stimulate economic growth and increase political participation.

Despite initial national and international enthusiasm, however, Konaré's decade was also characterized by an increasing fragmentation of Malian politics, which carried significant ramifications for the development of a cultural heritage with which the nation could identify. Konaré was initially committed to a project of national cohesion known as the Republican Pact (Diarrah 1996, 2000; Baudais and Chauzal 2006). His first two governments included a broad spectrum of parties in addition to his own party, L'Alliance pour la démocratie au Mali (Alliance for Democracy in Mali) (ADEMA), which was also the majority party. But the political opposition's growing demands for increased participation in and access to state resources, escalating violence and instability (notably on the part of the students), and the imposition of harsh economic measures by the World Bank and the International Monetary Fund (IMF)—one of the harshest was the 1994 devaluation of the CFA franc (the Malian currency) by 50 percent—led to an entrenchment of the ADEMA party's position and the radicalization of the opposition.

In particular, the strict application of structural adjustment programs by international organizations, such as the IMF and the World Bank, resulted in deep cuts to state expenditure budgets and to the privatization of the state-run economy at a particularly delicate phase of the Malian state's history. The state privatized most of its enterprises, most of which were then—in the absence of a strong private sector—acquired by foreign companies. Many of these foreign investments ultimately resulted in financial speculations and the dissolution or downsizing of formerly state-owned enterprises, a situation that escalated under Touré (see Beaudet 2006). Domestic and foreign factors conspired to promote the proliferation of parties (estimated to number more than a hundred in 2012) that competed for access to limited but more diversified resources. These factors included the reduction of the state budget for welfare spending in one of the poorest nations in the world, the allocation of funds to stimulate the growth of parties to strengthen civil society, and, as a result of the political expansion and economic contraction of the state, the increased presence of local and foreign NGOs (including the growth and rising influence of religious organizations, a theme developed in chapters 4 and 5). Cuts in state expenditures triggered cuts in state spending in education, health, and other areas addressed by often-uncoordinated foreign entities, NGOs, and their development projects. The actual condition of most Malians was misrepresented, in part because of overreliance by international aid organizations on limited measures of economic growth like GNP. The general population's standard of living declined as the socioeconomic gap among Malians widened.

In this changing economic and political context, the fracture between the government and opposition forces continued to grow—a situation that Konaré and his government were unable to overcome for most of his mandate (and one that escalated during his second term). Villalon and Idrissa (2005) articulate a political explanation that identifies in the specificities of the Malian electoral system a major motive for the opposition's growing dissatisfaction with ADEMA's rule. The Malian electoral system favored the hegemony of the majority party and left little room for opposition parties: "the majoritarian nature of the legislative electoral system in a context of a semi-presidential regime . . . produc[ed] the domination of a single large party" (Villalon and Idrissa 2005:58). As a result, opposition parties increasingly relied on popular revolts (e.g., the many student demonstrations) or boycotts to exert some influence on the government's decisions (2005: 61). The government's inability or unwillingness to broaden its coalition government led to the migration of opposition parties' members into ADEMA's ranks. It also led to party splits that enabled ambitious opposition politicians to work out political compromises with ADEMA and receive appointments in successive governments. These behaviors on the part of Mali's political class contributed to growing popular discontent vis-à-vis politics. Most local observers interpret candidate migration and party splits as examples of politicians' opportunism, corruption, and lack of significant ideological differences in their programs (Whitehouse 2015).

The renewal of cultural heritage occurred in the midst of the nation's major political and economic transformation, growing complexity, and escalating internal segmentation. For the state, heritage was intended to reground and reenergize Mali's heterogeneous nation—a particularly important project in light of the divisive tendencies of Malian politics.[12] The Konaré administration's unprecedented commitment to cultural heritage—and particularly material culture via the construction of monuments and cultural centers (mostly in Bamako but also in regional capitals)—sought to stress a shared historical past and suggest a common direction.

## The Konaré Years

In this context of political, economic, and social instability, the state and its representatives put an extraordinary emphasis on rebuilding national culture. The democratic state pursued a perspectival change to overcome the limitations of what Konaré defined as the monolithic ideology of the one-party state under the two successive governments from 1960 to 1991. Through the reinterpretation of the nation's past via official discourses, commemorative rituals, and the national heritage sector, the Konaré government sought to cultivate democratic values among Malian citizens. It sought to provoke public conversations around the past but also to remind citizens of their cultural roots and their creative potential as well as to counter the homogenizing forces introduced by economic globalization (Konaré 1995, 1999). To these ends, the hero narrative became a privileged medium for the articulation of the state democratic project.

From the beginning of his presidency, Konaré distanced himself from those politicians of the past who had used Malian artists—especially the *griots*, or *jeliw* (a semi-endogamous group of people specializing in music, praise giving, and family histories), and their arsenal of praises—to strengthen and legitimize the politicians' power. In a 1991 interview, he noted that some Malian artists (the jeliw, in particular) had put their art in service of the people in power, observing that manipulation of the arts was typical of "strong political entities [that] have always used artists to create a certain mystique and mystify power" (Pivin 1991).[13] Adame Ba Konaré, Konaré's wife and an esteemed Malian historian, further considered that Malian politicians and historians "had no sources other than the oral traditions of the *griots* and, to

FIGURE 2. Modibo Keita Memorial, Bamako, Mali, 2007. Courtesy of BluesyPete, licensed under CC-BY-SA 3.0.

a lesser degree, the traditions of the *marabouts*" (Muslim religious leaders) on the basis of which to reconstruct Mali's past in the immediate postcolonial period (2000: 17). In 1999, in response to growing popular dissatisfaction with "the flattery of the *jeli* [singular of jeliw] singers," Alpha Oumar Konaré's government "prohibit[ed] . . . any jeli praise on national media to further mark his distance from the forms of remembering that political leaders had exploited during the one-party era" (Schulz 2007: 198). Vouching his support for more critical forms of knowledge, Konaré (1999) described some of his counterinitiatives—notably, the construction of public spaces dedicated to the memory of past historical figures as a "temple of debates"—a space for the free articulation of opposing views seeking to clarify the past and draw new lessons for the future.

Konaré's presidency developed an extraordinary and unprecedented emphasis on visual culture—particularly monuments, museums, cultural centers, and memorials—as an important strategy in the representation of modern power, the cultivation of new forms of citizenship (Bennett 1995, 2006), and the transition to a more open and freely available national culture. It included not only the political leaders of the past but also the leaders of the student movement and the masses who had sacrificed their lives to overthrow Mali's military regime. Other monuments commemorate the

heroes of pan-Africanism, precolonial and colonial history, modernity, and aspects of Malian traditions and values (e.g., the tradition of hospitality, the importance of motherhood, and the centrality of farming).[14] The Malian media and government literature advertised monuments as a way to "cultivate a democratic form of citizenship" (Ly 2000), since they can be accessed and enjoyed by all segments of the public without restriction, as opposed to the "elitist and cliquish culture" of the past (Ly 2000; see also De Jorio 2003).[15]

The government's rehabilitation of the nation's fathers and the rhetorical tones of such an undertaking were established in Konaré's public speeches on the occasion of the first state commemoration of Keita's death (16 May 1995) and the inauguration of Modibo Keita Memorial (6 June 1999) (figure 2). In these speeches Konaré described his view of the recovery and the reassessment of the nation's fathers in light of Mali's democratic turn: the commemoration of the past was to be conducted with "thoughtfulness" and "distance to judge the facts and acts of the independence years" (1999; see also Couloubaly 1993, 2001). This approach consciously sought to avoid the tendencies to sacralize the past or establish a personality cult, a clear reference to the attempts by Keita's old comrades to do otherwise. The commemoration of Keita, Konaré clarified, was also the commemoration of a generation and its participation in the making of independent Mali, represented as the result of collective struggles (Arnoldi 2003).

In these two historic speeches, Konaré iterated the importance of recognizing other men and women who had contributed to Mali's independence. They included Keita's political opposition, Le Parti soudanais progressiste (Sudanese Progressive Party) (PSP), led by Fily Dabo Sissoko and Hamadoun Dicko. Konaré encouraged the recognition of both contributions and mistakes: "[T]he time, Comrades, has come, the time of maturity, where we have to face history and recognize every contribution to nation building, recognize also our gaps, our weaknesses, our mistakes and explain them to the new generations" (1999). Several of Konaré's collaborators echoed this position, including Modibo Diallo, director of the Modibo Keita Memorial, who conceived the memorial as a desacralized space for the study of Mali's postindependence history (M. Diallo 1997). The press close to the government further developed Konaré's message by more explicitly drawing the connection between democracy and truth-seeking dispositions: "The advantage of democracy is the possibility of identifying embarrassing truth, of deciphering it with as much objectivity as possible, of consciously integrating it into our collective experience" (Drabo 1999).

## Conflicts over Keita's Commemoration

Perhaps, the most significant change in the post-1991 period has been the proliferation and diversification of public memory. In the past, heritage was held tightly in the hands of state power, but after 1991, remembering and commemorating (which had always been contentious on the margins) became openly contested projects. Who should remember, what should be remembered, and how it should be remembered became highly debated topics during this time; one of the most contested and arduous heritage projects of the mid-1990s concerned the life and work of Mali's first president, Modibo Keita (De Jorio 2003). During Traoré's regime, students, union members, and teachers had all come to identify with Keita's message and work and claimed him as a source of inspiration in their struggles against the dictatorship. Keita's symbolic value and his status as father of the nation were undisputed, but his life and his legacy contained plenty of ambiguities.

Managing Keita's legacy in the post-1991 period was a challenging political act. Although he was popular in certain circles, he had left plenty of bad memories as well. As mentioned earlier, the older generations in the Ségou region still remembered with sadness Keita's brutal repression of the political opposition, namely, the UDS party and some of its supporters, as well as the brutality of the popular militia (B. Traoré, pers. comm.; Ségou 1994; Simonis 1995: 231). Such painful memories were rarely discussed, partly also not to reignite old conflicts as I learned in the course of my interviews with former USD party leaders' wives (e.g., Jagossa Sidibé, pers. comm., Ségou, 1994). In response to such mixed memories and the ambiguities of state power during Mali's First Republic, the state and its representatives endeavored to articulate a sanitized version of Keita, one with which a greater number of citizens could identify. Konaré stressed the need to establish some distance from the past in order to reckon openly with the shortcomings of the US-RDA party and thus recognize the struggles of a generation, without promulgating decidedly unrealistic and overly idealized depictions of the First Republic.

Furthermore, the neoliberal state and its representatives worked to downplay the socialist elements of Keita's thoughts to which certain segments of the country's political elites were still visibly attached. There was no mention of Keita's socialism in Konaré's 1995 and 1999 speeches, for example. In a later interview, Konaré described Keita as a liberal democrat, suggesting that Keita's alleged socialism was more a reflection of outside pressures, by such forces as the French Communist party and some of Keita's more radical party comrades, than of his own beliefs (Konaré 2010). Keita was described as a pious man, a father of the nation, and a respected pan-Africanist, rather than as a socialist thinker. The democratic and neoliberal state downplayed the socialist component of the First Republic, perhaps also in an effort to mend past wounds, and foregrounded select aspects of Keita's legacy: his nation-building efforts, his pan-African vision, and his ability to reconcile opposing views.[16]

The most vocal opponents of the state-led program to commemorate Keita's legacy were Keita's family members and his surviving party companions. This fringe of the US-RDA demanded more continuity with the past and hoped to resume some of their past political influence. Their position found expression, at least for some time, within the new logic of multipartism and the interparty struggles that came to characterize it. Some of Keita's family members and former political allies were committed to the rehabilitation of Keita's legacy and sought to correct some of the popular misrepresentations of his regime; they also hoped to resume some aspects of his socialist agenda.

Several of Keita's party companions had spent years in prison under Traoré's dictatorship, participated in the democratic movement that led to his overthrow, and resurrected the US-RDA party in the aftermath of the 1991 revolution. They had initially participated in Konaré's first two governments; indeed, they had supported Konaré's candidacy during Mali's first democratic presidential elections against a candidate fielded by dissenting forces within their own party (see De Jorio 2003). Following a brief period of participation in the government, the US-RDA leadership became dissatisfied with ADEMA's growing hegemony and their exclusion from projects in which they felt very much invested (such as the rehabilitation of Keita). US-RDA leaders decided to withdraw from the government and sided with the growing antigovernment opposition in an attempt to modify the terms of the political game and to widen political participation. Keita's vision came to drive intraparty struggles but also alternative social projects (see De Jorio 2003). As the country was experiencing drastic budget cuts, the dismantling of the welfare state, financial speculations, and rising economic disparity, narratives surrounding Keita reflected searches for economic and political alternatives to the current state of affairs (De Jorio 2009).

In this divided context, the rehabilitation of Keita's legacy was bound to be difficult work, and at first state representatives hesitated to take the lead in the process. When the government finally decided to proceed with its 1995 public commemoration of Keita's death and the 1997 construction of the Modibo Keita Memorial, these heritage initiatives ultimately failed to pacify the political field and, indeed, remained sparsely attended events or incomplete initiatives. For instance, after the disputed 1997 elections that led to the reappointment of Konaré as Mali's president, divisions between ADEMA and the opposition escalated. For the remainder of Konaré's presidency, Keita's family and the US-RDA leadership boycotted official state celebrations commemorating Keita's death as a critique of Konaré's presidency and the political hegemony of ADEMA. From 1995 onward, the state commemorated Keita each year in a brief flower-laying ceremony at Hamdallaye Cemetery at 10 A.M. on the anniversary of his death but with none of his colleagues or family members in sight.

By contrast, the US-RDA, aided by other forces of the opposition, instituted its own, more elaborate commemoration of Keita. On the anniversary of his death (May 16), the US-RDA and Keita's family organized their own daylong celebration that began with the reading of the Quran at his family compound early in the morning, followed by a funeral march to his grave in the afternoon. The parallel ceremonies by the state and the opposition both reflected and further articulated the fragmentation of the political field during Konaré's second term.

Such struggles over Keita's legacy had direct ramifications on the success of another, much more important government initiative: the Modibo Keita Memorial conceived as a cultural center for the study of Mali's First Republic and Keita's historical legacy (figure 3). The center, a major component of Konaré's plans to renovate and modernize Mali's capital, was completed in

**FIGURE 3.** Modibo Keita's statue, Modibo Keita Memorial, Bamako, Mali, 2005. Photo by the author.

1997 in only six months. The Chinese government largely funded the memorial in return for a trade agreement that lowered duties on imported Chinese commodities; the North Korean government also contributed by donating the statue of Keita for the memorial. The Malian state provided labor for the execution of the project. US-RDA members were initially under the impression that they would have some involvement in the administration of the memorial, in consideration of their personal experiences and knowledge of the period.

Although the memorial was completed in 1997, Konaré waited two years to inaugurate it in the hope of improving relations with the opposition. By the time of the inauguration on 6 June 1999, however, relations had not improved; indeed, the inauguration became a new point of contention between the government and the opposition. US-RDA leadership protested that several of its members had not been invited to the ceremony and responded to this slight by asking party members to participate "en masse" to oppose their exclusion. Things did not improve after the inauguration either as Keita's comrades were not given any formal role in the running of the institution.

Once more denouncing ADEMA's exclusionary practices, the US-RDA leaders refused to donate to the memorial their personal collections of documents from the first Malian republic. These historical records, which could not be found anywhere else, had been jealously preserved by US-RDA members who had managed to hide away party documents despite the arrests, incriminations, state violence, and army's destruction of documents in the wake of the 1968 coup d'état.

Given these fractures in the political-social fabric and limits on access to Keita-specific historical documents, proponents of the memorial were forced to redesign its mission. It was still an institution for the commemoration of Keita and his generation, but the research component was broadened to encompass the study of Mali's postcolonial history. The lack of overlapping perspectives on key aspects of Keita's commemoration (e.g., how it should be done, who should be in charge, who was the target audience) compromised the publicly stated goal of deepening the collective knowledge of Mali's recent history in order to learn from past mistakes.

As a result of these struggles, ADEMA resurrected an aspect of the one-party state: its autocratic face.[17] Malian cultural politics, particularly the construction of monuments commemorating the past, to a large extent became characterized by top-down initiatives.[18] Despite the narrative of inclusivity, the articulation and expansion of the hero narrative came to express divisions, political uncertainty, and the inability to realize effective forms of national reconciliation. By the end of Konaré's second term, there was uncertainty among representatives of the Ministry of Culture as to whether any of his "public work" would survive.[19]

## The Politics of Consensus and Reconciliation under Touré

Touré, who succeeded Konaré in 2002, inherited a divided political climate characterized by the overwhelming power of ADEMA as the majority party, the alienation of the opposition, the unequal distribution of state resources, and the often petty rivalries among members of the political elites. During his presidential campaign, Touré had openly addressed the divisiveness of the political field, presenting himself as the way out of Mali's growing political fragmentation. He was not connected to any specific party and thus was removed from the structures and institutions that had lost citizens' confidence due to politicians' opportunistic behaviors (notably, their frequent changes in party affiliations and political alliances). He was an independent candidate, although supported by a coalition of parties called Le Mouvement citoyen

(Citizens' Movement) (MC).[20] Touré positioned himself as a candidate outside all parties, presenting himself as willing to work with a variety of political entities and representatives of civil society on a common project of economic and political development (Chauzal 2011: 380, 383).

During the 1991 revolution, Touré, then a high-ranking army officer, had arrested Traoré to avoid further bloodshed and put an end to his twenty-three-year-long military regime. In the aftermath of the 1991 coup, Touré led the Transitional Committee for the Welfare of the People and withdrew from the political scene once Mali's first free elections—elections in which he did not participate—were completed, resulting in the election of Konaré as president. During the 1990s Touré took on various humanitarian functions, which included founding an organization for children's welfare and working as a United Nations special envoy to the Central African Republic. He was generally well regarded in national and international milieus and enjoyed great popularity in 2002 when he was elected president.

Once in power, Touré worked to pacify Mali's contentious political field. Drawing inspiration from Konaré's Republican Pact, Touré developed a model of democracy that he identified as particularly suited to the specificities of the African context. He called it a democracy of consensus based on "a consensual management of power" (Touré 2011). Years earlier, in a 1994 interview, Touré had criticized the African political leaders' uncritical adoption of Western democracy, later clarifying that "the confrontational character" of Western democracies was not a good fit for the African context, which was marked by a far greater degree of social heterogeneity (2011). Ideological confrontations in Africa, he warned, could easily degenerate into "confrontation between ethnic groups, regions, communities, with very dangerous consequences" (2011). His conception of democracy combined Western-derived liberal ideas and place-specific (albeit shifting) values—in particular, the belief that "we Africans, we seek consensus, we love mediations, we love to pass by the intermediation of another person" (2011). Based on these foundations, Touré declared his intention to work with "Mali's political class" around common objectives, proposing to take into account the country's cultural specificities but also democratic principles.

Touré's democracy of consensus was particularly well suited to the political context that emerged after the 2002 legislative elections, which did not result in a definite majority for any party. The votes were distributed among a number of parties as well as several independent candidates who had followed the seemingly successful formula of an independent president (Chauzal 2011: 390). The results of the legislative elections were read by Mali's political class as a further sign that the electorate was tired of party squabbles and supported the appointment of a broader spectrum of forces to the government (Chauzal 2011). From then on Touré worked to broaden Mali's coalition governments by including a wide range of political parties and independents.

The democracy of consensus diversified but also neutralized potentially contrasting political or social blocks. Touré and his political allies endeavored to contain the power of political parties and their representatives by inserting a growing number of independents, civil servants, and high-ranking army officers in the government (Chauzal 2011). Touré's goal was to create what he called "points of equilibrium that allowed each [entity] to play its role" (Touré 2011). During his ten years as president, Touré continued to work with heterogeneous forces (parties, independents, and army officials) and forged alliances between unlikely candidates in an effort to secure broad support around his presidency.

## State Commemorations under Touré

Touré and his political allies continued many of the new state rituals established by Konaré and maintained some of Konaré's previous commitments, such as Mali's participation in the 2003 Smithsonian Folklife Festival in Washington, D.C. (Barry 2004; Arnoldi 2012; see also Straker 2008). Touré put greater emphasis on rituals that promoted "national reconciliation" and reinforced his idea of a "democracy of consensus" that supposedly built on African traditions. One of his first actions, which he repeated at intervals throughout his presidency, was the orchestration of state rituals to celebrate the reunification of divided segments of Malian society and, in particular, to mend interparty divisions.[21] In the process, Touré further presented himself as an arbiter of Malian politics and a person above partisan fights, thus foregrounding his individual role in maintaining stability and peace, by capitalizing on—and further expanding—the reputation he had acquired in 1991.

Touré orchestrated the reconciliation between the state and the remaining representatives of the US-RDA (as representatives of Mali's First Republic). In particular, he sought to make the commemoration of Keita's death a more inclusive national celebration, one in which all political forces could come together to remember the nation's father. Following Touré's election, Keita's family and political comrades began attending the short flower-laying ceremony the state organized. The US-RDA has also maintained its daylong celebration, but the event has lost its oppositional character.

Touré was also behind the reunification of the US-RDA party, which had been weakened by more than a decade of internal fighting that resulted in the departure of dissidents who then formed new parties (Ouologuem 2010). On the fiftieth anniversary of Mali's independence, Touré orchestrated a ceremony that sanctioned both the return of dissidents to the US-RDA and the party's reconstitution as a greater "umbrella" party under a slightly modified name, L'Union malienne du rassemblement démocratique africain/faso jigi (Malian Union of the African Democratic Rally) (UM-RDA faso jigi). The celebration of more harmonious relationships between the US-RDA and the state, as well as reassertion of the US-RDA's party unity, was a further manifestation of Touré's reliance on public reconciliation rituals.

In his government, Touré included representatives from the first two major parties of Mali's modern history: the US-RDA and the PSP. The PSP had formally fused into the US-RDA around independence. The one-party-state model was then identified as the most suited political configuration to face the multiple challenges of the postindependence. Divergences from official US-RDA party lines were firmly repressed. When former PSP leaders had protested against the socialist economic policies of Keita's government, they had been incarcerated and ultimately killed in circumstances still not fully clarified. During the fiftieth anniversary of Mali's independence, Touré and his political allies orchestrated a peace ceremony between the PSP and the US-RDA/UM-RDA—Mali's oldest two parties and longtime rivals—to allegedly heal some of the still-open wounds.

The commemoration of the nation's heroes, the promotion of peace ceremonies between divided political forces, and the reunification of parties were avenues through which Touré and his political allies presented the objective of national reconciliation. Meanwhile, segments of the media and citizenry that were more critical of Touré's presidency started to take issue with his democracy of reconciliation and its selective recovery of the past. They began to weave a critical counternarrative that emphasized the emptiness of fake reconciliations in the absence of any serious historical clarification.

## Touré's Take on the Hero Narrative

In the process of articulating his narrative of reconciliation, Touré and his collaborators developed a narrative that foregrounded his historical agency—including the reassessment of his place among the nation's past and recent heroes—according to modalities from which Konaré had distanced himself. In an attempt during his electoral campaigns to leverage personally Keita's symbolic and historical capital, Touré had already presented himself as Keita's logical descendant and emphasized their similar roles in freeing their country from oppressive rule (Bussi, Lima, and Vigneron 2009).

Over the years, both Touré himself and representatives of the progovernment media continued to draw important connections between Touré and Mali's first president. Touré was presented as Keita's heir, "a spiritual son."

For instance, during the peace ceremony between the PSP and the US-RDA, Touré announced, "I am the child of the PSP and the US-RDA. . . . I was a young pioneer [socialist youth brigade] of the US-RDA" (A. Diakité 2010). He claimed connections to the PSP via kin relations on his mother's side, and recognized the US-RDA party's role in making "modern" education available to his generation, further highlighting his multiple filiations and his "above party lines" position.[22]

Touré's rituals of reconciliation and his vision of Mali as a democracy of consensus had clear political ramifications. Representatives of the PSP and the US-RDA were given important political appointments under his presidency. As an example, Oumar Hamadoun Dicko, president of an offshoot of the old PSP party, that is, Le Parti pour la solidarité et le progrès (Party for Solidarity and Progress, or PSP),[23] was first given a post as Minister of Malians Abroad and African Integration, then nominated as president of the committee in charge of organizing the fiftieth anniversary celebrations of Mali's independence in 2010. To complete the government reshuffle, Badra Aliou Macalou of the US-RDA was given Dicko's cabinet post. The politics of consensus translated into the co-optation of the political elites who were given positions in the government or administration and thus silenced (Baudais and Chauzal 2006).

In 2007 a pro-Touré party (known for its unconditional support of the president's politics of reconciliation), Le Front africain pour la mobilisation et l'alternance (African Front for Mobilization and Change) (FAMA), organized a public conference to celebrate Touré's reelection as president. In the course of the conference, which was suggestively titled "Modibo Keita and ATT: A Pan-African Vision," speakers commented on the human qualities of modesty and humility that Keita and Touré supposedly shared and pointed out similarities in the two men's political visions—in particular, their staunch support of pan-Africanism (Modibo Fofana 2010; F. Coulibaly 2010). They also made reference to a meeting that supposedly took place between Keita and Touré while Keita was in detention, thus highlighting the two men's immediate personal connection and mutual respect (Modibo Fofana 2010). In addition to reintroducing the celebratory tones from which Konaré had sought to distance himself during his mandate, such narratives of spiritual filiation further articulated Touré's projects of creating a culture of consensus and reconciliation to counter the fragmentation and proliferation of political parties. These narratives also contributed to a further personalization of the presidency, the magnification of his family name, and the presentation of public work (e.g., the construction of low-income housing) as presidential gifts to his people—all echoes of the techniques of power deployed by the political class during the one-party era (Amadou Beidy Sow, pers. comm., June 2012).

## The Return of the Griots

Touré's democracy of consensus is widely believed to have progressively quieted all political opposition (see Wing 2013). During this time, old forms of political flattery by Mali's so-called traditionists—the griots, or jeliw—were resurrected to the point that some local observers had begun to talk of Touré's presidency as the time of the griots' return (RFI 2012). The reliance on oral literature, the monopoly of the griots, or jeliw, for purposes of political legitimization is a well-studied trend in Mali's postcolonial politics.[24] Konaré had attempted to create some distance from the griots and their flatteries, but Touré's government mobilized forms from Mali's ancient past in order to anchor and justify present political choices. The deployment of Malian oral literature to legitimize Touré's presidency ultimately created a political culture that did not openly reject but did deemphasize the articulation of rational-critical perspectives vis-à-vis collective issues. One of the many instances in which this aspect of Touré's presidency is evident is the elaborate celebration his government orchestrated in 2010 for the fiftieth anniversary of Malian independence.

Touré's government scheduled a series of commemorations at Kurukan Fuga, a plain near the town of Kangaba in the Koulikoro region and a place of symbolic significance in recent intensely political reconstructions of the history of Mali's medieval empire (Amselle 2006; Smith 2007, 2009). According to this reimagined tradition, Sunjata Keita, the first emperor of the Mali Empire, in the thirteenth century, gathered his allies and issued a charter enumerating the principles guiding the lives of the diverse populations of his vast empire.[25] Some describe the charter as foreshadowing elements of Mali's recent political transformations, such as the advent of democracy—because of the charter's emphasis on peace and consensus-reaching efforts—and the decentralization of state institutions—because of the charter's alleged emphasis on unity in respect of differences. The celebrations at Kurukan Fuga iterated the message that neither of these transformations were new political constructs but had origins in Mali's illustrious past (Bagayogo 1987, 1992; Amselle 2006).

The 2010 visit of Touré and his entourage to Kurukan Fuga was the occasion for elaborate performances by representatives of the griots of the renowned griot school at Kela. The jeliw heaped most of their praises on Lobo Traoré, Touré's wife and a descendant of Tiramakan Traoré, one of Sunjata's most renowned warriors. The focus on Lobo Traoré ultimately gave prestige to the president for his association with a woman with such a reputable and noble family history. The griots also recognized Touré for his relentless work for the nation: "Amadou Toumani, we know why you are not sleeping; it is because of your hard work."[26] They praised Amadou Toumani Touré's family, the Touré, for their contributions as a marabout family, a family of Muslim teachers and leaders in the religious domain. Finally, the griots dedicated to Touré the *janjo*, a special song associated with Sunjata Keita, to celebrate the similarities in both men's qualities (and, in particular, their common bravery) and noteworthy initiatives for the well-being of the larger society.[27] Such practices constitute important ways by which the democratic present is seen as a continuation or transformation of Mali's foundational period—that is, the Mali empire from which aspects of the present political order are said to derive.

Touré thus drew from both Mali's recent and precolonial histories to create an arsenal of state rituals celebrating his role as mediator and pacifier of Mali's political field. In the process he maintained many of the state ceremonials developed during Konaré's presidency but also resurrected modalities of recollection and commemoration of the past that were popular during the one-party era. In particular, Touré and his political allies resurrected the tendency to personalize power, accompanied by a great emphasis on individual standing, family history, and patronage networks as crucial to the maintenance of the political order.

## The Countermemory Narrative of the Opposition

During Touré's presidency, particularly during his second mandate, the political opposition was almost nonexistent. One of the few parties that still played some opposition role was La Solidarité africaine pour la démocratie et l'indépendance (African Solidarity for Democracy and Independence) (SADI), whose vocal secretary general, Oumar Mariko, was a former leader of the student movement and an instrumental figure in the students' struggles that brought down Traore's military regime in 1991. In developing his political persona, Mariko has promoted a noticeably different version of Modibo Keita's legacy. According to Mariko, who has presented himself as the true heir of Mali's socialist tradition, both Konaré and Touré failed to realize the objectives and hopes of the 1991 "revolution" (Mariko 2010; B. Segbedji 2010). Mariko believes that the only period of Mali's postindependence history to warrant appreciation is the time of Modibo Keita and the US-RDA (A. Koné 2009; Mariko 2010). Since the military coup in 1968, he has suggested the "political discourse" of Mali's leadership "is at odds with President

Modibo Keita's vision, his social project, his commitment" (Mariko 2010). Mariko has continued to say that Keita, the US-RDA, and other "patriots" fought for Mali's independence in the hope of building a socialist society and laying the foundations for greater cooperation across the continent (pan-Africanism) and that SADI is the only party that can continue the US-RDA's legacy (Mariko 2010). Similarly, SADI's president, Cheick Oumar Sissoko, commented, "Our party's goal remains the recovery of the historical march of our people, by drawing lessons from the path already mapped out by our illustrious predecessors of the US-RDA, the late President Modibo Keita, and his brave comrades in struggle" (C. O. Sissoko 2010). For Mariko, SADI and his leadership have a "generational duty" to accomplish and redirect Mali's political course toward a socialist goal (Mariko 2010).

Parallel to his rereading of Keita's legacy and his self-fashioning as the most suitable candidate to represent that legacy, Mariko has also mobilized his ties to the student movement and revived his survivor narrative (previously deployed by the US-RDA leadership during Konaré's presidency), this time applied to the 1991 revolution. Mariko has condemned the state representations of the "1991 events" under Touré, which he prefers to call the "1991 Revolution" (Mariko 2010). The main point of contention here is over who (and what groups) brought down Traoré's dictatorship and made possible Mali's democratic turn: was it Touré, the representative of a dissident group within the Malian army, or Mariko, the leader of the student movement?

For example, during a 2011 conference-debate titled "March 26, 1991," Mariko discussed the trajectory that led Mali to the democratic turn of 1991. Offering a personal anecdote to corroborate his survivor narrative, he introduced Fatoumata Koné, a woman he called "the symbol of Mali's repression in March 1991" (Mariko 2011). He had first met her in 1991, a few hours prior to the military attack in which she lost a foot and the use of a leg. It was students like Koné and their personal sacrifices that made possible Mali's move to democracy, he suggested, because they reenergized the resistance movement in 1990 and were soon followed by women's groups as well as democratic organizations representing other segments of society (such as the professional urban class). The students' refusal (again) to compromise with the dictatorship precipitated the events that led to the ousting of Traoré.

Referring implicitly to Touré's version of the events, Mariko declared that March 1991 was the outcome of a "process" and "not a last-minute plot" (or military coup), as some would have it (Mariko 2011). His recollection of student mobilization against the dictatorship dated to 1980 when, as a high school student, he and other students participated in a number of strikes against the dictatorship, resulting in the military regime's decision to shut down all schools for two consecutive years. Students paid dearly for their

FIGURE 4. Statue of Abdoul "Cabral" Karim Camara (1955–80), in a square named after him in Bamako, 2008. Courtesy of R. Gaudin.

political participation; several lost their lives. One famous example of student sacrifice is Camara, the leader of the student movement, whom the Malian army ultimately killed in March 1980 during a time of intense confrontations between the students and the state. Other students also lost their lives in less-chronicled struggles against the dictatorship.

Building on this survivor discourse, Mariko has attacked the Third Republic (and Touré) for minimizing the role that student protest played in the overthrow of Traoré. Mariko has also denounced the removal of a portrait of Cabral and him from the walls surrounding one of Mali's new monuments, the Pyramide du souvenir (Pyramid of Memory), which in Mariko's mind symbolizes the political erasure of the youth from the official memory of the 1991 events (I. F. Sissoko 2010.). The portraits of Konaré and Touré remain, Mariko has pointed out, leaving Touré alone to symbolize the revolution of March 1991 (Mariko 2010). Mariko has repeatedly contested state interpretations of Keita's legacy and the erasure of students' history from public monuments and state discourse (I. F. Sissoko 2010).

In the process of articulating a countermemory,[28] SADI's leadership also has endeavored to construct its own public rituals to acknowledge and validate students' sacrifices for Mali's political progress. For example, the yearly commemoration of Camara's death takes place by the monument erected in his memory in 1996 and has acquired particular relevance in this process (figure 4). Mariko's re-reading of the hero narrative emphasizes his critical view of capitalism, his socialist project, and his critique of the democratic leadership, meanwhile staking his claim that the time has come for the generation he represents to take on the country's leadership and lead the country in a new direction.

## Unfinished Business

The commemoration of the heroes of the 1991 revolution came to constitute a new site of public debate and political confrontation (although less openly than during Konaré's decade). In such discursive contexts, the state, even under Touré, reclaimed a more rational, modernist stance vis-à-vis the past, revisiting rhetorical strategies already employed by Konaré during his tenure but reapprehended within the overarching frame of reconciliation.[29] State narratives criticized the mobilization of memory for particular political claims. For instance, on 26 March 2011, during the annual state commemoration of the martyrs of the 1991 revolution (the laying of flowers in front of the Monument aux Martyrs du 22 mars 1991), Touré declared, "26 March is not anyone's monopoly but a national heritage" (D. Koné 2011).

In this highly symbolic context, Touré reiterated his intention to proceed toward a more comprehensive national reconciliation, one significantly advanced by a full reconciliation of the Malian people with Traoré, whom Konaré had freed after his election as president. The fact that Malians have already accepted the presence of high cadres of Traoré's regime in various administrative and political posts today is a sign, according to Touré, of Malians' ability "to overcome themselves [and to manifest] solidarity" (D. Koné 2011). Touré had invited Traoré to attend the parades on Independence Day, the climax of the celebrations of Mali's cinquantenaire (fiftieth anniversary) on 22 September 2010. On the eve of the event, however, several commentators argued that reconciliation between Traoré and the Malian people should not occur in the absence of his public repentance. More than once he had been asked to contribute to the clarification of past horrors, but he had refused to participate in any such efforts. Ultimately, Traoré did not participate in the Independence Day ceremony, and neither did Konaré, who apparently questioned Touré's decision to invite the former dictator (e.g., Mamadou Fofana 2010). The Malian public remained divided on the appropriateness of Traoré's presence on the official podium, with some citizens further removed from the machinations and games of the country's politicians.[30]

In opposition to the distance and conciliatory rhetoric of state memory is the survivor narrative of the martyrs' families and political comrades. At yearly commemorations of the martyrs' deaths, the wounds are reopened; requests for further information about their deaths (requests that, sadly, go unanswered) are recorded by the press. These rhetorical confrontations are restaged at the commemorations of the deaths of all of the heroes mentioned in this chapter: Modibo Keita, Fily Dabo Sissoko, and Abdoul "Cabral" Karim Camara. Although no one doubts that these men were killed by the two previous regimes, the specifics of their deaths—that is, the circumstances of their deaths, the identities of their killers, and (for all but Keita) even the locations of their remains—are still unknown or highly disputed. Commenting on the emptiness of such efforts, more than one observer has invoked the South African Truth and Reconciliation Commission as a model for a more satisfactory resolution of societal conflicts. Some critics of Touré's democracy of consensus (e.g., Mariko and his political allies) have requested greater clarification of the historical past in order to engage in more genuine and long-standing forms of reconciliation.

The lack of recognition given to the "emotionality of memory" and the absence of any integration of more personal memories remain obstacles to the development of meaningful forms of public commemoration (White 2006). The reopening of past wounds is also a dramatic occasion for the political opposition and for segments of the general population to articulate their counterpolitical projects. For these groups, the revival of past injustices is an opportunity to denounce the continuities of the past in the present and to mobilize new energies for new political and moral projects. In the process, the remembrance of Keita's presidency in opposition discourse has also changed. It now increasingly emphasizes Keita's and the US-RDA's project of national economic independence, particularly in light of the recent and much-touted "savage" liberalization of the Malian economy, which has not brought the hoped-for improvements to most Malians' lives but has instead ushered in the demise of Mali's state economy, the hegemony of foreign capital, the rise of financial speculations, and the collapse of Mali's few existing industries (e.g., the blow to agriculture through the sale of farmers' land to foreign countries, such as Libya).

In her discussion of the constitutive links among citizenship, memory, and reconciliation, Rosemary Nagy comments on the importance of "'truth' processes ... to (re)construct a shared fund of moral intuitions by reinterpreting and condemning past events" (2004: 644). Without such processes, she argues, democratic citizenship cannot be realized. The persistent replaying of past traumas and the unsolved nature of most instances of state violence can be read as signs that such moral intuitions have not become—even temporarily—shared background and thus contribute to citizens' sense of restlessness and dissatisfaction with the present forms of democracy. One can also wonder whether requests for clarification about past crimes and injustices are evidence of the freeing of memory that Konaré had anticipated in his 1991 speech—even though such freeing is, perhaps, not always fully and productively channeled, given the culture of violence that has become ubiquitous in Mali's political life (see Lange 1999: 121). It remains that such contested memories have asserted themselves as powerful and complex sites for clashes and negotiations between conflicting political and moral projects.

## Conclusions

The chapter delineates core aspects of the heritage projects promoted by the Malian state in the post-1991 era as well as the proliferation of countermemory projects by the heterogeneous political opposition. The postcolonial state has invested substantially in renovating national culture to promote democratic values anchored in a new appreciation of (some) Malian traditions, in particular, the emphases on hospitality and conviviality, peace, and consensus building. Mali's democratic heritage includes the revaluation of Mali's recent history and its main actors, the development of new state commemorations, and the visualization and display of public culture as key strategies for the consolidation of modern power. The freeing of collective memory and its critical apprehension were seen as central to the formation of democratic subjectivities—particularly, during Konaré's presidency, when the state embraced a more decidedly rational-critical perspective that invoked distance and objectivity as keys to the resolution of past conflicts. Under Touré, commemorations of the past centered more on reconciling divided segments of the citizenry via an explosion of commemorative rituals—a process that, among other effects, led to what many decry as the banalization of state power (Mbembe 2001; Le Sphinx 2006, 2007).

Partly in response to these state practices, the political opposition deployed sensibly different counterdiscourses, particularly as seen in the articulation of their survival narratives. Under Konaré, one segment of the opposition emphasized its close adherence to Keita's "true" message, which was embedded within a survivor's narrative and thus highlighted the sacrifices endured by his political allies and family members for the Malian nation. On these foundations, the political opposition articulated its right to represent Keita's legacy in the present. Under Touré, fewer individuals and groups publicly objected to the state appropriation of Keita's legacy (and when they did, as in

SADI's case, they focused on the importance of Keita's program of economic development and did not deploy, also because of generational distance, a survivor narrative), thus further reflecting the co-optation of the political class under Touré and the containment of public debates in which the democracy of consensus had ultimately resulted. At the same time, however, opposition members also increasingly questioned Touré's historical significance in the 1991 revolution, from which Touré garnered so much of his national and international prestige. In response to what was perceived as Touré's inaccurate or opportunistic representations of the past, some opposition leaders (e.g., representatives of SADI) rearticulated a survivor narrative, this time emphasizing their personal sacrifices for the advent of democracy. In this discursive context, they questioned Touré's reconciliation efforts in the absence of any commitment to achieve clarification of some of the violence of the past. By the end of Touré's mandate, heritage initiatives and public debates on heritage matters increasingly reflected people's dissatisfaction with twenty years of democracy and its limited results (see also epilogue, current volume). The coup d'état of March 2012, from which Mali is presently slowly rebuilding, brought sudden international attention to the limits and contradictions of Malian democracy, which had, with a few exceptions, been undetected or unreported by the international media.

## 2. Remembering the Colonial Past

IN JANUARY 2009, just before the start of the fifth Festival sur le Niger (whose attendees were mostly Western tourists), the statue of French colonial officer Louis Archinard was reinstalled near the Niger River in Ségou, based on a unilateral decision by the region's governor, Abou Sow (figure 5). The reinstallation was critically reviewed by the Malian press, which did not support the commemoration of Archinard, the man who led the conquest of Ségou and the surrounding region in 1890 (Samba Sow 2009). The governor's decision was not challenged, however, and in June 2014 (during my last visit to Ségou), the Archinard statue, still standing, was a recognized historic site and tourist destination.

Nearly a decade earlier, an attempt to remove the statue from its current location sparked a popular revolt in Ségou. In January 2000, President Alpha Oumar Konaré had ordered the transfer of the statue from Ségou to the national capital, Bamako, to be exhibited there. The truck sent by the presidency had arrived at the regional branch of the Office of Public Works (Travaux Publics) after rush hour, allegedly so it would not be noticed.[1] Despite such measures, the arrival of a truck from Bamako and the resulting activity surrounding the Archinard statue awakened the interest of nearby street vendors, who hurried to the statue's location. Radio Kaira, a local radio station and a forceful voice of the opposition, soon learned of Konaré's initiative and began alerting the population to what the station portrayed as a presidential scheme. People from nearby neighborhoods gathered by the entrance of the building, determined to oppose Archinard's departure from Ségou. In the days that followed, students organized a strike to protest the statue's removal, and under the approving gaze of most of the population,

**FIGURE 5.** Statue of Louis Archinard, 2014. It was relocated in 2009 by the Niger River in Ségou to valorize the area's historical past and promote it as a tourist destination. Photo by the author.

they occupied main roads, burned old tires, and surrounded the police office. Faced with such a unified opposition, Konaré abandoned the project, and the statue was left in Ségou.

Such a strong popular response to the attempted removal of the Archinard statue warrants some explanation. In the past, Ségouvians had not shown great interest in preserving the statue (or most other monuments of the colonial period). A representation of Archinard in his uniform and cane, the statue had been inaugurated in Ségou on 27 December 1933, the fiftieth anniversary of the French arrival in the Soudan and one year after Archinard's death.[2] Originally, it stood in front of the home of the *commandant de cercle* (the highest-ranking colonial official in residence) of Ségou, near the Niger River. After independence, the statue was removed from its original location:[3] in a public display of anticolonial and anti-Western sentiments, the statue was toppled, dragged behind a car, and dumped in the backyard of the Office of Public Works, where it remained until 2009 (M. O. Coulibaly 1999;[4] Samba Sow 2009). When I first visited the statue in 2001, I was surprised by the number of visitors near it—and, in particular, the children who, under the approving eyes of their fathers, were climbing on the statue or throwing the occasional stone at it. Archinard had not left positive memories among the citizenry, and such memories had oriented the symbolic disposal of his statue (as well as the mode of its preservation) after independence (Simonis 1994; Samba Sow 2009).

The struggle over the preservation of the Archinard statue, one of the most heinous reminders of the violence of French conquest, is a complicated affair, with multiple ramifications. It shows the resurgence of the state's autocratic practices, as manifested by the executive power's single-sided decision to remove part of the city's colonial heritage (that is, the statue of Archinard) without any attempt to properly inform or publicly discuss this (presidential) decision prior to its execution. It also clearly indicates some breaks with the past in the increasing role that multiparty politics came to play on heritage work, particularly during the Konaré's administration.

Furthermore, the state's attempted removal of the Archinard statue in 2000 unleashed memories of the colonial past that the elder generations (Nora's milieux de mémoire) had tried to suppress and silence. As Cole suggests in her study of the Betsimisaraka of Madagascar, "Historical consciousness—memory itself—is always produced by particular social practices and it is always socially occasioned" (2001: 101). State threat awakened Ségouvians' memories of past political defeats and destruction. It provided a continuous narrative plot through which to make sense of yet another episode of state violence. Indeed, people's shifting representations of the state emerge in the course of their more or less banal encounters with the state. As Sharma and Gupta remark, "States . . . are produced through everyday practices and encounters and through public cultural representations and performances" (2006: 28).

Resistance to the removal of the Archinard statue (and also critiques of the state's memorialization of the colonial past) came from the political opposition but also, more broadly, by peripheral urban groups who felt abandoned by Bamako and sidestepped by political dynamics and development initiatives. Public debates and conversations on whether to represent French colonization (and how to do so) became sites of individual and collective critical engagement with the heritage projects and memorialization of the past spearheaded by the state (and, more broadly, on the meanings of democracy and decentralization from the perspective of the city's inhabitants). The debates and conversations revealed some of Ségouvians' preoccupations with state power, dissidence, and their search for meaningful ways of representing and commemorating their past.

The 2000 incident also contributed to the development of a new interest on the part of the citizenry in reclaiming and valorizing their historical heritage, with some seeing these actions as opportunities to restore their families' past prestige and relevance (Ceuppens and Geschiere 2005; Geschiere 2009; Schulz 2007). Debates on local radio programs, in newspaper articles, and in casual conversation manifested growing attention among segments of the Ségouvian population (and not just at the government level) in preserving aspects of their heritage and realizing its potential for the city's economic development.

This chapter is divided in three parts. First, I briefly describe some of the ways in which French colonization was represented during the period of the one-party state (1960–1991), using them as a benchmark against which to gauge changes in those representations by the democratic and neoliberal state that followed. Second, I examine the state memorialization of French colonization since 1991, focusing on the Koulouba monument complex in Bamako, the largest series of monuments dedicated to Mali's colonial history. Here I detail the emergence of a new narrative of colonization that suggests contacts, hybridity (e.g., Bhabha 1994; Canclini 1995; Liebmann 2008), and cross-feeding—a representation reflecting some of the experiences and narratives of Mali's cosmopolitan political and cultural elites. Third, I analyze Ségouvian citizens' perspectives on the government's memorialization project in light of their experience with state encroachment on their city's patrimony. This final section centers on the confrontation between the state and peripheral urban communities over the management of the colonial heritage and explores some of its political and cultural implications, including the embryonic development of a few private heritage initiatives in Ségou.

## The Colonial Past in the Immediate Postindependence Period

The First Republic of Modibo Keita set the tone for the ways in which the Malian state represented the experience of colonization until 1991. Immediately after independence (1960), the First Republic of Keita tended either to glorify episodes of resistance by the Malian people or to deemphasize the impact of colonization (Snyder 1967: 84). Colonization was often represented as a historical accident (Cutter 1968). Other representations emphasized local resistance to colonization, as in the 1965 play *The Lesson of the Past*, performed by the Regional Art Company of Sikasso—which, according to Sada Sissoko, was one of the best performances ever presented at the youth and sport festivals known then as Les Semaines nationales de la jeunesse (1995: 30). The primary focus was on nation building, for which the precolonial past was a continuous source of inspiration. As Schulz observes, "Although the regimes of Keita and of Moussa Traoré founded their rule on institutions and principles modeled after a Western system of representation, the political leaders were anxious to endow themselves with the symbols of traditional rule" (1997: 456).

In contrast to Senegal, where major French colonial monuments were preserved as an integral but not uncontested part of the national patrimony, Malians removed the most obvious markers of the colonial presence, such as statues of explorers and conquerors (McLaughlin n.d.). The project was not carried out comprehensively, however, and most monuments were dismantled and abandoned on the grounds of governmental buildings or in the storage facilities of the presidential palace. Several geographical locations, such as neighborhoods, roads, and squares, were renamed (Y. Coulibaly 2001), and administrative boundaries were redefined, as marked by the dissolution of the chefferies de canton and the constitution of new administrative territorial units, the *arrondissements* (Meillassoux 1970: 107). In the process, family histories of betrayals and alliances with the colonizers were temporarily put to rest, only to resurface in moments of political crisis (such as during the post-1991 electoral campaigns). The removal of colonial monuments, a process that characterized the aftermath of independence, was completed during the Active Revolution (1967-68), whose excesses contributed to the end of the First Republic in 1968.

A few colonial monuments remained. For example, the monument commemorating Sudanese soldiers' sacrifice during the world wars was left partly because it was reinterpreted to signify local resistance to colonization; to many Bamako city dwellers, the Archinard statue portrays Samory's army and its fierce struggle against French invaders (A. Diallo 1993; Klimkeit 1997; Arnoldi 2003; Mann 2005). Another colonial vestige, the Gallieni Monument—a monument erected in Ségou in 1926 in memory of Joseph Gallieni, an architect of French conquest—was not destroyed either, probably because it lacked distinctive features (it was a column with a dedication plaque). It was rededicated twice: in 1962 to the memory of Patrice Lumumba (a symbol of anticolonial struggle) and then again during Konaré's presidency to the martyrs of the 1991 revolution (to commemorate their sacrifice for the construction of a democratic Mali) (M. B. Keita n.d.). Also, most colonial buildings (houses and public buildings), which were erected in the neo-Sudanese style, became the residences or the workplaces of the Malian bureaucracy, thus providing continuity to the geography of power after independence.

## Representing French Colonization in Democratic Mali

Konaré's cultural politics sought to break with the destructive logic and the anti-memory work of the one-party state and to create "a national harmony, to fill the cracks of a broken memory" (P. B. Couloubaly, interview with author, 7 December 2004). The new state memory discourse introduced new interpretive paradigms—new ways of conceptualizing the past—to acknowledge traumatic episodes of Malian history but also to claim the heterogeneity of historical roots as a constitutive trait of the Malian nation.

The most impressive material expression informed in part by this new vision of the colonial past, which claims French colonization as a key component of national patrimony and questions easy dichotomies between the colonized and colonizer, tradition and modernity, is the Koulouba monument complex. The monuments gathered here and the criteria behind their display invite multiple readings of core episodes of the Malian past. In particular, they suggest unprecedented ways of coming to terms with the traumatic collective experiences of French colonization. Parallel to the contrasting themes of national identity building as antithesis to a period of domination and belittlement and as colonial nostalgia lies evidence of a postmodern claim to hybridity, which "foregrounds the issues of power and inequality inherent in colonial societies, highlighting the empowering nature of hybrid forms that often make space for anticolonial resistance through the challenging of binary categories" (Liebmann 2008: 83). The hybridity narrative challenges simple and often limiting oppositions (such as the one between tradition and modernity) and creates new opportunities for experiments in identity, space, and history for contemporary Malian citizens.[5] Mali's history of intersections with France is increasingly apprehended by Mali's political elites within a broader historical narrative that emphasizes the sudden and unexpected turns of history by which people alternatively experience periods of freedom and periods of conquest. Within this framework, French colonization is boldly claimed as an intrinsic part of Mali's postcolonial history.[6]

The Koulouba monument complex is situated on the top of Koulouba Hill, where the presidential palace (the former residence of the colonial governors of French Soudan), a few administrative buildings, and a school stand. The hill is a scarcely populated and relatively remote area of Bamako. With the exception of people who work or attend school there, most of the city's residents are unlikely to have seen these monuments, although over time they seem to have become more known, at least among the educated population. Because of their location, their intended audiences are local or foreign delegations visiting the presidential palace. They provide visitors with a comprehensive view of Mali's history, including some of its most recent political achievements, as indicated by the significantly titled monument Le Mali Nouveau (the New Mali), which consists of a map of Mali's new administrative structure since the implementation of the program aimed at decentralizing state institutions—one of the most important political results of Malian democracy (Amselle 2006).

Most of the monuments on Koulouba Hill represent old and new political leaders; some include maps, flags (the Square of Nations), historical scenes, and traditional symbols that have acquired a national character (Klimkeit 1997). Most of the monuments seem to connote power—which reinforces an already popular association, as this location is commonly known as "the hill of power." The hill features a few references to both old and new symbols of power, such as a *bâton de commandement* (baton of command) that stands in the middle of the traffic circle in front of the presidential gate (Barry 2004: 187), and a statue dedicated to the importance of literacy, represented by a girl and a boy reading books (a reference to the importance of formal education for the development of an informed citizenry and for the exercise of modern power) (figure 6).[7] Most of the new monuments are built in the socialist-realist style and are made of cement and marble (Arnoldi 2003). A few are influenced by the neo-Sudanese style (a mixture of Western, Moroccan, and western Sudanese styles). These include the baton de commandement; the Koulouba door (through which one must pass in order to reach the presidential palace); four *ciwara* (stylized representations of antelopes) depicting a male, a female, and two calves and symbolizing dedication and hard work (figure 7);[8] and some of the murals.

The design and location of the Koulouba monument complex were not chosen arbitrarily. Most of the monuments representing French colonization are located there, and they disclose more than one reading of colonization, as I learned in the course of my conversations with some of the state actors behind the development of this complex as well as thorough analysis of media coverage and work by Malian scholars on the new monuments. These monuments provide examples for each of the three narratives mentioned earlier: the anticolonial stance, colonial nostalgia, and the hybridity narrative that claims colonization as an integral part of Mali's history.[9]

**FIGURE 6.** Statue of Literacy, Place des explorateurs, Koulouba, Bamako, 2003. Photo by the author.

**FIGURE 7.** Statue of Ciwaras, Place des explorateurs, Koulouba, Bamako, 2003. Photo by the author.

FIGURE 8. La Place des Cités et Villes Martyres (the Square of Mali's Martyred Cities and Towns), comprising two cement structures: a large colored map of Mali and a plaque listing various towns and cities and the date of the French colonial army conquest. Koulouba, Bamako, 2003. Photo by the author.

The anticolonial stance emphasizing the violence and devastation brought about by the French is distinctively represented in La Place des Cités et Villes Martyres (the Square of Martyred Towns and Cities) (figure 8), which is almost entirely occupied by two cement structures: a large colored map of Mali and a plaque specifying the dates on which the French colonial army conquered certain towns and cities (e.g., Ségou, 6 April 1890). Projecting contemporary national boundaries back in time, the map shows the complex geography of Mali before colonization (with varieties of centers ranging from villages to cities). As its title suggests, this monument is a tribute to the suffering the Malian people endured during the conquest period, although the mention of martyrdom suggests that their sacrifice was not in vain and that they have, indeed, contributed to the emergence of the independent nation of Mali. A more recent analogue is the Monument to the Martyrs of 1991 in downtown Bamako, which honors Malians who sacrificed their lives to overthrow Moussa Traoré's dictatorship and put Mali on the path to democracy

*Remembering the Colonial Past*

(Arnoldi 2003). This is the only Koulouba monument that unambiguously portrays the horrors of colonization, and it is a permanent reminder of the suffering the local populations endured under French rule.

Other monuments pay tribute to Malians' anticolonial struggle but also present a few heterogeneous elements. For instance, the History Wall (Les Fresques Murales de Koulouba), the murals analyzed in depth by Arnoldi (2003), represents some of the most celebrated heroes of the resistance to French conquest, including Almami Samori Touré, "the most difficult opponent the French faced in Africa" (Klein 1998: 52), and al-Hajj Oumar Tall, who built a powerful theocratic state in the region at the end of the nineteenth century. The History Wall also includes portraits of major figures of the French colonization of the French Soudan (present-day Mali), such as Gustave Borgnis-Desbordes and Louis Faidherbe, and scenes from the colonial conquest. The series of murals ends with two panels portraying two of the most iconic leaders of the anticolonial struggle and the first postindependence period: Aoua Keita,[10] the first woman deputy of Mali, and Mali's first president, Modibo Keita. The representational style of these scenes is generally homogeneous, with both indigenous and foreign chiefs represented in equally dignified ways.

Historical themes from Mali's rich history provide the organizational scheme for other clusters of monuments. Such is the case of La Place des Explorateurs (the Explorers' Square), which combines precolonial, colonial, and postcolonial themes. This is a heterogeneous square that includes bronze busts of renowned nineteenth-century explorers, such as Alexander Gordon Laing and René Caillé, who epitomize Western fascination for Timbuktu, the mysterious city. Also included are busts of Eugène Mage and Pierre Soleillet, who both visited Ségou during its rule by the Toucouleur invaders (De Benoist 1989).[11] All of these explorers left behind memoirs and reports of their travels, writings that constitute important references in the study of precolonial history and the initial phases of French conquest. Added to this cluster of monuments is the towering statue of Borgnis-Desbordes, guarding an entrance to La Place des Explorateurs (figure 9).

The redisplay of some of the colonial statues that were removed in the aftermath of independence from French rule was without doubt a highly contested aspect of Konaré's initiative. The reinstallation of the statue of Borgnis-Desbordes (a French military officer known for his brutal methods of conquest and proponent of harsh strategies of colonial rule), in particular, has not been fully embraced by some Malian observers and has been the object of severe critiques from the political opposition, which accused Konaré of expressing the resurrection of the assimilation dream (a powerful strategy of

FIGURE 9. Statue of Gustave Borgnis-Desbordes, built during the colonial area and relocated in 2000 to Explorers' Square. Koulouba, Bamako, 2003. Photo by the author.

French colonial domination). This perspective found vocal expression in the work of Malian writer Doumbi-Fakoly, who criticized Konaré for his "admiration . . . for colonial France" and deemed the display of statues, such as the one of Borgnis-Desbordes, "a permanent insult to the memory of African resistance fighters [and] . . . a major shame for Mali" (2002: 111–12; see also Barry 2004: 36). Also opposed to the display of these French colonization vestiges were the few surviving women and men who had actually experienced French colonization, who could not easily disassociate such statues from the historical conditions in which they were created and displayed (see also Stoller 1995: 31). More than one elder I interviewed suggested radical ways to dispose of these monuments, which were originally built in order to glorify French colonization.

Less problematic for Malian observers is the representation of the colonial period via newly constructed monuments, as in the case of Governors' Square, for which—unexpectedly—I could not collect or find any critical assessment (figure 10). Located behind the National Archives (the main depository of colonial documents), Governors' Square is dedicated to the memory of the French governors who ruled the French Soudan from 1880 to 1960. Each governor (or lieutenant governor) is represented by a white-

**FIGURE 10.** Governors' Square, Koulouba, Bamako, 2008. Courtesy of R. Gaudin.

marble column, decorated with a medallion representing his portrait and a plaque specifying the length of his service in the country. The columns are arranged in chronological order in a semicircle oriented toward the center of the square, where an octagonal enclosure carries the inscription "La Place des Gouverneurs."[12] A similar row of monuments honors the presidents.[13] Although the two series of monuments are physically separated (the presidents' columns are located on the sides of the New Mali's Square farther away from the presidential palace), the representational choices—white columns, each with a portrait and a plaque—are exactly the same, although the presidents' columns are slightly larger. Both the style and the chronological organization create the impression of continuity between the two series.

The Koulouba monument complex is an eclectic, postmodern assemblage of old and new symbols of power—a sort of laboratory for exploring new ways of representing the past in the light of the turn to democracy. The monuments displayed there suggest multiple readings of the colonial past, including anticolonialism and colonial nostalgia. However, the dominant discourse that finds material actualization there is a "hybridization narrative" that represents the colonial past as a violent and painful experience that was fiercely resisted but also was constitutive (along other histories) of postcolonial Mali (Bhabha 1994; Morton 2000). The wall paintings, the Explorers' Square, and the Governors' series are all material expressions of this discourse. Evidence that "the hybridization narrative" was one intended interpretive scheme came from my conversation with Konaré's cultural adviser (and one of the main ideologues behind Konaré's cultural initiatives) and Mali's former minister of culture, Pascal Baba Couloubaly, who remarked, "Alpha Oumar Konaré's politics is a politics of rupture [in relation to Mali's previous governments]; it is a politics of renewal and psychological redistribution of the course of Malian history" (interview with author, 7 December 2004). For Konaré, heritage initiatives held the potential to redress the collective imaginary of the Malian people. Indeed, heritage sites are not always meaningful to their intended audience but sometimes succeed in constituting "privileged space[s] in which the sense of loss and disruption can be contemplated and assessed and finally cured" (Rowlands and de Jong 2007: 17).

Couloubaly, Konaré, and their intellectual milieu challenged constraining dichotomies (such as the opposition between colonizer and colonized) in an effort to widen the conceptual framework within which postcolonial narratives of the nation are articulated (see also Liebmann 2008: 83). They foregrounded the disruption brought about by colonization but also claimed modernity not just as a Western imposition but constitutive of the Malian nation. Couloubaly argued that the colonial past was no longer France's but was, at least, a shared past: "[T]he history of the colonial state is Mali's history. It is not France's history: it is the history of France and Mali" (interview with author, 7 December 2004). The events that surrounded the statue of Archinard further support this interpretive line: when the inhabitants of Archinard's native town, Le Havre, petitioned President Konaré to authorize shipping the statue back home (because the French copy had been destroyed during World War II), Konaré is reported to have said something like, "It is out of the question. . . . Archinard belongs more to Senegal and Mali than to France, in any event, at least equally" (Couloubaly, interview with author, 7 December 2004). In this hybridity narrative, heritage projects provided an important space in which to experiment with new and also more empowering readings of the past.

Konaré's vision was also rooted in his training as a historian but also reflected popular understandings of the courses and recourses of history and a profound awareness of history's steep turns in which all people alternatively experience cycles of freedom and subjugation. Couloubaly further clarified, "Alpha Oumar Konaré is, first and foremost an historian. . . . He understands the dynamics of history very well" (interview with author, 7 December 2004). Konaré's professional background, his temporal distance from colonization, and his awareness and inclusion of widely distributed conceptual frameworks led him to situate the colonial experience in a broader historical perspective in which the Malian people had also been conquerors.

These observations and the cultural realizations that ensued reveal the complexity of contemporary leaders' assessment of the colonial experience, aspects of which certain sectors of the population may not necessarily share. There is the recognition that one may retrospectively identify formative aspects of colonization despite its overwhelming violence but also a sense that it is in relation to the colonial experience that Mali developed its identity as an independent, modern nation. Couloubaly explained, "We have emerged out of this painful history, and it is precisely in this historical context that we have become aware of our identity, of our difference, to the point of struggling for our independence." The display of monuments representing French colonizers can re-create that originating or identifying sentiment. Ultimately, this representation of the colonial past asserts that modernity is internal to the nation's formation and moves beyond the simplistic oppositions between traditions and modernity that formerly led to cultural and political impasses.[14]

In addition, the assertion of historical intersections as constitutive of contemporary Mali can be seen as a reminder to France of its responsibilities toward Mali.[15] This interpretation would seem to be supported by the construction of yet another critical monument to French colonialism, La Place des Martyrs de Thiaroye (the Square of the Martyrs of Thiaroye), located in downtown Bamako and dedicated to the memory of African soldiers (many of them Sudanese) who served in the French army during World War II. At the end of their service, they claimed their overdue salaries and other compensation. During a confrontation between insurgents and the French colonial army, several African soldiers were killed or wounded at Thiaroye, near Dakar, in 1944. In addition to Sembène Ousmane and Thierno Faty Sow's film *Camp de Thiaroye* (1988), recent newspaper articles have covered this episode of French colonial history. Malian historian Bakary Kamian, who dedicated a voluminous publication (2001) to the study of Malian involvement in the world wars, has postulated a connection between this episode and the callous treatment of Malian immigrants in Paris. His work and its political repercussions have received wide coverage in the Malian press. The monument and Kamian's scholarly work stand as a reminder to France's historical responsibility vis-à-vis Mali.

The Koulouba monument complex presents diverse representations of the colonial experience. It includes references to the anticolonial struggle and chronicles the birth of Mali as an independent nation but also positions the French conquerors in a national narrative that presents freedom and subjugation as inescapable movements of history. It ultimately represents an attempt to account for the diverse roots of the Malian nation, in which both African and European histories are seen as mutually implicating.

## Multiparty Politics and State Memorialization of the Archinard Statue

I have addressed the study of the state's memorialization of the colonial period and considered some of the responses this project elicited among the cultural and political elites in Bamako. I now examine Ségouvians' responses to the state's attempted removal of the statue of Archinard from their city. In this analysis I further investigate their perspectives on the state-promoted memorialization of the colonial past.

There is no doubt that the opposition of some political parties to government initiatives often found symbolic expression in the rejection of the heritage work promoted by the central government (as discussed in the previous chapter). The dispute over the Archinard statue occurred at a particular historical juncture, from 1997 to 2002, that was dominated by struggles between the government and opposition parties, with the latter questioning the increasing power of the majority party (ADEMA) and the limited role given to the opposition.

Government representatives have interpreted Ségouvians' response as an attempt by the opposition to destabilize the government: "We have led this country for ten years in an extremely hostile context," considered Couloubaly (pers. comm., 7 Dec. 2004; see also Couloubaly 2004). Representatives of one of the main opposition parties in Ségou, the Congrès national d'initiative démocratique (National Congress for Democratic Initiative) (CNID), admitted that they took this opportunity to undermine the government by joining with other Ségouvian groups in reclaiming the Archinard statue as an essential part of the city's heritage.

The opposition's unwillingness to work with the central government often resulted in the latter's enforcement of top-down decisions. Konaré's decision to move the Archinard statue to Bamako in 2000 was made without formally consulting the citizens of Ségou. Apparently, only the governor of the region was notified of the initiative, but he did not attempt to inform the population. Even some representatives of the regional branch of the Ministry of Culture admitted that they had not been informed, although responsibility for protecting and valorizing the city's patrimony falls squarely to them.

Besides opposition-party representatives, the most vocal opponents of the Archinard statue's departure included students, who were caught up in party struggles. Their intervention must be understood as part of an ongoing confrontation between the students and the government that dated back to the late 1970s but became more prominent in the mid-1980s, when the state could no longer afford to employ graduates of different levels of schools (Imperato 1996: 19; Bagayogo 2007).

Students had been essential to the fall of Traoré's regime, but their hopes for a democratic Mali and social changes had soon been frustrated, and they made up the bulk of antigovernment demonstrators during Konaré's presidency (Bagayogo 2007). They were dissatisfied with school reform and the government's failure to address their needs (although Mali did make substantive headway by developing a university system starting in 1996; see Bagayogo 2007: 19), complained about the lack of financial support from the state, and contested the criteria for student assessments and the lack of adequate infrastructure (De Noray and Maiga 2002). The students who participated in the 2001 demonstration in Ségou were also painfully aware of politicians' instrumental use of the students' cause. The students criticized the state and the opposition forces for their opportunistic understanding of democracy; they also questioned the arbitrariness of state power as well as the opposition's tendency to manipulate them without ultimately defending their interests.

I discussed the events that surrounded the Archinard statue with a youth grin of the Deuxième Quartier, one of the oldest neighborhoods in Ségou.[16] Several of its members had participated in the student demonstration in protest of the statue's removal. They knew little about their grandparents' experience of colonization, and although they claimed to have learned some stories from their families, when invited to provide examples, one of them replied, "At that moment we were too little; when my grandfather was still alive, we had not learned much" (interview of 11 July 2003). Later, some of their grandparents explained the limited intergenerational transfer of experiences as the result of the grandchildren's lack of interest and the grandparents' own reluctance to talk about what they perceived as a humiliating past. What the students knew came mostly from their schooling, as Cole (2003) also found with Malagasy students. Malian students' narrative became more detailed when they described the last phase of colonization, the creation of indigenous parties in 1946, and the struggle for independence, reflecting the narrative of the nation promoted during most of Malian postcolonial history, with its emphasis on Malians' struggles for independence and nation building.

When we discussed the events surrounding the statue, the students argued that Konaré had claimed the statue for his birth city, Kayes, where he allegedly wanted to create a museum of colonization. But its inhabitants knew nothing of Archinard, the students claimed, and the attempt to move the statue was just another manifestation of the arbitrariness and capriciousness of power: "He is the president of the republic; he has got the power," they told me. When we discussed events in the years since the statue controversy, they revealed a deep awareness of their position: they felt that the opposition parties were stirring up the students and encouraging them to fight for their rights, but they also felt that the opposition did not necessarily have the students' interests at heart. The students were angered by the disarray of Malian schools, as they realized that years of strikes (and several *années blanches*—years when school had been canceled because of the frequency and length of student strikes) had put them far behind in the standard curricula and delayed their graduation and that this situation was going to limit their chances of finding employment.

They were aware that the children of the cosmopolitan elites were not hampered by the school crisis. They observed that politicians "send their children abroad to study. And we learn nothing here; they push us to strike; they refuse to pay our rights [students' unmet request for scholarship raises], so that we stay at home without studying." Students recognized the absence of real alternatives and the lack of committed political allies. Their critique of state power and politics in general found articulation in the work of a famous rap group of the late 1990s. In their song "Cikan" (Message), Fanga Fing addressed the lack of government concern for the fate of the Malian youth and the youth's feelings of powerlessness and lack of prospects. Students also questioned their own understanding of democracy and the democratic process, suggesting that "people"—a category in which they included themselves—had not fully understood the concept of democracy and alluding to the fact that the confrontations were often inconclusive and involved some level of violence.

In January 2000, protesting students received ample support from the population (i.e., a support that superseded party squabbles), including some of the leaders and key actors during Mali's independence struggle and Mali's first postcolonial regime, who apparently cheered the marchers and engaged in civil disobedience with them. Some commented that the students had played their role (in Bamana, *joyoro*) by publicly manifesting wider popular dissatisfaction with the central government. Many sectors of the Ségouvian population praised what they described as the youths' valiant effort to save the city's honor. The old people could not have done anything, they claimed, and if it were not for the young, the statue would have left. Students' efforts allowed the city to reassert ownership and control over its past and simultaneously expressed a critique of state power. In their dissatisfaction with democracy, the students were joined by many Ségouvians who, until that moment, had seen very little investment in the socioeconomic development of their city.

## State Heritage Initiatives and Public Culture

Despite the deployment of undeniably questionable autocratic techniques, the government initiative to memorialize the colonial past did lead to a widening of debates on the colonial past as well as to the unleashing of memories that had been repressed and silenced (for a similar point, see Cole 2001, 2003). Rowlands and de Jong suggest that heritage initiatives may loosen the circulation of memory flows and open public discussions on people's past (2007: 13; see also De Jorio 2006b; Schulz 2007). Heritage is an important site for the development of public culture—that is, a culture that does not lie solely in the hands of the state but sees the emergence of new actors and groups who take an active role in the management of culture (Appadurai and Breckenridge 2004: 407; see also Appadurai 1988; Rowlands and de Jong 2007).

The attempted removal of the Archinard statue triggered important reflections on French colonization and how to better represent and display it. A group of Ségouvian journalists described the dilemma as involving "where to place [the statue] so that it does not inconvenience anybody, because one needs to remember, Archinard reminds us of the gloomy pages of our history" (Coulibaly, Coulibaly, and Koné 2000). Several observers noted that the responses to the president's memorialization of the colonial period varied depending on people's temporal distance from it: "It is perhaps with the passing of time that people have realized that really colonization had some positive aspects. Otherwise during the colonial period, people were so oppressed that they did not see a point in it" (M. B. Keita, pers. comm., 13 July 2003).

In addition to temporal distance, the generational gap emerged as a significant element. Several elders (many of whom had rejoined their original party, the US-RDA, after it was reconstituted in 1991 and sided with the opposition forces during Konaré's second mandate) found the redisplay of the Archinard statue deeply offensive. As members of the generation that had struggled for independence, the *milieux de mémoire*, the "real environment of memory," resisted the memorialization of the traces of colonization promoted under Konaré's presidency (Nora 1989: 7). For them, the statue could not be easily recycled as a vestige from a past worth remembering or even as a tourist attraction; it remained what it was meant to be: a celebration of French colonization. The fathers of independence—under whose impetus the statue had been removed to an out-of-the-way place—vented their viewpoints in occasional conversations but also in radio interviews. In the days that followed the revolt over the Archinard statue, Radio Kaira hosted a series of debates on the statue and its destination. Some older listeners who called in expressed their shock at the idea of reinstalling it in Ségou. Others suggested radical measures, such as melting it to erase the heinous memory of the colonial past once and for all. Not all elders agreed: for some, the statue was an important trace of the past—a vestige of Ségou's better days and greater renown—and should not be removed.

Some middle-aged educated professionals expressed support for Konaré's cultural politics but not necessarily for their implementation. They judged it important to preserve and display the Archinard statue, although they opposed its transfer to Bamako. Thiero, a middle-school teacher, attempted to find a middle ground to take into account the sensibilities and experiences of the generations involved. He reckoned that "the leaders who have experienced colonization . . . do not even want to see the statue of Archinard" and suggested a feasible alternative: "I would like for it to be preserved here, but not in public, because for some, it brings shame to the city; for some, Archinard committed here lots of crime. . . . But our generation, . . . we do not want the disappearance of these remnants, because [colonization] is part of the history of our country" (Thiero, pers. comm., Ségou, July 2003). Others, like Keita, stressed how "when one takes [a monument] away from its original intended location, . . . it loses part of its meaning" (M. B. Keita, pers. comm., Ségou, 13 July 2003). In light of the state's alleged decentralization project, it was suggested that the management of the city's patrimony be left to the Ségouvians.

Among some long-term residents of Ségou, the modalities of state appropriation of a remnant of the city's once-prestigious past brought up memories of the violent and destructive face of previous powers (on this trope of state violence, see Bagayogo 1989, 2007). Events such as the statue controversy are occasions for old historical disputes to resurface and for displaced elites and defeated party leaders to reexperience the past. Representatives of one of Ségou's oldest families, the Diarra (descendants of a Ségou royal family that had led the powerful Bamana state of Ségou in the eighteenth and nineteenth centuries), perceived the decision to remove the statue of Archinard as a replay of historical experiences. In our 2001 conversation, it became clear that, in their memory, every new power had asserted itself by destroying the vestiges of the previous power. After al-Hajj Oumar Tall's conquest of Ségou in 1861, the Toucouleurs destroyed several of the Diarra's venerated tombs and most of the places where the family had kept its sacred objects (in Bamana, *boliw*) and made sacrifices and offerings. The destruction of such sites of collective memory continued under French colonization when most of the French colonial buildings along the Niger River were built on top of preexisting buildings and significant locations. Relatively close to the river were the mosque and the massive palaces that al-Hajj Oumar Tall and his son Ahmadou had built, for example, where hundreds of people (including the Tall spouses and the slaves they had captured during the wars) had lived in proximity (Brasseur 1968). During French colonization, these buildings were destroyed to make space for urban development. To the Diarra, the government's attempt to appropriate the Archinard statue without consultation and at a strategic time (after the end of the workday) was just a reminder of the destructive force of state power and its continuity over time.

## State Heritage Politics Reconsidered

Parallel to a critique of state memorialization of the past, several Ségouvians were beginning (at the time of the statue of Archinard affair) to frame their historical legacies and family memories within the context of heritage initiatives. Heritage is not just about identifying and reclaiming the past. Rather, it produces new practices, sensibilities, and objects: "It is a mode of cultural production in the present that has recourse in the past" (Kirshenblatt-Gimblett 2004:1, 2006b).

The state politics of comprehensive remembering and its emphasis on *le devoir de mémoire* (the duty of memory) were triggering new public interest in the past, which was increasingly reappropriated within the global language of the heritage industry. The same Diarra family members who had developed a critique of the destructive side of state power mentioned to me several activities they were undertaking in an attempt to rescue their family's patrimony from oblivion.[17] For example, they had created a loosely organized family foundation to help them with the valorization of their family history and sites of memory. By 2014 they had acquired a piece of land in Ségou (close to the administrative quarter) and were hoping, eventually, to build a museum and cultural center there (see chapter 3), an increasing popular undertaking among Mali's elite families, who enjoy prestige because of their histories and not necessarily because of their economic status.

In 2001 the Diarra family members' memory of French colonization shifted significantly once we moved to discuss their family foundation and cultural projects. They related that once the conquest period was completed, the French had developed some measures to protect the city's patrimony. The Diarra referred to an area (*wulafèbarokèyòrò*) that kings had used for afternoon socializing and conversation, an area that the French had apparently enclosed. It is a space where Bamana petty traders still convene on Monday (Ségou's big market day) to sell calabashes and leaves used as herbal remedies and cooking. The Diarra family is still struggling with the city's authorities to have that location recognized as part of the city's patrimony and thereby restored. This is one of many culturally mediated activities that the family is organizing to counter what they called the monopoly of money-driven *griots* (bards) and modern scholars, some of whom, they felt, were contributing to the misrepresentation of past events. Initiatives such as the Diarras' signal an increasing tendency on the part of local families to take history into their own hands.[18]

The narratives presented here allow us to understand some of the readings that motivated Ségouvians' protest in January 2000. It is clear that the city's population experienced President Konaré's decision as an arbitrary one: it served as evidence that despite its democratic claims, the state was continuing to act despotically (even though it ultimately withdrew from this initiative—when faced with popular opposition). In this regard, the students acted in unison with the rest of the population, showing that their discontent was a sign of much wider societal concerns. This situation led people once more to wonder about the meaning of democracy and its attainability—ideas that were already challenged by dissatisfaction with the limited results of democracy for most of the population and concerns about the excessive power of ADEMA (Villalon and Idrissa 2005). Despite or, perhaps, because of such debates and confrontations, certain sectors of the city's population (e.g., the Diarra) came to express a growing interest in the valorization of their city's history and, most of all, a firm conviction in the rights of local communities to have their say in the representation and management of their own cultural heritage.

## Conclusions: Early Phases of Privatization

Under Konaré's presidency, a number of cultural heritage projects endeavored to spearhead changes in Malians' representation of the colonial past. Prior to the democratic neoliberal turn, state narratives tended either to minimize the effects of the colonial experience or to emphasize people's struggles in the pursuit of freedom. Heritage initiatives and the culture of memory promoted under Konaré mark important changes from that pattern in that they reflect a substantive commitment to rescue from oblivion the forgotten or willfully erased. During this period, the duty of memory (le devoir de mémoire) was raised to the level of a national value. Massive investment in the rehabilitation of public memory and heritage initiatives has called into question former representations of French colonization.

The Koulouba monument complex represents a privileged arena for observing and reflecting upon how the new cosmopolitan elites view colonization (and some of the debates that such initiatives have generated). With the highest concentration of monuments from the colonial era and several new monuments covering Mali's colonial and postcolonial history (as well as a few monuments representing precolonial symbols of power), Koulouba's eclectic assemblage represents varying periods of Mali's history. Several of the monuments manifest diverse and partly contradictory readings of colonization, some of them reflect a classic anticolonial stance, and others elicit colonial nostalgia; increasingly, they evoke cultural hybridization. My analysis takes into account the motivation of Mali's intellectual elites and their attempts to accommodate the French colonial experience and to rebuild the nation with a new historical consciousness that is more aware of its diverse, hybrid roots. The representation of colonization as a complex experience reflects an attempt to overcome limiting dichotomies, such as the oppositions between colonizer and colonized and between modernity and tradition. Similarly, several years earlier, Malian anthropologist Shaka Bagayogo argued for overcoming an ill-conceived opposition between "national culture (lost heaven)" and imported culture, seen as a synonym of "loss of national identity" (1987: 91)—an opposition that, in his view, hampered much-needed social and political changes.[19]

Opposition to state memorialization of the colonial past arises in part from underlining political and social dissatisfaction with the promises of democracy. It reflects interparty struggles, the lack of popular participation in this as well as other cultural initiatives, and the lack of the government's effective communication of its objectives to civil societies (as highlighted by the Ségou episode, in particular). However, some of Konaré's politics could also be interpreted as attempts to provoke discussion, as they challenged established representations of the past. They generated lively public debates that have contributed to the development of a less-ephemeral public sphere—a late appreciation of Konaré's presidency made even by members of the opposition just a few years after the end of his mandate (see De Jorio 2013).

Popular responses to government-promoted cultural initiatives have been scarcely investigated, and this chapter is a first step in further research on this topic. The past and its representations constitute an arena for the definition of power struggles between the majority party and the composite opposition bloc but also between different generations. Elders who had participated in the independence struggle and Mali's first postcolonial regime were horrified by the sudden inclusion of European explorers and French governors in the pantheon of national heroes. The forms of state retrieval of vestiges of the colonial period have rekindled old preoccupations with the nature of power, its destructiveness, and its apparent arbitrariness. The refusal to commemorate Archinard in the forms chosen by the government reflects political opposition but also city pride and (perhaps unexpectedly) citizens' growing commitment to their family heritage. Increasingly, individuals and groups are invested in the promotion of initiatives via which they reclaim their own past and explore new ways of representing and displaying their heritage.

## 3. The Women's Museum Muso Kunda

*Citizenship, Gender, and Social Memory*

I FIRST VISITED the women's museum Muso Kunda (in Bamana, literally "on the woman's side") of Bamako in 1999 and returned to conduct ethnographic research in 2001 (De Jorio 2002b). My following visits to Mali centered on other research projects, but I continued to inform myself about the museum. The institution appeared well-established and had become a recommended tourist destination in travel guides. I was both astonished and saddened to learn during my last visit to Mali in June 2014 that the museum was closed for renovations (figure 11). When I investigated the reasons behind its closing—the last reported activity goes back to March 6, 2011—plans to improve and expand the facility were mentioned as well as lack of funds to ultimately complete the work undertaken.[1] Deeper reasons were alluded to but never fully explained.[2] Muso Kunda was an ambitious enterprise that reflected hopes for a greater inclusion of women in all domains of social life in the age of democracy. At the same time, though, it was also marred by a number of contradictions and ironies, as this chapter illustrates. The museum's closing (after years of uncertainty) was a clear indication of the laissez-faire that had dominated Amadou Toumani Touré's administration.[3] It also further showed Touré's mild commitment to women's emancipation, exhibited above all by the government's handling of the new family code that ultimately led to the ratification of a corpus of law that further limited women's freedoms.[4] The commitment of Ibrahim Boubacar Keita's administration to culture and to women's role in cultural initiatives appears very limited, based on politicians' speeches and state investment in the domain of culture.[5] State cultural policies more than ever seem to be determined outside Mali and center on the reconstruction of UNESCO World Heritage

**FIGURE 11.** Unfinished renovation and expansion of the women's museum Muso Kunda, Bamako, 2014. Courtesy of Iris van Hall.

Sites and the valorization of the cultural patrimony of the northern regions (see chapter 5).

Even though its fate remains uncertain, the museum disclosed some important aspects of Mali's female cosmopolitan elites' history and aspirations for women's development and therefore warrants inclusion in this work.[6] The museum mirrored the cosmopolitan elites' efforts to challenge victimizing or exoticizing readings of Malian women by educating national and international audiences about selected aspects of women's lives. It reflected a particular phase of Malian democracy, Alpha Oumar Konaré's presidency, during which efforts to include women in the political process and improve women's rights were most prominent. Finally, examination of the Muso Kunda experience illustrates some of the political and economic challenges private heritage initiatives face in today's Mali. Muso Kunda's format as a multipurpose center—combining, in addition to the exhibit space, a small library, a restaurant, a museum shop run by female artisans, a center of ethnomedicine and traditional healing, and a cultural center with a pronounced civic mission—represents a model many heritage preservationists seek to emulate, whether consciously or not. Today, state and international entities encourage the privatization of the heritage sector, conceived as one major axis for the economic development of the country; analysis of some of the contradictions and challenges Muso Kunda faced offers valuable insights.

## The History of Muso Kunda

The 1998 creation of Muso Kunda reflected a growing effort on the part of state and quasi-state organizations to integrate women into democratic processes (figure 12). The exhibits celebrated historical and contemporary aspects of women's lives but also situated Malian women's experiences in a broader context, in an imaginary conversation with transnational and international women's organizations and aid entities. The construction of the women's museum—the first of its kind in Mali and one of the few women's museums in the world—was one of the many cultural initiatives promoted during the ten-year presidency of Konaré, from 1992 to 2002. Although formally a private institution, Muso Kunda was part of a larger government effort to democratize Mali's political and cultural institutions by giving voice to traditionally marginalized strata of the population, in this case, women (Ba Konaré 1998a, 1998b, 1999a). Malian women's participation in politics, the formal economy, and education was (and still is) limited, although women remain central to the household economy. Under Konaré's presidency, a number of steps were made to integrate women into the state apparatus: in particular, by creating a ministry for women's and children's affairs and by nominating more women representatives to high government positions.[7] The establishment of Muso Kunda was an initiative promoted by Adame Ba Konaré, a prominent Malian historian and Konaré's wife, and was grounded on her historical work on women's formal associations and her dictionary of notable women in Mali's history.[8] Muso Kunda aimed to instruct both national and transnational audiences about women's specific heritage and historical contributions.

In consideration of its many and, at times, divergent objectives, Muso Kunda embodies especially well what Foucault defined as heterotopias—that is, spaces characterized by the simultaneous presence of heterogeneous "slices of times" and multiple organizational criteria (2008: 20). Muso Kunda manifests different techniques of appropriation and representation of women in time, at once extolling a return to secular feminine virtues and promoting a progressive reading of selected past traditions. Its exhibits celebrate women's rich clothing traditions, creatively reinterpreted in light of contemporary aesthetic and religious sensibilities, particularly, in its emphasis on women's modesty and propriety. The exhibits also include some of the forward movements of history and celebrate women's contributions to independence from

**FIGURE 12.** The women's museum Muso Kunda, Bamako, main entrance, 2000. Courtesy of Maria Luisa Ciminelli.

colonial rule and nation building as well as women's work for the improvement of women's rights.

Muso Kunda's classic educational mission is designed to enfold the preservation of what are perceived as disappearing traditions. At the same time, this institution aspires to forge a new political and social consciousness for women and the youth who were called to participate more widely and effectively in the democratization process (Bennett 1990, 1998, 2006). The museum attempts to counter some of the homogenizing effects of globalization by creating awareness of Mali's cultural heritage and by reasserting the centrality of women in preserving culture and educating the younger generations.

This chapter looks at Muso Kunda as a place of interactions and exchanges. The focus is not limited to the politics of representations—that is, the decoding of meanings behind the selection of objects and their meaningful arrangements—but also includes the interactions between people (as museum representatives and museum visitors) and people and objects within the highly regulated space of museum exhibits (Reed 2005). Accordingly, this chapter focuses on the diverse modes of organizing artifacts, their capacity for disclosure of complex world orders (see, for instance, Errington 1998), and the intended objectives of the museum's organizers. It also refers to some of the conversations and negotiations of cultural meanings taking place within the museum, particularly through snapshots from guided tours and a public debate that disclose some of the conflicts, contradictions, and consensuses surrounding the roles of women and men and of younger and older generations in contemporary Malian society.

## Heterotopias of Time

Muso Kunda aims to contribute to the revaluation of women's status in Malian society. In the words of the museum director, Diarra Marie Goundiam, "Muso Kunda [is] . . . a women's institution, a representation for women's rehabilitation" (pers. comm., 8 June 2001). The museum brings together seemingly incommensurable aspects of women's past and present, thus manifesting some of the defining traits of Foucault's heterotopia. Muso Kunda is a space where "all the real emplacements, all the other real emplacements that can be found within culture, are simultaneously represented, contested, and inverted" (Foucault 2008: 17). The museum invokes a return to secular virtues and selected cultural traditions; at the same time it promotes women's greater political participation and economic empowerment. It chronicles the early phases of women's national associations and the legislative changes in support of women's rights while distancing itself from what are perceived as the confrontational tones and the egalitarian ideology of Western feminism (see also De Jorio 2001).

Focusing on women's portrayal as mothers and educators of the new Malian generations, the museum emphasizes some of women's fundamental commonalities. The museum's displays and literature available suggest that Malian women, regardless of their social and economic backgrounds, share the burden of marriage and motherhood—one that simultaneously draws on and enhances what are perceived as women's specific values, such as patience, sacrifice, and endurance.[9] This is a widely shared, recurring narrative by the cosmopolitan female elites, reflecting their effort to overcome class and status distinctions and to foreground communalities with their women constituencies (De Jorio 2009, 2010). Misunderstandings across class lines, in addition to rivalries between women's groups (often fueled by men),[10] have been endemic since the early beginning of the Malian women's movement in the late 1950s. Such divisions, as also recognized by female cosmopolitan elites,[11] have further weakened women's ability to generate substantive changes in Malian society.

The appreciation of women's "secular virtues" and the centrality of the family in Malian society are accompanied by "a more progressive and supportive perspective" (Ba Konaré 1999b: 3–4). This theme, which recurs throughout the museum, is articulated more extensively in discourses surrounding one of the most popular displays in the museum: a fountain dedicated to Faro, a goddess of the Niger River who has a semi-human appearance. Faro also lends her name to the museum's magazine. In an early issue, Ba Konaré expands on Faro's symbolic meaning: "Faro has the power to order and classify; she embodies the good mother's consciousness, always willing to alleviate children's sufferings. . . . The magazine *Faro* promotes a return to women's secular virtues, but also a more progressive and supportive perspective [to women's issues]. We can assert, without falling into the traps of a differential approach, that each gender has got its assets, that deserve to be made public and enhanced" (1999b: 3–4).

Faro thus symbolizes women's specific strengths and evolving responsibilities in Malian society. Faro is also one of the objects from Mali's pre-Islamic past;[12] her presence in the museum suggests women's link to esoteric powers. According to Goundiam, Faro is connected to the Bamana conception of power (*fanga*) and the role of women as either sources or mediators of power (pers. comm., 8 June 2001). In the museum director's version of the Faro legend, Ba Faro (Mother Faro) provided Biton Coulibaly, the founder of the powerful Bambara kingdom of Ségou in the eighteenth century, with the powers needed to achieve political and military success. Goundiam also presented Faro as a goddess who reintroduced order within Bamana society by teaching humans the arts of agriculture, fishing, and metalwork, thus countering the disorderly forces the male god Pemba introduced.[13] As a constant reminder of women's contributions to all worthwhile endeavors, Faro symbolizes the unity and strengths of women on which they can build as they develop new forms of civic engagement.

Muso Kunda's emphasis on women's secret powers was also the focus of a temporary exhibit (open from 1999 to 2001), a significant portion of which consisted of a series of wooden masks and statues that, according to Ba Konaré, exemplified "the *occulte* (secret) power with which women are endowed" (1998a: 271). In a provocative talk at a CODESRIA (Council for the Development of Social Science Research in Africa) seminar a few years earlier, Ba Konaré had invited local women to resume witchcraft practices as a means of self-empowerment (1991); this exhibit at Muso Kunda echoed her emancipatory reading of women's esoteric knowledge. But in 2001 the masks and statues were replaced by an exhibit on women's work and their tools, reportedly because most of the objects in the temporary exhibit had to be returned to the National Museum collection from which they had been borrowed. The elimination or reduction of references to Mali's "pre-Islamic" religious practices was also intended, however, as a preemptive effort to minimize clashes with opposition forces that had mobilized Islam, among others, to express their political and moral dissatisfaction (Goundiam, pers. comm., 8 June 2001; De Jorio 2003; Barry 2004; Soares 2009). Indeed, some of the heritage initiatives undertaken under Konaré were criticized on religious grounds. For example, the cross on the top of the Monument de l'Indépendance (Independence Monument) was criticized because, as a Christian symbol, it allegedly offended the sensibilities of the majority Muslim population. In a few instances, monuments that pertained to Mali's pre-Islamic beliefs and practices were destroyed during popular revolts triggered by the opposition and were no longer rebuilt (see Barry 2004).

## A History of Household Technology and Women's Activism

Parallel to the revaluation and rearticulation of women's traditions, sections of the museum more resolutely seem to embrace an ideology of progress and technological advances. An exhibit that opened in 2000 documented transformations in women's work and the tools and techniques they employ. According to the exhibit designer, Malian anthropologist Salia Male, Ba Konaré had initially suggested organizing the exhibit displays around a list of verbs describing women's work. One display, for example, presents grinding tools in an evolutionary progression. It begins with a Neolithic stone, followed by a mortar and pestle, and concludes with a picture of a mill, which my male guide praised as a major advance because it provided women with more time for other domestic chores (sic!). Other parts of the exhibit display artifacts specifically used by the women of some of Mali's ethnic groups. Thus we admire Bozo women's tools for fishing and fish preservation, as well as the tools and containers used by Peul women to collect, transform, and sell milk.

The exhibit also juxtaposes "traditional" objects of everyday use with their more modern variants. For example, the three-stone fire appears with the *foyer amélioré* (improved stove), which L'Union nationale des femmes du Mali (National Union of Malian Women) (UNFM) consistently promoted between 1974 and 1991 as a device to preserve energy. Also present are Chinese imports (e.g., large bowls to serve food) and modern appliances (e.g., a refrigerator, represented in the exhibit by a photograph). This section of the exhibit is clearly educational in its promotion of the use of energy-saving devices (e.g., the foyer amélioré). And although it reinforces women's associations with the domestic sphere, it also acknowledges women's increasing use of modern technology.

The museum also includes references to women's engagement with nation building and development efforts. A small display deals with the early history of women's national associations, mostly in the form of the great-hero narrative. It includes a few photos of some of the most famous women of the First Republic (1960–68): Aoua Keita, the only woman representative in the highest organ of the US-RDA party structure during these years and the general secretary of the Commission sociale des femmes (Social Commission for Women), the only official women's organization between 1962 and 1968; Fanta Diallo, member of the Commission sociale des femmes and one of the wives of Modibo Keita, Mali's first president; Marie Diarra, the first woman teacher; and Fanta Damba, one of Mali's most well-known women singers and a political campaigner for the US-RDA.[14] The display also includes some of the legislation in support of women's rights, dating from the colonial period to the early years of the twenty-first century.[15]

This section of the exhibit simultaneously celebrates the heroic beginning of women's formal associations and recognizes their selfless participation in independence struggles and nation building. Implicit contradictions exist, however. The emphasis on the early beginning of women's national associations may be read as an attempt to bring some legitimacy to the disputed trajectory of women's organizations in the postcolonial period. By focusing on the foundational narrative of the postcolonial state—with its emphasis on the anticolonial struggle and the early phases of nation building (Arnoldi 2003)—women scholars and activists counter and correct some negative images of women's groups, such as their staunch support of Moussa Traoré's dictatorship until its final days and the general stereotype of women as naïve followers of shrewd politicians who typically forget their campaign promises after being elected.

Significantly, the few references to the history of women's associations in the museum exhibit do not cover women's history during the twenty-one years of Traoré's dictatorship, even though women's associations were incorporated into Traoré's state machinery and, in fact, became an effective tool of the dictatorship (Ba Konaré 1998a, 1998b). The exhibit also leaves unaddressed the debates on the new family code. These debates deeply polarized the Malian population for more than a decade and ultimately ended in December 2011 with the ratification of a corpus of laws sanctioning the victory of a coalition of religious and conservative social forces. The inclusion of such controversies would have hampered the unifying and legitimizing perspective privileged at Muso Kunda.

Muso Kunda situates Malian women within the wider international women's movement. The museum was formally opened on 8 March 1998, International Women's Day, thus marking Malian women's participation in celebrations that unite women worldwide. The museum echoes Malian women's own brand of women's emancipation and their critique of what they see as Western feminists' antagonistic approach to gender issues—a theme consistently articulated from the 1960s onward. As stated in the museum's literature, this institution promotes the complementarity of gender roles, not necessarily equality or interchangeability between women and men (Ba Konaré 1998a, 1999b). Women's central role as mothers and wives is not disputed; on the contrary, women's emancipation is to be rooted in an appreciation and revaluation of selected women's secular traditions. An increase in women's political, social, and economic participation is justified as a key step toward improving the quality of life of Malian families. Muso Kunda expresses a celebratory and selective return to traditions, one that takes into account the country's general political and cultural climate and its attempt to forge an original path to democracy.[16] Muso Kunda is at once a venue for defining women's specific historical trajectory and a means of repositioning Malian women's trajectories within globally circulating gender discourses.

## Representing and Reappropriating Time in Fashion

Muso Kunda aims to overcome stereotypical representations of women in the colonial iconography. Ba Konaré comments on the colonizer's fascination for women's bodies as evident in postcards from the colonial time, some of which are posted on a museum wall: "The colonizers were, in their way, hunters of images. They were particularly captivated by morphological considerations. In their representations, we have the women *stéatopyges*, women with a big bust and short legs, [an obsessive fascination for] flat noses, thick lips, large and carnivorous teeth, frizzy and woolen hair" (Ba Konaré 1998a: 271). In its reconstruction of ethnic and historical outfits informed by the dicta of contemporary fashion, the museum also counters the silence on women's dress in much of the available literature as well as in European museum collections. For instance, in his monograph on the West African *boubou*, a long, loose tunic with embroidery, Bernhard Gardi observes, "The boubou is especially a man's dress, but it is not rare that women wear it too" (2000: 10). His rich and informative book is, still, dedicated primarily to the classification and study of men's boubous in historical perspective. As it documents women's past and present experimentations with clothing, Muso Kunda deploys diverse representational strategies to overcome stereotypes and fill the gaps in the existing literature, not only relying on criteria of historical or ethnological accuracy but also using fashion as a discursive frame to reinterpret and represent the past in the present.

In Mali as in Senegal, emphasis on external beauty is seen as a reflection of inner qualities (Mustafa 1997: 19). The museum's dresses suggest first and foremost a sense of decorum and elegance. This aspect also emerged from most Malian students' written responses to the museum visit, where they expanded with obvious pride on the beauty and elegance of their foremothers. Muso Kunda challenges some of the biases (informed by the idea that art per se was exclusively a Western achievement) of colonially derived ethnographic museums by favoring an aesthetic perspective over historical and ethnographic accuracy.

Fashion represents one privileged idiom that mediates Malian women's contemporary search for identity and recognition. It is "a domain for the negotiation of changing social relations, local institutions, and transnational connections" (Mustafa 1997: 15). By subsuming the language of fashion as one of the ordering criteria, the museum recognizes the centrality that being well dressed assumes in women's circles. Dresses display women's inner values, mediate their identity searches, and exhibit their intended or achieved status. The adoption of fashion also provides curators with greater latitude as they construct models of ethnic outfits that incorporate dresses and accessories of different time periods—thus reinforcing not only the function of the museum as a site for the accumulation of time-related artifacts and visual narratives but also for the reimagining and, possibly, reordering of the social order that lies outside the enclosed museum space (Foucault 2008; Lang 2008).

Muso Kunda presents a rich collection of women's clothing, such as dresses worn for major events in a woman's life cycle (e.g., marriage, the birth of a child). Also presented are dresses worn by two women characters from the Bamana theatrical tradition: the slim woman (*Pékélé*) and the opulent woman (*Yayoroba*); the latter embodies in her fuller figure the affluence of her household.[17] Of particular relevance here is a group of fifteen mannequins displayed along the walls of the main display room. Fourteen represent various ethnic styles from different regions of Mali, and one represents the attire of the contemporary Malian woman. This is, without doubt, one of the most popular sections of the exhibit. The mannequins were specially made for the museum by a North Korean firm.

The museum aims to avoid some of the gaps or imbalance noticed in colonial ethnographic collections in which certain ethnic groups (e.g., the Bamana, the Dogon, and the Senufo) were overly represented (Arnoldi 1999: 28). All major ethnic groups are included here, including those of the northern regions of Mali like the Tuaregs, with whom the Malian government has had a turbulent relationship since independence. The relationship has been marked by endemic rebellions and searches for greater autonomy on the part of the Tuaregs, as also more recently shown by the short-lived secession of the north led by Tuareg-Islamist groups in 2012. Furthermore, by inserting in the series of ethnic dresses the mannequin of an urban woman wearing a modern boubou, Muso Kunda overcomes the typical limitations of ethnographic exhibits with their exclusive attention to the exotic and the remote.[18]

Despite their regional and ethnic differences, these ethnic outfits reveal important similarities. The dresses displayed at Muso Kunda represent an idealization and homogenization of ethnic dress. They are the outcome of a retrospective look informed by contemporary taste and sense of propriety. The Abbé Henry, one of the few authors to record data on women's dress practices at the beginning of the twentieth century, reports that the preferred dress of wealthy Bamana women was either a *duloki* (the Bamana term for boubou) or a *tafé*, a large piece of cloth fastened, according to the fashion of the day, under the armpits so as to leave the left breast uncovered (Henry 1910). In the exhibit all mannequins are dressed so that their bodies are fully covered, thus revealing an attention to contemporary fashion trends and expectations of women's modesty (rather than to historical accuracy) and inclusivity of various dress forms.[19] Similarly, the mannequins representing young, unmarried women are not dressed in traditional clothes but modern boubous. According to Henry (1910), young women used to cover only the lower part of their bodies with the so-called *cache-sexe*. In the exhibit young women are represented as wearing boubous, although they rarely wear them today, instead limiting their use to special occasions, such as "traditional" weddings and religious celebrations.[20] Furthermore, there is no mention of the contemporary experimentation with style and the playful subversion of moral taboos in which the younger generation engages today. In Mali, as Mustafa observed in Senegal, young women often sport more Western-inspired outfits until the arrival of their first child, when they switch to garments of African fashion (Mustafa 1997).

In the museum, there is an overrepresentation of the boubou—and a particular recent stylistic variant—as a woman's dress of choice. Several of the mannequins in the exhibit sport a demi-boubou, which is currently more fashionable than the grand boubou and also more practical (and perhaps more economical) because it requires less cloth and facilitates a woman's movements (Gardi 2000: 10). The boubou is a highly symbolic garment conveying "local ideals of successful adulthood: piety, prosperity, and deep roots in regional culture" (Rovine 2011: 59). The garment was associated with the elites of Mali's northern region, particularly in the religious urban centers of Timbuktu and Djenné (as shown by the mannequins representing women from the northern regions). Over time the boubou became popular among younger and older women alike as shown by the mannequins representing young and contemporary women all wearing demi-boubous.[21] The museum thus subtly documents not only ethnic differences but also the emergence of a national and transnational culture of dress centered on the boubou and its variants (Rovine 2011).

The adoption of the idiom of contemporary fashion gives greater representational freedom to the curators and allows for the simultaneous display of accessories and items of clothing from different periods. Mannequins of present-day women stand beside mannequins sporting outfits and accessories from the precolonial and colonial periods. There is no clear demarcation of the time frame this display aims to cover.[22] This perspective finds further articulation in the fusion of historical and ethnological perspectives as manifested in individual outfits. Mannequins portraying ethnic groups fixed in the ethnographic present also wear a multitude of accessories covering several historical periods. The Soninké mannequin, clothed in a way intended to typify the dress of women from this ethnic group and thus defined as atemporal, is wearing a blue boubou (attributed to no particular period). Her boubou is decorated with coins (a practice of wealthier women in the early colonial period, according to the guide), and she wears a pair of leather shoes typical of the precolonial period. Similarly, a few mannequins away stands the Kassonké girl from Kayes. She is wearing a modern boubou but with a coiffure typical of the colonial period. This specific hairstyle, which represents in a stylized form the locomotive of a train, offers a social commentary on the changes and transformations generated at the local level by construction of the railroad connecting Bamako to Dakar via Kayes (begun in 1881 and completed in 1924). This hairstyle was apparently selected to highlight the centrality of the train for the economy of the region, especially for female petty traders who make a living by selling food and other local merchandise to train passengers, some of whom are traders themselves.[23] The adoption of the idiom of fashion foregrounds similarities among women and acknowledges the body as one major site for women's identity searches and self-fashioning while granting a certain playful representational freedom to museum curators.

## The Logic of Consumption and Status Display

The outfits displayed at Muso Kunda are those women wore (or still wear) on special occasions, from collective celebrations to the weekly market (Ba Konaré 1998a). Furthermore, most of the dresses displayed are by no means representative of the average woman's status. The exhibit of ethnic dresses portrays the image of wealthy women who signified the power of their households via their body ornaments and dresses: "Here you have the Sonrai woman. This Sonrai woman is also from Timbuktu. She wears a boubou with embroidery done by hand.... There were no sewing machines at that time, and so to wear a boubou like this, one needed to be very, *very* wealthy" (museum guide, 8 June 2001). In his commentary, the guide unpacked the grammar of status distinctions by directing visitors' attention to the length of a string of pearls, the display of gold and amber jewelry, the voluminosity of a head scarf, and the use of coins as decorations in women's coiffures during the early colonial period when the French franc was still a rarity. This ostentatious dimension is best embodied by the mannequin portraying the Senufo woman, who wears the jewels that once belonged to the last queen of Sikasso, and the Bobo woman, who sports a hairpin that, according to the guide, was exclusive to the wife of a chef de canton (museum guide, 27 May and 8 June 2001).

In this sense the museum adopts and magnifies the logic of consumption and status display of contemporary Malian society and confers to women's past a new foundational dignity. The transformation of the Bobo woman into the wife of a local political representative during the French colonial period constitutes a way to unite all women by articulating a narrative of the past in which women can positively identify themselves. The idiom of fashion further contributes to the production of an idealized past because it allows the erasure of time depth and the syncretic reappropriation of clothing items from different periods—for instance, the parallel display of demi-boubous, coiffures, and jewels from different times. Within the museum display, the contemporary search for women's identity is simultaneously—and not unambiguously—carried out in a perspective of negotiation with contemporary religious sensitivities, competitive status display, consumerism, and the search for women's self-empowerment.

## Museum Tours

Tony Bennett focuses his work on the disciplinary and educational functions of the museum in the history of Western societies (1990, 1998, 2006). In his discussion of the history of Western museums—which have their antecedents in private collections of elites—Bennett emphasizes their contributions to the broadening of the public sphere by the progressive inclusion of the working classes, children (seen as future citizens), and women (in their role as educators of the younger generations).[24] Museums contributed to the creation of what he calls a "regulated restlessness," particularly among the white male audiences—in other words, in "forming and shaping the attributes of citizens" (Bennett 1998: 150). Museums promoted bourgeois values and practices among the populace, including the value of self-improvement and continuous self-progression (Bennett 1998: 157).

Bennett's studies center on the history of Western museums but are, nonetheless, helpful in framing some fundamental questions and in providing useful interpretive perspectives on Malian contexts. Bennett sees museums as people movers in that "museums have proven themselves to be highly productive machineries in their capacity to transform modes of thought, perception, and behavior—in short, ways of life" (2006: 57). Museums disclose the more appealing side of power because of their ability to inspire social changes. They are not just experienced as imposing control upon or constraining individuals' behavior. In this respect, Muso Kunda is an ambitious enterprise targeting multiple and diverse audiences and endeavoring to inspire significant perceptual and institutional changes. Its desired audiences are both specific segments of Mali's population (e.g., women and youth) but also international and transnational actors (e.g., tourists, Malians in the Diaspora, representatives of aid agencies, political delegations, and scholars). The museum provides a framework for the expansion of the notion of citizenship to encompass marginalized segments of the Malian population: youth and women. It is a site for articulation of and education about fundamental ways of being in Malian society. In particular, it attempts to reassert the value of respect for elders (also seen as representatives of a vanishing world order) amid the intense crisis of the Malian youth that has arisen, in part, from the many problems of the Malian school system, the lack of job opportunities, and Mali's weak economy. At the same time, it is a space that celebrates women's role in maintaining stable households and contributing to the education and cultural grounding of their children. It is also a place to situate Malians, particularly, women, as engaged in global discussions on women's opportunities and challenges in postcolonial societies.

The museum literature suggests that increasing global interdependency requires that citizens think beyond the restrictive boundaries of the nation-state and embrace new forms of global connectednes. The museum fosters forms of citizenship and belonging that are not simply national but also global.[25] It also strives to cultivate a new awareness of women's rich and diverse heritage while encouraging critical engagements with modernity and development. The museum articulates many Malian women's view of development and women's emancipation by presenting a world order based on gender complementarity, family values, and women's centrality in the transfer and transmission of regional and ethnic cultures. It acknowledges the influence of Western feminist movements but reinterprets them to reflect Malian women's culturally grounded repositioning—what Ba Konaré defined as neofeminism in a 2010 interview with a French journalist of *Après-Coup*: a feminism revisited in light of a renewed appreciation for Malian women's specific heritage and history.[26]

## Muso Kunda and Its Publics

In addition to the museum's displays and literature, its guided tours enable contemporary audiences to experience additional key aspects of Muso Kunda, and in particular some of the institution's internal contradictions. I analyze here some of the ways in which museum displays are narrated to visitors in the course of guided tours (including a consideration of the guide's narrative shifts to accommodate diverse publics) as well as some of the conversations that took place after the museum visits. On two of my several visits to the museum, I was accompanied by the museum's only guide at the time, an educated man in his thirties who was also a highly pious man from the Wahhabiyya (an Islamic reform movement).[27] His appointment as the museum's guide reflected an attempt on the part of the museum staff to divert criticism from increasingly vocal segments of the society who reject Western feminist perspectives. In order to get a sense of how Muso Kunda was presented not only to international audiences but also to another of its intended targets—the Malian youth—I sought the help of S. Diabaté, a professor of art and drawing at a lycée in Bamako, to arrange a group of young museum visitors. Diabaté helped me identify approximately twelve male and female students who were either in their last year of high school or in their first year of university studies.

The typical guided tour follows an established pattern. It departs from the fountain dedicated to Faro and ends near the large wooden statue of an idealized "traditional" woman placed in front of the main exhibit's entrance—both symbolic references to women's esoteric powers. The organization and general content did not vary much between the two guided tours I analyze here. The guide's emphasis and some of his examples, however, varied significantly in response to his audiences.

On one day I toured the museum with an Italian female friend from an Italian-Malian NGO. When we stopped to examine the recently added exhibit on women's work, the guide described in a matter-of-fact tone the various objects and their use, limiting to the bare minimum his discussion of the disciplinary implications of women's work. About the basketry he observed: "Here you have the Kassonké woman of the first region [Kayes]. She sports a boubou with embroidery done by hand by the women. This is a specialty of Kassonké's women. These are very *interesting tasks for the women, because they can stay at home and do not go out a lot*" (27 May 2001, my emphasis). He added that a full collection of baskets was an integral part of the trousseau that a woman brought to marriage. On the day of this tour, I did not pay much attention to some of the guide's brief references to the moral implications of housework. His comments eventually became very meaningful.

The guide's description of this very same class of objects underwent a significant transformation the day of the Malian students' visit (8 June 2001). When we reached the section dedicated to women's work utensils, the guide spoke for some time about the moral implications of the tedious work of eliminating the impurities from flour. He expanded on the virtues of patience and endurance that women learn through the repetition of measured acts like sifting flour. To the guide, the museum space had been transformed into a valuable occasion to remind female students of women's proper behavior. Switching intermittently between "they" and "we," the guide underscored Malian youths' lack of knowledge about their cultural traditions and the museum's importance as a site for the transfer of such knowledge. He lamented that Malian youth knew very little about past traditions and illustrated this concept by referring to Fily Dabo Sissoko's shoes, which he had shown the group earlier in the visit. Sissoko, a writer and a major political figure in the 1950s and 1960s, used to wear sandals made of recycled tires; because of his example, such footwear became very popular in the 1950s. According to the guide, the museum enables the young generations "to know the tradition, what our mothers wore, the cultural values . . . to make sure that we do not abandon them all. It is to sensitize ourselves, to wake up our interest in our culture, to avoid just throwing ourselves at the European culture" (8 June 2001).

To this guide the museum seems to echo a certain world order that supposedly has been challenged or forgotten outside the museum walls. The museum's function then is to remind the young people of that order and to inspire a return to certain traditions (albeit, shifting ones). The guide highlighted—in a manner much in accordance with the museum's emphasis on women's clothes—the ambiguities of female students' contemporary outfits. Half jokingly, he kept noticing how the female students' clothes differed from those of their "mothers." He remarked, "When you see a woman whose head scarf is this voluminous, it means she is important . . . [but] today you go out without wearing a scarf." By pointing out this distinction, he intended to impress upon the youths that it was no longer possible to determine a woman's status just from the way she dressed. A similar message was iterated a few minutes later, when he showed certain bracelets that in the past were worn only by married women and commented, "You wear things any which way. ... [We no longer understand] who is married and who is not." The students either laughed at or challenged some of his statements. "I bet you cannot cook couscous," retorted the guide. A female student responded vehemently that she could—thus denying the lack of competence among younger women that the guide was suggesting. The guide's promotion of a return to traditions and the centrality of women's role in preserving such traditions—a recurring theme in political speeches since independence—went without being directly challenged.

Later on during the students' visit, it became clear that female museum staff did not necessarily share the guide's interpretation of the exhibit. During the post-tour discussion with the students, other museum representatives—who typically are removed from everyday contact with the museum's visitors—articulated their vision of the museum and departed from some of the guide's narratives. Significantly, the guide was not present during this final phase of the visit, and his absence created a space for some of the museum representatives to speak more openly than they would have otherwise. Here some of the differences and the similarities between their view and the guide's began to emerge. In his presentation of Faro, for example, the male guide had asserted that women do not autonomously search for power but that women's help and support are necessary for men's success, suggesting also that women should be content with their behind-the-scene role.[28] Museum director Goundiam held a different opinion. She clarified that Muso Kunda did not simply celebrate women's role within the family and men's need for women's support to succeed but also aimed to empower women to seek public recognition for their own contributions as independent persons (pers. comm., 8 June 2001).

In spite of the differences just highlighted, there were also points of convergence among perspectives held by the guide and the rest of the museum staff. During the discussion, the museum representatives all agreed, for instance, on the inadequacies of Malian youth and the corrective role that the museum could and should play in their education. They lectured the young crowd on the inadequacies of their generation in comparison to past generations. They expanded on the deep changes (including a return to "traditions") that institutions, such as the museum, were supposed to inspire in the younger generations: the reinstatement of values of respect and self-knowledge based on a solid appreciation of one's past (the well-known Mande imperative "*I yere don*" [Know yourself]). The elders expressed their disappointment with the younger generation for their fascinations with Western lifestyles and accused the latter of neglecting proper forms of respect in intergenerational exchanges.

None of the students, even those more rhetorically skilled, challenged their elders' accusatory tones. Indeed, some joined their elders in an autocritique of their own generation. Various causes were suggested, but the one most recursively mentioned was the lack of parental investment—women's especially—in children's education due to the difficult economic conditions experienced by many Malian households. The museum, supposedly a site for women's emancipation, had unexpectedly turned into a disciplinary site for the youths and the women. The tensions running through the museum's displays—and, in particular, the disjuncture between conflicting women's agendas—had suddenly precipitated (at least temporarily) a univocal message to the youth: one that unexpectedly pointed to women's failures in educating young people about fundamental social values.

The museum aims to reroot the young generations in their national and regional heritage while it endeavors to open them up to selected aspects of modernity. It constitutes a space for expressing and sorting out some of the contradictions and ambiguities running through Malian society: in particular, societal tensions between youth and their elders and between women and men in this age of neoliberal democracy. The attempt is not itself without contradictions, as the museum displays—without necessarily resolving—the tension between an emancipatory program and one that reasserts selected traditions. It is from the delicate balance of these contradictory tendencies that a modern and gendered Malian self should, ideally, emerge.

## Conclusions

Muso Kunda was founded with the objective to preserve and celebrate some of women's traditions and practices and to challenge women's economic and political marginalization (Ba Konaré 1993). The goal of women's empowerment fits squarely within the democratizing effort pursued under Konaré's presidency. It takes place in a more or less imaginary dialogue with regional, national, and transnational audiences in the attempt to define a culturally rooted yet progressive role for Malian women today. The museum stresses women's similarities and continuities with the past, reinforcing women's privileged association with fertility, childrearing, and household chores. On the other hand, the museum also promotes a progressive agenda by encouraging women's participation in all aspects of national life while taking a stance against Western feminism, whose objectives of gender equality are seen as too radical.

In building on Foucault's seminal work on heterotopias, I have proposed an interpretation of the museum as a privileged arena for the simultaneous display, deconstruction, and reassembly of multiple temporalities (further enabled by the adoption of the idiom of fashion) and social orders that are at times both divergent and conflicting. This recombinant aspect of the museum was particularly evident in the display dedicated to women's clothes, which conveyed women's often-contradictory searches for recognition, propriety, and empowerment. Adopting the language of fashion allows for the erasure of time depth and the free assemblage of clothing items and accessories from different periods. The resulting collage ultimately reduces variations in style and form within and among ethnic groups and simultaneously incorporates contemporary religious sensitivities. For example, most mannequins, regardless of their purported age group, are shown wearing the iconic boubou, though many of them wear a type (a demi-boubou) that fits contemporary taste and moral and practical concerns. Fashion also mediates the creative attempt by the female cosmopolitan elites to re-read the past in light of contemporary sensibilities and to articulate empowering historical narratives with which contemporary women can positively identify. The exhibit of women's dresses, with its creative combination of old and new clothing styles and accessories, challenges the sexualizing and diminishing gaze of the colonial propaganda. Muso Kunda seeks to cultivate audiences' perceptual changes and inspire projects of social change (Bennett 2006).

The delicate balance of positions that Muso Kunda ultimately aims to attain is a rather tenuous one. Some of the more emancipatory aspirations of Muso Kunda are challenged within the institution itself, as illustrated by the analysis of the guided tour and post-tour debates. The museum then comes to mirror some of the internal conflicts experienced by Malian citizens—and women, in particular—among various forms of preservation of (however shifting) traditions and the crafting of modern selves in a global context. Ultimately, this case study shows numerous discrepancies between institutional goals and institutional practices. These internal inconsistencies parallel some of the accommodations female cosmopolitan elites had to make early on in the history of Malian democracy to avoid antagonizing vocal (yet heterogeneous) social forces with conservative agendas on gender issues. The museum thus came to reflect the many struggles, attempted negotiations, and ensuing contradictions that characterize the discursive construction of gender in contemporary Mali. Ultimately, its very existence as a heterotopic space—that is, as a space carefully separated from the everyday and from which to initiate social change—has come to be disputed in the wake of the (temporary) closing of this institution.

## 4. The Heritagization of Islamic and Secular Architecture
*Djenné*

IN 1988 THE CITIES of Djenné (that is, the modern city of Djenné as well as the surrounding archaeological sites, the most notable of which is Djenné-Jeno) were inscribed on the prestigious UNESCO list of World Heritage Sites, following a request initiated by the Malian state almost a decade earlier (in 1979). This designation recognizes Djenné's architecture as the highest manifestation of the Sudanese style, characterized by the use of mud bricks, monumental facades, and interior courts (Maas and Mommersteeg 1993: 478). Djenné is also an exceptionally well-preserved "pre-colonial sahelian city, born out of the contact between Africa and the Arab world" (Bedaux, Diaby, and Maas 2003: 1). Since joining the UNESCO list, Djenné has attracted international aid (primarily from the Dutch government and the Aga Khan Trust for Culture) for the restoration and valorization of the city architecture and the promotion of economic development.

Djenné is a celebrated site of Sudanese architecture and Islamic learning, and analyzing this case sheds lights on the many dimensions—local, national, and transnational—of the process of heritagization of Malian heritage. The Malian government; transnational organizations, such as Djenné Patrimoine; foreign entities, such as the Netherlands, France, and the European Union collectively; and international organizations, such as UNESCO and the Aga Kahn Trust, are simultaneously engaged in transforming a number of sacred sites into public patrimony. This process is modeled after what Tony Bennett (1988, 1995, 2006) originally described as the exhibitionary complex—that is, the emergence of new discursive formations and techniques of vision (as manifested by museums, exhibits, arcades, and department stores) that articulate modern forms of governmentality. The exhibitionary complex is "a network of institutions in which earlier practices of exhibition were significantly overhauled in being adapted to the development of new forms of civic self-fashioning on the part of newly enfranchised democratic citizenries" (Bennett 2006: 48). Building on the Djenné case, I contend that the construction and articulation of the exhibitionary complex are not limited to the action of the state and that in the age of transnational governmentality, the state is, in fact, no longer the sole producer (if it ever was) of cultural heritage. The heritagization of Djenné's heritage documents the emergence of new—and equally stringent—forms of (transnational) governmentality (Ferguson and Gupta 2002; Sharma and Gupta 2006; Collier and Ong 2005; De Cesari 2010, 2012). In the process of state deregulation (also accompanied by the decentralization of state institutions), some of the regulatory functions of the state are exerted by a plethora of national, international, and transnational organizations: "Although this move to neoliberalism has often been understood (and variously celebrated or lamented, depending on one's politics) as a 'retreat' or 'rolling back' of the state, Barry et al. stress that it has, rather, entailed a transfer of the operations of government (in Foucault's extended sense) to nonstate entities, via 'the fabrication of techniques that can produce a degree of "autonomization" of entities of government from the state' (1996: 11–12)" (Ferguson and Gupta 2002: 989).

While the entities involved in the articulation of the exhibitionary complex are multiple and often in conflict with one another (and reflect not only the capillarization but also the fragmentation of the political), the heritagization of Djenné still presents some resemblances to the trajectory of the exhibitionary complex. Two aspects of the exhibitionary complex are particularly relevant in this case: for the exhibitionary complex to develop, the modern state had to transform formerly private space (here defined as space inaccessible to all but discrete segments of the population) into public space (e.g., the national museum) and diversify the body of heritage to be preserved and valorized to appeal to wider constituencies.[1] In Mali the transformation of formerly private space into public space is conducted simultaneously by a multiplicity of entities, national, supranational (UNESCO), and transnational. Recognition as a UNESCO World Heritage Site and the insertion of Djenné in touristic circuits have produced greater visibility and scrutiny in the ways in which the Djennenké use their lived-in space and resulted in deep contestations (De Jorio 2006a, 2009; Joy 2007a, 2007b, 2012; Rowlands 2007).[2] Furthermore, the heritagization by national and transnational entities has resulted in the diversification of the architectural patrimony to be preserved in and around Djenné. This move confers an aura of impartiality and distance to the state and its partners and conveys the state's commitment to protect and valorize the heritage of various segments of the population. The patrimony to be preserved is thus not limited to that of Islamic derivation (and, particularly, Islamic architecture) but is discursively expanded to include monuments, rituals, and know-how associated with the non-Islamic (what was formerly known as "animism") and has been recently reconceptualized as a key component of the secular patrimony.[3]

## Colonial Representations of Sudanese Architecture

Western discourse on Sudanese architecture has a complex history, beginning with its original denial of the indigenous roots of such an architectural tradition (e.g., French journalist Félix Dubois's 1897 thesis that Sudanese architecture originated in ancient Egypt) and continuing to its present emphasis on the authentic sub-Saharan origins of Sudanese architecture, often conceived within the romantic scope of ethnology. Following work by Labelle Prussin (1977, 1985, 1986, 2007), Michael Rowlands (2003, 2007), and Charlotte Joy (2007a, 2007b, 2012), I focus instead on the regimes of representation and regulation of Djenné enacted by the colonial and postcolonial states and by international organizations, such as UNESCO. Such perspective acknowledges the "Creole" character of all cultural heritage and the greatly political dimensions of its representation and preservation. Furthermore, this perspectival shift holds important practical implications. It can help promote new forms of heritage preservation where heritage sites become "site[s] of engagement, . . . space[s] of questioning and interrogation," as is the case of Cape Town's District Six Museum, described by Ciraj Rassool (2006: 290). Preservation work can become a site for a greater participation of local populations; for the critical examination of local, national, and transnational entanglements; and for the development of a transnational public sphere (Fraser 2007).

As part of this critical reflection on heritage work in Djenné, I turn now to a study of different forms of representation of Sudanese architecture by some of the main regimes of power and knowledge characterizing Mali's complex colonial and postcolonial history. I start by examining some of the French colonial representations of Sudanese architecture and some of their changes over time. Sudanese architecture—and, particularly, what has since been perceived as its highest manifestation, that is, the Great Mosque of Djenné, rebuilt by Djenné masons under the French in 1907—became a symbol of French imperial possessions in West Africa and also a major reference in the canonization of the Sudanese style by the French in both

**FIGURE 13.** Great Mosque of Djenné. Courtesy of Toin van Haeren.

the French Sudan and France (e.g., in the context of colonial exhibits) until the mid-1940s (figure 13) (Prussin 1985: 215; Ralph 2005).

The reconstruction of the Great Mosque of Djenné must be understood within the broader field of French colonial intervention in the domain of Sudanese architecture (Prussin 1977, 1985, 1986, 2007). During the initial phases of conquest and expansion, French intervention in Sudanese architecture was limited, consisting primarily of the facilitation and standardization of this style and, some argue, the introduction of some architectural innovation (e.g., arches, according to Domian 1989). Prussin reports that in the early 1890s the French had already overseen "the reconstruction of the Palace of Ahmadou at Ségou by Underberg and its conversion into a residence for the commandant of the Cercle" (1985: 226).

The French had also commissioned the reconstruction of the Aguibou Tall Palace after their conquest of Bandiagara in 1893,[4] thus showing how "this first example of colonial architecture in the region is incredibly respectful of local building traditions."[5] The construction of the Aguibou Palace was also realized "in authentic Sudanese style" and built by the "well-respected Djenné masons."

From 1889 to 1937, the organization of various colonial expositions in France and abroad more decidedly constituted an arena for French involvement in Sudanese architecture. Since the late 1870s, "colonial sections were included in all of the French universal exhibitions and in most of the French sections at the foreign world's fairs. By 1900, they had become extremely popular entertainments" (Morton 1998: 76). These colonial exhibits constituted sites of architectural experimentation, where the French incorporated Sudanese design elements in the architectural representations of their overseas empires. Informed by well-known travelers and reporters (notably, Dubois), French engineering firms helped develop hybrid forms, incorporating elements of Sudanese architecture within the neoclassical template of the Beaux Arts architectural style.[6] Such architectural experimentations ultimately led to the development of a neo-Sudanese style in French West Africa (Prussin 1985: 220).

According to Prussin, the Great Mosque of Djenné is the first expression of the neo-Sudanese style. Prussin contends that several aspects of the Djenné mosque reveal clear signs of French influence, such as the mosque's similarities to other buildings constructed under the French (manifesting the presence of a consistent design paradigm informing French architectural interventions in their overseas territories) and the use of "fake" forms to accentuate the building's overall symmetry. Prussin's position has been criticized by, among others, Jean-Louis Bourgeois (1987), who argues that the French merely authorized the mosque's reconstruction. Bourgeois denies any French influence and foregrounds instead Djenné masons' skills and creativity (see also Marchand 2009). Regardless of the degree of architectural innovation introduced by the French (probably very limited to none), the Great Mosque of Djenné remains "an architectural creation, because the masons did not have any documents depicting the façades of the old mosque, and many memories had faded in seventy years" (Djenné Patrimoine, n.d.). Despite specific objections, Prussin's work contributes to the clarification of French interest in the preservation of Sudanese architecture and their progressive appropriation and transformation of this architectural tradition.[7] According to Prussin, the rationale for the regime of representations the French instituted is mostly celebratory: the progressive appropriation by the French of the Sudanese style aimed to celebrate the success of French imperialism and to suggest the many economic and political opportunities expansion offered in French Sudan (and, particularly, the Niger Valley).

Gwendolyn Wright (1991, 1997) further explores the meanings of French colonial architecture and urban design until the 1930s, particularly in North Africa, where French architectural intervention was much more extensive.[8] According to Wright, French interest for local architectural traditions represented an important dimension of the articulation of colonial imagination; whether reconstructed (according to the "original") or newly constructed in the regional style, early French colonial architecture aimed to represent "colonization as a nondisruptive force often involved protecting the 'historic traditions' and 'economic climate' that they [the Europeans] had helped create" (1991: 54).[9] The preservation of "historic traditions" also constituted a powerful strategy of colonial administration by informing the very organization of urban space under colonial rule. Wright (1997) examines the separation of the city space in native and European quarters,[10] through which a form of urban apartheid was instituted (J. Abu-Lughod 1981).

In French West Africa, the French contributed to the standardization and canonization of Sudanese architecture (through the construction of the Mopti mosque, for example) on the basis of what they recognized as its most remarkable expression—that is, Djenné's architecture, in general, and the Great Mosque, in particular. French interest in actively preserving Sudanese architecture also mediated important French colonial policies. Known as the *politique des races*, this policy—of which William Ponty, an influential French colonial administrator, was a major promoter—was based on the belief that distinct and irreconcilable cultural differences among various African ethnic groups required different techniques of colonial intervention. This policy sought to discourage interethnic or intragroup alliances that could potentially threaten French control of the region. However, as Jean-Louis Bourgeois (1987) shows, Djenné individuals (e.g., religious authorities) and groups (e.g., the Tukolor and the Songhais) also strategically used the policy to increase their power within the colonial system relative to rival ethnic groups (e.g., the Peul).

Marcel Maussen (2007) highlights additional aspects of French intervention in West African architecture. He describes the reconstruction of mosques (both in the métropole and in West Africa) as part of a complex and not always successful strategy to establish some control over the practice of Islam, perceived simultaneously as an asset and as a threat to the stability of the French presence in the region. Black Muslim populations, considered "superior" to the "animistic" populations, according to dominant tenets of cultural evolutionism (Brenner 2001: 154), were seen as potentially facilitating France's civilizing mission. At the same time, black Muslims were feared because their transnational connections could threaten the stability of the empire. The French feared "the spreading of anti-colonial Muslim movements and . . . pan-Islamist ideas" among them (Maussen 2007: 984). In response, the French lent their support to a particular form of Islamic practice they called Black Islam (*Islam noir*), which they represented as a syncretic formation integrating Islamic and "animist" practices (and which they saw as less threatening to their own imperial interests).[11] The rebuilding of the Great Mosque of Djenné (framed as a reconstruction of Koi Konboro's thirteenth-century mosque) and the tearing down of Sekou Amadou's nineteenth-century mosque and the construction in its place of a Franco-Arabic school constitute early manifestations of this key French Islamic policy (see also Rowlands 2007), further demonstrated by the care with which the French colonial administration ensured the annual replastering of the mosque following its reconstruction (Prussin 1986).[12]

Colonial France became involved in the representation and transformation of Sudanese architecture during the decades of colonial expansion by facilitating the reconstruction of old and new buildings in the Sudanese style as well as by progressively forging new hybrid forms (within the frame of both colonial exhibits in France and urban development in West French Africa). Prussin (1985) points out that colonial exhibits became obsolete by the late 1930s at the conclusion of the expansion period.[13] According to R. F. Betts, the neo-Sudanese style became the dominant architectural style in French West Africa between World Wars I and II (Betts 1985: 199). As its hold over its West African empires grew stronger, colonial France became more obviously involved in the codification and transformation of the Sudanese style—from the modification of construction techniques (e.g., the replacement of traditional round Djenné bricks with square bricks called *toubabou ferey*; Maas 2011: 2) to the emergence of the neo-Sudanese style (particularly, in Bamako and Ségou). Through the reconstruction and progressive appropriation of elements of Sudanese architecture, the French aimed to convey their respect for local cultural traditions as well as to manifest—using new technologies of vision—the modernizing influence of France. According to Betts, the neo-Sudanese style "quietly left the scene after World War II" (1985: 200).[14]

## Postcolonial Representations and Global Recognition

The reevaluation of Djenné as a historical and archaeological site in the postcolony is intertwined with the process of recognition by UNESCO initiated in 1979 during Alpha Oumar Konaré's two-year tenure as minister of culture and continued during his presidency (1992–2002).[15] Although a coherent preservation policy of Mali's tangible heritage is rather recent, Djenné (symbolized by the Great Mosque) has been identified as a national symbol since the first years of independence, and the Great Mosque of Djenné has appeared on the coat of arms of the Republic of Mali since the early 1960s. In 1979 Mali submitted a request for the city of Djenné to be inscribed on the list of UNESCO World Heritage Sites. Acceptance by UNESCO was deferred on the grounds that the proposal did not include information on the conditions of the site or on the measures in place to preserve it. On the basis of UNESCO's feedback, Mali adopted laws in 1985 to address protection of its national heritage. A few years later, Mali successfully submitted a modified proposal to include the archaeological sites surrounding Djenné, a move recommended by UNESCO's consociated organization the International Council on Monuments and Sites (ICOMOS) on the grounds that it would help Mali curtail real-estate speculation as well as ensure the protection of Mali's rich archaeological past.[16] Djenné was finally included in UNESCO's World Heritage List in 1988. Following the country's neoliberal and democratic turn, Mali's government began compiling its own list of nationally recognized heritage sites in 1992, which included the city of Djenné. Since then the state has instituted cultural missions (*missions culturelles*), organisms in charge of carrying out Mali's preservation policies as well as overseeing and facilitating the execution of specific preservation projects, most often in cooperation with various international partners, at the local level. Under the Third Republic (1992 to present), the Great Mosque of Djenné remains one of the key symbols selected to convey the richness of Mali's historical past, the originality and richness of its cultural traditions, and the relevance of Islam in the lives of many Malian citizens. This symbolism is further manifested in a scale model of the Djenné mosque that was constructed in 2007 next to the National Museum of Mali (and was annexed to the National Park of Mali when the park was created in 2010). The iconic centrality of the Sudanese mosque (of which the Great Mosque of Djenné is the recognized model) in representations of Mali and its cultural patrimony is evident, too, in use of a mosque to showcase Mali's artisanal and artistic production in international exhibits.[17]

Western fascination with Djenné and its architecture has thus a long and tortuous history. The inclusion of Djenné on the list of UNESCO World Heritage Sites followed decades of Western interest in Mali's monumental past. Rowlands and Joy observe, "There is really no question that the world heritage list has had a significant effect in Africa—through promoting the recognition and documentation of cultural properties, preserving and restoring of heritage sites and the training of a new body of professionals committed to the recognition of the value of their cultural patrimony" (2011: 1). The UNESCO decision also poses a number of challenges, partly because the romantic notion of culture that informs such recognition also implies a view of culture as neatly defined, distinct, unique, and fundamentally unchanging (Eriksen 2001). Such a perspective does not sufficiently acknowledge the hybrid and Creole character of all cultural constructs. Most of all, it does not reckon with the political dimension of all cultural acts.[18] The recognition by UNESCO creates a new regime of vision, where the formation of a patrimony not only generates a new awareness and new practices on the part of the cultural producers (e.g., the masons of Djenné) vis-à-vis the artifact being produced (Kirshenblatt-Gimblett 2006b) but also exposes people (and things) to new forms of visibility and self-regulation of their conduct (Bennett 1995). The imposition of these techniques results from a multiplicity of political and cultural entities of various scales that have embraced the scopes and strategies of modern power. The transformation of an entire city into a permanent museum also transforms people's relationship to their living space by creating new forms of visibility and control that are on occasion fiercely resisted by the citizenry.[19]

## Restoration of Djenné

The inclusion of Djenné on the list of UNESCO World Heritage Sites imposes numerous constraints on the city inhabitants. For example, "UNESCO has decreed that the whole town should stay materially the same and rejects new technologies that would help home owners cope with the yearly cost of maintaining their homes" (Joy 2007b: 3). UNESCO literature reiterates the importance of keeping intact a certain town atmosphere and does not restrict the restoration to individual monuments. Following the Venice Charter and its reformulations (Joy 2007b: 3), of which Mali is a party, the restoration of Djenné must conform to the aesthetic criteria of Sudanese architecture (e.g., imposing facade, a certain decorative pattern), maintain the spatial organization of the lived-in space (e.g., an interior partitioned into small spaces arranged around an interior courtyard), use local materials (mud, karite, rice shaft, etc.), and use specific construction techniques—mastered by a specialized group of masons.[20] UNESCO does not directly contribute funds for the maintenance of World Heritage Sites, though UNESCO representatives do participate in decisions pertaining to the restoration of such sites (Joy 2007b). Financial aid and professional expertise for the restoration of Djenné are provided mostly by translocal and international entities in cooperation with the Malian state.

To date, the largest project of restoration of Djenné architecture was financed by the Netherlands from 1996 to 2012. It was run by a distinguished group of Dutch and international scholars with the participation of Djenné-based organizations and the Malian ministry of culture. During the first phase of this project, fewer than 10 percent of Djenné houses were selected for restoration because the application of such stringent restoration criteria to the whole city was considered unfeasible (Schmidt and Fané 2013; Maas 2011). It was suggested that the remaining 90 percent of the houses be built of traditional construction materials but without striving to maintain architectural "authenticity," thus providing greater latitude to the city inhabitants in terms of the organization and use of space. The restoration objective was "to retain the atmosphere of the city based on its location, with its typical structure of narrow streets and small squares and, especially, the monumental mud-brick houses with decorated façades, plastered by hand" (Maas 2011: 4). On the basis of "architectural criteria . . . 168, mostly monumental houses, were selected for restoration" (Maas 2011: 4). A few less monumental houses were also chosen to ensure greater social inclusiveness, due to the fact that the monumentality of the facade is typically a manifestation of a family's wealth and prestige. Representatives of the Dutch Housing Restoration Project recognized that because of the perishable nature of the materials utilized, most buildings were of relatively recent construction and decided to restore them to their precontact conditions. Maas explains, "The architecture and the city's atmosphere of around the turn of the century are taken as an arbitrary model for the restoration," a choice facilitated by the abundance of photographs from that period but also because it reflects the image of Djenné (both nationally and abroad) "that is most famous and forms the basis of the so-called 'style soudanais'" (2011: 6). The project also aimed to include and sensitize the population "to the importance of cultural preservation and cultural promotion of their architecture" as well as to revitalize the profession of masons, the expert builder on which Sudanese architecture rests (Rowlands 2007: 134; Marchand 2009).

## Preserving a Lived Patrimony: Djennenké Perspectives

Following UNESCO guidelines (and the Venice Charter of 1964), the Dutch-led preservation of the city patrimony is informed by the criteria of authenticity (of materials and techniques employed, for example) but also—in a departure from UNESCO's totalizing approach—by significance, as the entire town cannot feasibly be preserved (Bedaux, Diaby, and Maas 2003: 50). The application of international preservation guidelines has engendered various episodes of resistance on the part of the Djennenké, who did not necessarily identify with the forms and modalities of heritage preservation promoted by international organizations, such as UNESCO. In Djenné there were already established place-specific preservation practices (e.g., of the Great Mosque), and the new heritage regime threatened to displace collective forms of participation to the upkeep of Djenné's architecture as well as personal and group interests (A. F., pers. comm., Bamako, June 2014). Many Djennenké also came to perceive heritage initiatives as essentially benefiting a handful of secular and religious city authorities to the exclusion of the majority (De Jorio 2009; Joy 2007b, 2012; Rowlands 2007).

Many homeowners who agreed to participate in the restoration project complained that it did not permit architectural innovations to reflect their current needs and aspirations. A number of household heads among those solicited refused to participate in the restoration project altogether, fearing a reduction in their authority (Rowlands 2003).[21] To sensitize the population to the objectives of the restoration and valorization of the city patrimony, the ministry of culture and tourism organized a town meeting (*tuguna*) in 1998, during which some citizens expressed their reservations with the scale and form of the restoration. Sirandou Bocoum, a representative of a women's group, explained: "Difficult restoration rules are imposed on us. We are not allowed to change the present dimensions of our houses, but they are very small. Today we need spacious living rooms to entertain guests. The old entrance halls just won't do any more. A little modernity won't make our architecture any less authentic. . . . The rules are forcing the townspeople to live in a 'perpetual ghetto'" (qtd. in Kiabou 1998: 70). Women, in particular, voiced their desire to furnish their houses with modern fixtures, such as the armoire, an item not only functional but also symbolic of one's social status (B. A. Cissé 1998). The small windows and doors as well as the small rooms of the classic Sudanese house prevent the introduction of modern furnishings and the creation of living spaces to accommodate changing ideas of cleanliness, hospitality, and prestige. Indeed, generations of authors have commented on the contrast between the beauty of the exteriors and the unsanitary conditions of the interiors (Monteil 1903; Rowlands and Joy 2011). In response to some of these concerns, the Dutch Housing Restoration Project compromised with a few homeowners. In the case of a homeowner named Islamila Maiga, for example, Rowlands (2003) reports that the house facade was restored to resemble the depiction of this house in an old photograph, and the homeowner was given greater freedom in terms of material and organization of the interior space.[22]

The restoration of Djenné ultimately altered the delicate equilibrium of social forces and produced a series of popular revolts culminating in the events of 20 September 2006,[23] when the youth of Djenné attacked the Aga Khan Trust for Culture restoration team and demonstrated through the streets of town, burning cars of key city representatives, destroying the fans donated by the U.S. embassy for use in the Great Mosque, and committing other acts of protest (A. P. Cissé n.d.). The public saw the trust team's work as another episode in a series of interventions of which local residents had not been sufficiently informed (or even consulted) and that they perceived as benefiting the town elites.[24] Seeing these demonstrations as evidence of communications failures, the state administration and Djenné-based cultural associations made a significant effort to better inform and involve a broader spectrum of the town population. The collapse of one of the mosque's towers in 2009 also precipitated these initiatives. The outreach efforts ultimately yielded some positive results, and renovation work on the Great Mosque was successfully completed in 2011.[25]

## Conflicts Surrounding the Preservation of Djenné's Architectural Heritage

Both foreign and local experts criticize the use of modern material and modest technological innovations in Djenné restoration projects. These experts argue that such inclusions either contradict UNESCO guidelines or serve as expressions of bad taste and view them as contributing to the city's cultural decline. The pages of *Djenné Patrimoine Informations*, the online bulletin of the cultural association Djenné Patrimoine, recursively criticize several of these modern practices, such as the use of neon pipes to decorate a side of the Great Mosque, the placement inside the mosque of one hundred fans donated by the U.S. embassy, and the use of plastic pipes instead of ceramic.

The use of modern construction material (e.g., cement, ceramic tiles, and plastic pipes) and techniques is also increasingly popular, following trends that arch back to the French colonial period and the introduction of square bricks often made with a less expensive and durable mixture (toubabou ferey). The introduction of new materials is a particularly controversial issue, as UNESCO guidelines state that the use of traditional materials is a condition for the retention of World Heritage Site status. According to a 2002 study by a French engineering student Marie-Laure Villesuzanne, however, a considerable number of Djenné residents prefer constructions in concrete, which they consider more durable and modern than the traditional banco building material (Villesuzanne 2002).[26] Covering the exterior walls with ceramic tiles is another popular practice—and a solution that eliminates the need for the annual replastering of traditional houses. This innovation, however, is not only criticized for aesthetic reasons but is also considered of limited practical consequence: a number of experts argue that it represents a more expensive and temporary fix because water creeps in between the banco base and the tiled external surface, ultimately weakening the house structure (Scherrer 2009).[27]

The construction of a new school (replacing one built under the French in the Sudanese style) constituted a renewed occasion to observe the perspectival discrepancy between the preservation discourse of the modern state and the modernization discourse of segments of the Djenné population.[28] The new school, financed by the Banque Islamique de Développement (functionally similar to the World Bank but for the Islamic world), was realized in concrete with ceramic tiles and in a style some preservationists deemed to be "certainly foreign to Djenné's architecture" (Djenné Patrimoine 1998a).[29] The school had been built on the site of Sekou Amadou's mosque at the beginning of French colonization but was poorly maintained, and the roof eventually collapsed, harming some of the pupils (Charlotte Joy, pers. comm. 23 Jan. 2015). The renovation project found support among the pupils' families (who aspire to more modern, secure, functional, and durable housing), city authorities, and teachers. The construction of the new school (circa 1998) that violates international preservation guidelines also highlights some of the state administration's challenges in executing UNESCO's preservation program and in developing a coherent urban-development plan, partly because of the weakening effects of decades of structural adjustment programs and increased dependence on external donors.

A number of scholars have observed that Djenné's inscription on the list of UNESCO World Heritage Sites has created a difficult situation for the city's inhabitants, as the resulting museological approach in the handling of the city patrimony freezes a lived patrimony in constant transformation (e.g., Marchand 2009; Joy 2012). In short, the Djennenké have been condemned to live in the ethnographic present. They are now restricted to forms of life that they find confining owing to economic difficulties further heightened by the near-total lack of tourism revenues due to continuing insecurity in the north; changes in taste, family size, and family dynamics (resulting from immigration and shifts in gender dynamics, among others); and contemporary aspirations. In the words of its own citizens, Djenné has been reduced to a sort of living museum—that is, to a spatial arrangement scarcely responsive to its inhabitants' rapidly changing needs and aspirations.[30]

## Diversification and Secularization: The Saho Case

The valorization of Malian cultural heritage aims to encourage and strengthen the region's economic development while preserving the cultural diversity of Mali's populations (B. A. Cissé 1998). Both the state and its international partners contribute to the transformation and diversification of the region's patrimony, striving to preserve Djenné's Islamic architecture as well as its secular architecture. In particular the *saho*, or youth house, has attracted preservationists' attention. The architectural tradition of the saho was originally introduced by the Bozo, a population of fishermen and among the first inhabitants of the region. The saho was also appropriated and transformed by other social groups, such as the Somono (a professional group of fishermen) and the Marka (a group of Muslim traders of diverse ethnic origins) (Mommersteeg and Pedrocco 2013; Schmidt and Fané 2013: 10). The diversification of the region's patrimony has materialized in two parallel heritage projects, both of which take the vernacular architecture of the saho as their point of departure: the construction of new public buildings, such as the Museum of Djenné; and the preservation of sahos in the Djenné region.[31]

When the project of a museum in Djenné was initially presented and discussed in 1998, the connection between the preservation of the saho and the construction of secular buildings was immediately drawn (figure 14). An article in *Djenné Patrimoine Informations* states, "For the style of the facades, the architect [of the museum] drew inspiration from a *saho* in the proximity of Djenné, because these buildings represent the only example of public nonreligious architecture in the surrounding of Djenné" (Djenné Patrimoine 1998c). Although more-recent descriptions of the museum no longer make an explicit connection to the saho—perhaps in response to critiques by some religious authorities—the museum vision as articulated by architect Abdoulaye Touré (2008) rests on the figurative tradition and the construction techniques of Sudanese architecture and includes elements of the saho's decorative tradition (through the prudent use of sexual symbols). Descriptions of the museum continue to stress this institution's unprecedented secular character. One writer at *Djenné Patrimoine Informations* states, "The museum of Djenné will be the second-largest building in the city, it will be like the mosque in the center of town, and it will be the first public building," and further argues that if the building were to successfully embody the originality and adaptive capacity of Sudanese architecture, it would "bring to the city an air of modernity that it currently lacks" (Djenné Patrimoine 2006).[32] Started in 2008, the museum (the largest secular public space available) was completed in 2010 with European Union funds (Berthé

**FIGURE 14.** Musée de Djenné, 2015. Courtesy of Mamadou Samaké, the Cultural Mission, Djenné.

2014). As of late 2015, the museum remains closed because it lacks the funds to build any collections or exhibits. It is due to open with an ornithology exhibit on West African birds, in partnership with Goldsmiths College of the University of London and the Horniman Museum and Gardens in London.[33]

Malian preservationists identified in the Bozo youth-house restoration one of their most pressing objectives in the larger Djenné region. Yamoussa Fané, the former head of La Mission Culturelle de Djenné, relates, "For decades, new saho have not been built, and those remaining are either abandoned or disfigured by cursory interventions" (2011: 3). Commenting on the restoration of the saho, the then-minister of culture, Boubacar Hamadoun Kébé, clarified that it should not be seen "as a rejection of modernity . . . but [as a response] to an urgent need to provide cultural references to a youth [facing a profound] identity crisis" (2013: 5). The saho restoration, sponsored by the Netherlands and overseen by the Ethnology Museum of Leiden, "is

*The Heritagization of Islamic and Secular Architecture* 109

an integral part of the broad program of restoration and preservation of Djenné's architecture" (Kébé 2013: 5). References to the saho in both government documents and *Djenné Patrimoine Informations* highlight its secular character and downplay its connection to "pre-Islamic" religious traditions. Indeed, the restoration encountered various challenges, partly because of the more individualistic ethos of the Malian youth, the youths' conflicting views of modernity and democracy (often resulting in the rejection of practices and logics the youth perceive as constraining), and opposition from certain religious representatives who see in the saho a place of sexual license and improper behavior (Mommersteeg and Pedrocco 2013: 28). Fané emphasizes the saho's secular and monumental dimensions: "In the Bozo villages of the interior Delta, two social centers coexist: the religious, symbolized by the mosque, and the laïc [secular], represented by the saho, the house of the young men [or adolescents]. The saho, is a true monument, on equal footing with the mosque" (2011: 3).

Sebastiano Pedrocco (2003) distinguishes two types of saho: the saho of the villages (monumental and central) and the saho of the fishing posts (simpler and peripheral). According to Pedrocco, the saho of Bozo villages is profoundly influenced by Sudanese architecture (2003: 167). The rural Bozo appropriated the Sudanese style (viewed as urban and cosmopolitan) to express their specific ethnic identity, as evidenced by the saho's decorations, whose "forms recall some fishing and hunting instruments, representations of the cosmogony . . . [as well as] male and female sexual symbols" (Pedrocco 2003: 166). The continuity and exchange of style and motives are evident in the fact that Djenné masons (many of whom have Bozo origins) were recognized for their artistry and were invited to build their sahos in the surrounding Bozo villages.

As the house where young men lived from puberty until marriage (when they moved out in order to assume their responsibilities as adults), the saho constituted a site for regulated romantic encounters but also for the inculturation of the male youth (Pedrocco 2003: 163; Mommersteeg and Pedrocco 2013). Pedrocco explains that "the Islamic authorities strongly oppose these buildings, which they see as an expression of the strong animist traditions and of the free premarital erotic practices" of the Bozo (2013: 175; Mommersteeg and Pedrocco 2013: 28). A similar critique was developed in response to the initial presentation of the museum project in 1998, when the saho model was first discussed. The classificatory shift of the saho from a monument shaped by "pre-Islamic" beliefs to an example of secular architecture in the government literature is a further manifestation of the state commitment to diversifying its cultural mandate and circumventing some of the predictable obstacles (e.g., religious objections to the incorporation of certain architectural elements). The diversification of the objectives of the restoration confers a certain distance and neutrality to the Malian state and its partners. The restoration of the regional architecture is not limited to Islamic architecture but also protects a more heterogeneous architectural patrimony, even if strategically reconceptualized as secular. The construction of secular buildings, such as museums and heritage sites, further completes the inclusion of Djenné within the circuits of modern power, strengthened by the extension of the exhibitionary complex to Mali's regions.

## Making Religious Heritage Public

The Malian state, transnational organizations, such as Djenné Patrimoine, and international partners are promoting new patterns of the circulation of knowledge and use of space. The modern state encourages the free circulation of knowledge and free (in the sense of public) access to Djenné's cultural heritage. The regulation of Djenné's architecture (to a large extent of religious significance) becomes a venue via which the state further cultivates forms of religiosity that are deemed compatible with its secular option. For instance, a number of cultural entities, such as Djenné Patrimoine (but also the Malian press and representatives of the ministry of culture), campaign to open the Great Mosque and Quranic schools to the public—in particular, to foreign tourists and visitors (A. F., pers. comm., June 2014). Thus members of Djenné Patrimoine expressed their satisfaction with the decision by L'Association Malienne pour l'Unité et le Progrès de l'Islam (Malian Association for the Unity and Progress of Islam) (AMUPI) to open the Great Mosque to official delegations.[34] Similarly, Djenné Patrimoine stresses the importance of informing the public (particularly, travel agencies and potential tourists) well in advance of the date of the mosque's annual *crépissage* (replastering), an event in which the entire town participates. In spite of growing awareness of the connection between widespread announcement of this date and an increase in tourism (and tourism money), in 2001 one of the most influential members of Djenné Patrimoine, French economist Joseph Brunet-Jailly, noted, "Djenné inhabitants have not yet decided whether to share such occasion of intense festivity with foreigners; whose participation presupposes that they be informed well in advance" (2001). Because the preparation of banco requires several weeks, it should be possible for the organizers to schedule the date of the crépissage in advance. Unfortunately, "the date of the crépissage is kept secret until the last minute and without any valuable reason" (Brunet-Jailly 2001). Four years later, Amadou Cissé, a leading organizer of the cultural festival Djennery, reported that after numerous discussions, he was able to persuade the city elites to make the date of the crépissage public months in advance (qtd. in Touré and Sissoko 2005; Joy 2012).³⁵ As Christopher B. Steiner observed, within a nation, "the transition from artifact into art—from object of religious veneration to object of aesthetic contemplation—is not always acknowledged universally at the same moment in time; it is a process that is at once reversible and incomplete" (1995: 4). The transformation of the crépissage into an aestheticized form to be accessible to other publics than the Djennenké themselves was a process ridden with conflicts between state representatives, on one hand, and religious and traditional authorities, on the other, the latter resisting the forms of memorialization promoted by the state (Gatti 2006; Rowlands 2007; Joy 2012).

Furthermore, the state, various cultural associations, and international entities not only encourage free access to Djenné architectural patrimony (including sacred sites) but also actively promote forms of religiosity deemed compatible with the secular option of the Malian state.³⁶ These techniques are reminiscent of French Islamic policies and their conspicuous interventions in the religious sphere. The French intervened heavily to control what they deemed as threatening tendencies within Islam and to promote French culture and values (Soares 2013); accordingly, they built their first West African *médersa* (Islamic school) in Djenné in 1906 (closed in 1913) to promote Franco-Arabic education. Governor General William Ponty declared that the teaching of French in Islamic education was to be interpreted as "the most effective cure one can employ against [religious] fanaticism" (qtd. in Brenner 2001: 41). Simultaneously, the French encouraged local forms of religious expression, particularly the so-called Islam noir, which was seen as more tolerant and syncretic.³⁷ The reconstruction of the Djenné mosque under the French—its placement on the site of Koi Konboro's mosque, a symbol of a tolerant Islam vis-à-vis the rigid and severe Islam promulgated by Sekou Amadou and symbolized by his more austere and simpler mosque—was an early manifestation of French support to certain movements within Islam. The French colonial state was heavily invested in the construction of mosques and the appointment of loyal religious authority as a strategy of colonial domination (Maussen 2007). Many of the French Islamic policies (and their contradictions) have continued in the postcolony; indeed, "one of the truly striking continuities from the colonial period until the present age of neoliberalism is how Islam and Muslims are almost invariably assumed to be among the most significant potential problems for governance" (Soares 2005b: 83).

A number of articles in *Djenné Patrimoine Informations* reflect a certain normative anxiety vis-à-vis the forms of Islam practiced in Djenné. For instance, Boureima Touré, independent researcher in Djenné, foregrounds the unifying role of Islam, on which basis the Djennenké overcame ethnic divisions and came to claim a shared identity. The form of Islam practiced in Djenné, he contends, manifests "a certain particularity," in part due to the "long survival of animism" (2004). Touré recognizes the ambiguous nature of Islam that he sees simultaneously as a source of and an obstacle to the city's "progress." Islam can be mobilized as a source of unity and citizen empowerment, as, for instance, when the Djennenké successfully opposed the first project for the construction of a new dam, the *barrage de Talo*, that would have had detrimental effects on the populations of Djenné and made them more susceptible to drought (2004).[38] Simultaneously, Islam is presented as a barrier to "the city's progress" because it may hamper citizens' full participation and identification with state institutions. Indeed, Touré points out, "The Islam practiced in Djenné rejects the idea of secularity when the Malian state asserts itself as a secular entity" (2004).

The practice of Islam that is praised and encouraged by some of the contributors to *Djenné Patrimoine Informations* is one that does not threaten the secularity of the state and its regulatory function. Thus in their reporting on the 2004 election results, the editors of that publication underline how the religious authorities did not recommend any party or candidate. Even the position taken by an Islamic association, the Association pour le Développement de l'Islam à Djenné (Association for the Development of Islam in Djenné) (ADID) against ADEMA is explained as the result of personal rivalries (or, at most, conflicting aesthetic projects) more than explicitly political motivations: "Only the Association pour le Développement de l'Islam à Djenné (ADID) carried out a campaign against the ADEMA candidate, because the latter had opposed the installation of iron doors at the Great Mosque that ADID's generous patron had commissioned and transported to Djenné" (Soumaila Sow 2004).

In 2001, on the occasion of religious celebrations marking the birth and naming ceremony of the Prophet Muhammad, the editorial board of *Djenné Patrimoine Informations* commented with satisfaction on the "studious and tolerant" atmosphere that characterized the celebrations by the two main marabout families, the Traoré and the Gaba. Less glowing tones colored the reportage of the Islamic organization Ansar Dine's celebrations. According to *Djenné Patrimoine Informations*, the organization's representatives occupied the square in front of the Great Mosque (a "symbol of the unity of Islam") and attracted a negligible crowd comprising mostly curious passersby and children, trying to convince them to embrace "a pure and uncompromising Islam" to which the more tolerant versions of local religiosity were juxtaposed (Djenné Patrimoine 2001). At that time the leader of this organization, Ousmane Madani Haidara, "was (and still is) perceived by many government officials and representatives of the Muslim establishment as a fundamentalist threat to Mali's secular constitution; despite the fact that Haidara vehemently opposes the agenda of the *intégristes*, that is, the Muslims who since 1991 have called for the establishment of the shari'a" (Schulz 2003: 147).[39] Boureima Touré also comments with some anxiety on the increasing popularity of the organization in Djenné and refers to the "heated debates among the population" following the last visit of Ansar Dine and concludes that the Islam practiced in Djenné "is not safe from outside threats (including American influence)" (2004).[40] The critique of a more literal Islam with perceived translocal connections is accompanied by an endorsement of place-specific Islamic practices, represented as syncretic and more tolerant (and also portrayed as more open to the new demands of the heritage sector).[41]

## Conclusions

The heritagization of Djenné is the work of multiple political entities that have taken on the functions and attributes of the state, here analyzed from the perspective of the technologies of vision they deploy. Paradoxically, the neoliberal turn (as shown in the reduction of the state budget and the privatization of previously state-owned enterprises, among others) and the so-called program of decentralization of state institutions (supposedly aimed to empower local communities and their elected representatives) have resulted in the strengthening of modern forms of governmentality. In the past the state was often an intermittent presence in the form of delegations, visits, and the like. Local state representatives had rather limited functions, mostly activated by the discontinuous flow of the "party words" emanating from the center. The international recognition of Djenné as a national and global heritage site results in multisited processes of heritagization that promote the diffusion of techniques of vision associated with modern power. Despite the conflicts and differences, national, international, and transnational entities participate in the transformation of Djenné into an exhibitionary complex—that is, in the transformation of Djenné into a public space, regulated by UNESCO guidelines and with varying degrees of participation from the Djennenké, who, consequently, experience a reduction in their ability to make choices pertaining to the use and organization of their lived space.

However, the heritagization process is far from linear, as the entities involved in the restoration and development of Djenné express partly conflicting visions of the city and sponsor contradictory projects. A case in point is the American embassy's gift of electrical fans to the Great Mosque of Djenné—a gift meant to indicate the United States' tolerant attitude toward moderate forms of Islam in the wake of 9/11. Such initiatives diverge from UNESCO-informed guidelines for the preservation of Djenné, creating conflicting development policies. Furthermore, UNESCO's decision (at the request of the Malian state) to inscribe the cities of Djenné on the World Heritage Site list is seen by many as problematic because of the top-down forms of heritagization it promotes with limited returns for the population, despite citizens' hopes that the nomination would bring in tourism revenues (Brunet-Jailly 2002; Joy 2007a, 2007b).[42] Prior to the 2012 political and security crisis, Djenné's growing notoriety had been attracting tourists and development money, thus theoretically opening new opportunities for economic development. On the other hand, tourism revenues were still very limited and did not offset the disadvantages of living in a town turned into a museum as recognition of its "outstanding value to humanity" (Joy 2007a: 147, 2012).[43] Despite the formal resolution in 2013 of the political crisis (and the election of a new government), tourism in Djenné, as elsewhere in Mali, still struggles because of the continuing insecurity in the northern regions.

Manifestations of the multisitedness of modern power also include Djenné-based organizations with strong transnational links (notably, Djenné Patrimoine) that emerge as important forces in the heritagization of Djenné, in terms of both the more inclusive initiatives they promote and their dissemination of knowledge about the city. The development of grassroots organizations, such as Djenné Patrimoine, aims to counter the top-down forms of heritagization promoted by the state and UNESCO. This organization is contributing to the broadening of the debate and circulation of information via the publication of an informative bulletin that provides new opportunities for citizens to voice their concerns about the forms of preservation promoted by UNESCO. In 2015 Djenné Patrimoine was able to complete its center, La Maison du Patrimoine, from which to launch initiatives to facilitate citizens' preservation of their built space and promote the preservation of place-specific knowledge and know-how but also to mobilize the population to pressure the state to spearhead changes to the classification (*révision du classement*) of Djenné as a World Heritage Site.[44] The construction of a Maison du Patrimoine and its ambitious programs, if successful, could represent a site of empowerment for the population, breaking the spatial dichotomy between the state (museum) and religion (Great Mosque) and spatially inscribing the presence of a growing civil society in Djenné.

## 5. The Fate of Timbuktu's Sufi Heritage

*Controversies around Past Traces and Current Practices*

THE FATE OF THE cultural heritage of the legendary city of Timbuktu and, particularly, the destruction of saints' mausoleums under the occupation of an unstable alliance of Tuareg and Islamist extremist groups sparked unprecedented media attention due to the mausoleums' highly symbolic character as UNESCO World Heritage Sites.[1] The destruction of Timbuktu's mausoleums in the last days of June 2012 came to symbolize the occupants' obscurantism and absolute disregard for place-specific forms of religiosity,[2] such as people's pilgrimages (*zyhara*) and veneration of saints. Because some of the Timbuktu-based elites draw their status and livelihood from the management of the mausoleums, the destruction of such ritual sites undermined the very foundations of Timbuktu's social order, resurrected within a neoliberal scape in which tourism and culture function as vehicles for economic development.[3]

Saints' remains and mausoleums and the cemeteries that developed around some of the mausoleums are distinguishing features of Timbuktu. Indeed, Timbuktu is known as the City of 333 Saints, a reference to the central role it played "in the development and diffusion of Islamic thought in the Saharan region" (Ghetti et al., 2011: 18), and its mausoleums and mosques are tangible traces of the enduring power of a "religio-learned hierarchy of scholars and jurists" and its transformations over time (Saad 1983: 14). In fact, the history of the city—particularly, memories of the city's golden age under Songhai occupation (ca. 1468–1591)—"lies at the fulcrum of the city's own consciousness of its history" (Saad 1983: 10). The revitalization of the city's heritage in recent years through the renovation of mosques, the opening of private libraries, and the inclusion of the mausoleums in tourism circuits has opened new opportunities for the (re)deployment of a heritage elite rooted in pliable memories of Timbuktu's rich history (see Molins Lliteras 2013).

Analyses of the conflict have thus far focused mostly on the more visible political dimensions of Mali's crisis, citing the global war on terror, Tuareg irredentism, the fall of the Muammar Gaddafi regime in Libya, and the Malian state's loss of legitimacy as factors that contributed to the March 2012 coup d'état in the south and the secession of Mali's north under a short-lived alliance of Tuareg and Islamist extremist groups. I focus here on the preservation of cultural heritage in Timbuktu, the city's recent history, and some of the debates surrounding its heritage. While much of the press has quickly dismissed the destruction of the mausoleums as evidence of the Islamist extremists' "barbaric" form of Islam (about which very little is known) and the act of mostly foreigners with scarce (or even nonexistent) roots in Malian society, I examine the deeper reasons behind the mausoleums' destruction (see also O'Dell 2013; Soares 2012). In particular, I explore whether the destruction of the saints' mausoleums and the discourses surrounding these events may be at least partly indicative of conflicts and antagonism triggered by the forms of heritage preservation that were pursued by the state, foreign entities, and the heritage elite in Timbuktu (and accompanied by state or statelike interference in the religious field) prior to the occupation. More broadly, I view heritage matters as a lens through which to examine the broader workings of modern power and its internal tensions in the present era.

I also reflect on some of the divisions pertaining to the reconstruction of the mausoleums—divisions that are emerging within the Malian religious sphere in the postconflict era and are largely ignored by the entities who are promoting the reconstruction work. Yet, the expansion and diversification of the religious sphere, the shifting of boundaries between the secular and the religious, and the complex entanglements of those two realms have been recognized as major developments of the neoliberal era (Soares 2005a, 2005b, 2007, 2013; Holder 2014b; Holder and Sow 2014). As discussed in further detail below, Muslim leaders and Malian citizens have different views of the mausoleums' reconstruction, especially as envisioned by representatives of UNESCO and other heritage entities. In order for more-enduring forms of postconflict reconstruction to take place, "negotiations" about the reconstruction of the mausoleums among UNESCO, the state, and the Timbuktu's population should consider broader debates (both those in Timbuktu and those in wider Malian society, which reflect transregional factors) about the preservation of the Islamic heritage (e.g., O'Dell 2013). The reconstruction may then become a site for more-inclusive conversations and questionings on the forms of preservation of the religious heritage (and their multiple and, at times, contrasting meanings) in present-day Mali.

## The Mausoleums and Their Relevance to the Religious Economy

The mausoleums and tombs of saints and scholars and the cemeteries that developed around some of them are distinguishing features of Timbuktu, reflecting on the city's centrality in the history of Islam in Africa.[4] The tombs are located not only all around the city but also inside the old town center. Some mausoleums are contiguous to or in proximity to historic mosques or the houses of prominent families; these include the mausoleums attached to the external walls of Djingarey Ber (the great mosque in the dialect of Songhai spoken in Timbuktu) and the Sidi Yahya Mosque. Saints are even buried inside some buildings, as in the case of the twin saints buried beneath one of the pillars of the Djingarey Ber itself (figure 15).[5]

In 1988 a number of Timbuktu's sacred sites—sixteen mausoleums (including the cemeteries surrounding some of them) and the three historic mosques of Djingarey Ber, Sankoré, and Sidi Yahya—were added to UNESCO's list of World Heritage Sites. But recent studies convey some uncertainty as to the number of actual mausoleums:[6] of the sixteen listed in the original request for World Heritage status, six can no longer be identified (Ghetti 2014: 22).[7] Information varies also as what saints are the most venerated, reflecting the speaker's situated position and preferences.

Most saints' burial places share a common design: five stones indicate the saint's body, and a terra-cotta pot indicates the head, which is oriented toward the Kaaba in Mecca, as is common in Islamic burials (Ghetti, Bertagnin, and Antonelli 2002: 76). There are also a few larger tombs, known as mausoleums because of their symbolic relevance.[8] At least one of the larger mausoleums, that of Muslim scholar Cheick Sidi Mahmoud (1498–1548), was originally the entryway (vestibule) of the saint's home and was turned into a burial place at his death. Several other mausoleums have been elevated or even rebuilt on top of existing mausoleums. In the mid-1950s, it became fashionable (as a sign of "the modern") to cover the mausoleums' mud structures with alhore stone blocks and cement, which conferred a more angular structure to the buildings (Direction Nationale 2014: 39).

The city's saints are said to protect Timbuktu's inhabitants from outside incursions. In this expression of Sufism,[9] certain individuals present "special gifts of intimacy with the Divine," by virtue of which they are recognized

FIGURE 15. Djingarey Ber Mosque, Timbuktu. Courtesy of Toin van Haeren.

and sought as spiritual leaders (Howell and van Bruinessen 2007: 6). Many Malian Muslims are not members of specific Sufi orders but follow "certain practices closely tied to Sufism, Sufi orders, and their leaders, including the veneration of certain persons with reputations as saints and the use of the Islamic esoteric sciences ('marabouts' and 'maraboutage' in the French colonial lexicon)" (Soares 2007: 79). Entire cemeteries developed around several of these mausoleums (including the one of Cheick Sidi Mahmoud), because proximity to a saint is believed to protect the deceased "from the dangers of the afterworld" (Becker 2009: 429).

In Timbuktu the mausoleums are the property of individual families that claim descent from those saints or have acquired the right to represent their legacy. Male elders attend to the upkeep of the mausoleums; this task is often reserved for Friday mornings prior to going to the mosque, although the tombs of some of the most revered saints (e.g., Cheick Sidi Mahmoud, Alpha Moya, and Cheick Mahmoud Tamba-Tamba) are visited daily (C. M. Haidara 2012: 28).

Saints are also buried under Timbuktu's three World Heritage mosques: Djingarey Ber, Sankoré, and Sidi Yahya. In times of crisis, people often visit the mosques and seek saints' intervention. For instance, those people with problems related to the conquest of power are advised to go to the Djingarey Ber Mosque, those seeking resolutions to family problems and marriage issues and the attainment of knowledge usually visit the Sankoré Mosque, and people who wish to succeed in business might conduct their prayers at the Sidi Yahya Mosque (Senou Sidi, pers. comm., 2014).[10]

Mausoleums are visited mostly by Timbuktu residents (T. Maiga, pers. comm., 2014). However, nonresidents, too, visit the tombs, particularly during the Mawlud (the celebrations surrounding the birth of the Prophet Muhammad), when many Timbuktu natives return to the city. When tourism was still flourishing in the region, roughly between 1994 and 2004, mausoleums also became preferred tourist destinations. The promises of revenues from tourism led to the commodification of the saints' tombs, adding further dimensions to the transformation of the religious economy in the neoliberal era.[11] Tourists could go inside the mausoleums in exchange for a monetary donation (T. Maiga, pers. comm., 2014). Tour guides competed with one another for exclusive rights to specific mausoleums, negotiating special arrangements with a mausoleum's owners to ensure the presence of a family representative (typically, the male family head or, in his absence, one of his older sons) when the guide brought tourists there. Such visits were made even more "authentic" by a short presentation delivered by the saints' descendants at the mausoleum site.

The mausoleums and the practices surrounding them are central to the formation and articulation of group identities, because genealogical or spiritual descent from certain saints confers religious authority to groups and individuals within the highly stratified (though far from cohesive) society of Timbuktu.[12] Furthermore, their association with certain Sufi tombs enables some families to partake in the heritage industry as owners of sites of touristic and religious interest and to position themselves as potential recipients of funds earmarked for heritage-preservation initiatives.

The veneration of Sufi saints is an important religious practice, but dispositions vis-à-vis these saints vary throughout the population. The 2012 Tuareg-Islamist occupation of the north, continuing insecurity in that region, and the postconflict government's lack of credibility have together produced a sizable shift in perspectives about the veneration of saints.[13] In particular, the heritage elites have a more cautious approach toward what they describe as more popular forms of religiosity in which people venerate the saints in hopes of obtaining certain material or spiritual rewards in return. At most, the heritage elites concede that the saints are surrounded by an aura of sacredness conducive perhaps to more efficacious communication with God while still maintaining that the saints have no actual power per se (Senou Sidi, pers. comm., 2014).

## Heritage Work in the North before 2012

Some of the initiatives in the field of heritage preservation and valorization carried out by the state and other entities in Mali's northern regions were partly the result of decentralization policies, that is, concerted efforts to promote greater regional autonomy and economic development. At the same time, these initiatives (several of which had to do with the preservation of Mali's Sufi heritage) also reflected increasing preoccupations with the rise of Islamist extremist groups in the north. In this context, state and statelike organizations expressed open support for what they identified as moderate and tolerant forms of Islam.

Under Amadou Toumani Touré, the revival of Timbuktu's heritage became a government priority, with greater attention to the city's cultural and economic development reflecting "the president's personal attachment to the religious patrimony of the city" (Holder 2014b: 442; De Jorio 2009). Touré put greater emphasis on the preservation of Mali's religious heritage than did his predecessor, Alpha Oumar Konaré, who stressed "the archaeological, historical, and intellectual heritage of Mali," though his government did establish some of the infrastructure for later heritage work development in the north (Holder 2014b: 497).[14]

During Touré's administration, a number of initiatives for the preservation of the Islamic heritage in Timbuktu were implemented. They centered on the preservation and valorization of the important collections of Arabic and *ajami* documents (written in African languages, using Arabic characters), the restoration of the city's architectural buildings, and the preservation of traditional know-how (e.g., masonry). During a 2005 visit to Timbuktu, for example, Touré reportedly commented on the state of disarray of religious sites, particularly those endowed with World Heritage status (Séméga 2012). He subsequently secured the financial support of the Aga Khan Trust for Culture for the renovation of Timbuktu's Sudanese architecture. The AKTC also committed important human and other financial resources to restore the great mosque of Timbuktu (and the mosques of Djenné and Mopti, too), work that ultimately took place between 2006 and 2011.

Under Touré's presidency, a productive partnership with South Africa was also developed, resulting in part in the 2009 inauguration of "a new state-of-the-art facility built with South African help to house and preserve the Timbuktu Manuscripts" (SAinfo Reporter 2009).[15] Due to a lack of funding for the transfer, however, most of the manuscripts were still housed in the old headquarters of the Ahmed Baba Institute of Higher Islamic Studies when the Tuareg-Islamist occupation took place in 2012—circumstances that saved many of the manuscripts because the Islamists made the new facility their headquarters, although they left it in disarray and burned several manuscripts as they fled.

Touré also lent state support to religious celebrations that uniquely characterize the cultural heritage of renowned religious centers, such as Timbuktu and Djenné, perhaps also in response to criticism of the excessive role monuments played in the preservation work promoted under Konaré (Ouallet 2002). The Mawlud became an official national holiday in 2005, with government workers receiving a two-day holiday to celebrate the birth and baptism of the Prophet Muhammad (Holder 2014b). Some religious communities celebrated the entire one-week period between the Prophet's birth and his naming (and some celebrated even longer).[16]

In Timbuktu the Mawlud is the occasion for numerous celebrations, both religious and secular, punctuated by visitations to religious sites (including the famed mausoleums, a tradition known as *zyhara*), readings of the Quran, and the recital of panegyrics dedicated to the Prophet. During the Mawlud, many immigrants from the diaspora return temporarily, and linkages of friendship and kinship among the population are rekindled (T. Maiga, pers. comm., 15 February 2014).

The nationalization of this holiday was supposed to have significant ramifications for the economic and cultural renaissance of Timbuktu, one of the main religious centers in Mali and the site of one of the most elaborate Mawlud celebrations. As a representative of Timbuktu's heritage elite recently clarified to me, the nationalization of the Mawlud was seen as Timbuktu's unprecedented opportunity to become a major religious destination, with the hope that "after the pilgrimage to Mecca, the Mawlud of Timbuktu could become the most important form of religious tourism, surpassing in importance the Magal of Tuba" (Senou Sidi, pers. comm., 2014). In short, Mawlud-related festivities and the attraction of pilgrims from all over Africa (and beyond) were to ensure a more enduring renaissance of Timbuktu.

In 2006, one year after its nationalization, the Mawlud was organized with greater care and at a much-larger scale than in previous years and saw the participation of several African political and religious leaders.[17] The event was mostly sponsored by Muammar Gaddafi, who at the time was orchestrating similar celebrations all over West Africa and beyond (e.g., in Uganda).[18]

Through his participation, Gaddafi sought to enhance his prominence in sub-Saharan Africa, particularly in the Muslim countries (Ronen 2011; Holder 2014b). According to Yehudit Ronen, "since seizing power in 1969, the regime of Mu'ammar al-Qadhafi has devotedly wrapped itself in the banner of Islam, giving it pre-eminent status among the values of its 'revolution'" (2002: 1). Beginning in the 1990s, Gaddafi publicly supported a moderate form of Islam, a position that further marked his move away from his previous pan-Arab stance (and away from Saudi Arabia's support for reform Islam). At the 2006 Mawlud,[19] Gaddafi delivered a long speech on African unity under Islam and reiterated the commitment of the desert peoples (which, he clarified, included the Peul and the 'Bambara' people) to fight Western encroachment in the region (2011).[20]

The 2006 Mawlud also acquired significance for the Malian government.[21] As radical Islam was on the rise, particularly, in the north (as proselytism successfully targeted the lower echelons of the population and Islamist extremist groups increasingly engaged in criminal activities), the secular state once more abandoned its alleged position of nonintervention in the religious and openly supported the more moderate and tolerant forms of Islam that were represented by the celebration of the Mawlud.[22] Timbuktu was not chosen casually as a site for renewing and extending local and regional alliances; rather, its selection drew on the city's historical and religious capital as both a center for the propagation of Islam in West Africa and a cosmopolitan center known for the piety and education of its scholars. As implemented in Timbuktu, the government's cultural policies sought to strengthen Mali's (Western-induced) role "as a bulwark against radical Islam in Africa" (Soares 2005b: 78).[23]

Not all Malians agreed with publicly celebrating the Mawlud at all, and even fewer approved of its nationalization. The Mawlud is, indeed, a contested celebration in Mali, particularly, as a result of the growing relevance of the (albeit heterogeneous) Islamic reform movement there (Kassim Koné, pers. comm., 2014).[24] The government's support for the Mawlud raised some concerns as to the secular character of the Malian state. The anonymous writers of ATT-cratie—a group opposed to Touré and his policies—writing under the collective pen name "Le Sphinx," presented the decision to make the Mawlud a national holiday as one of the president's many political miscalculations (Holder 2014b; Le Sphinx 2006).[25] The government of a secular state should not take sides in religious matters, wrote Le Sphinx, especially given the controversial status of the Mawlud within the Muslim community. Illustrious religious leaders in the Sufi traditions, too, criticized the government's interference, warning the state to let individuals choose for themselves and not to stir dissent among Malian Muslims by interfering in religious matters (Holder 2014b). Some reformist leaders, for example, rejected the Mawlud as *bid'ah*, or innovation in religious matters.[26] Participants in the lively discussions on the Maliweb website forums offered further rationales for uncertainty about the legitimacy of the Mawlud, as well as thoughts about the proper protocol and conduct for its celebration. Some Maliweb participants exhorted people to participate with moderation, thus at least avoiding some of the reportedly criticized behaviors (e.g., commodification of the event).[27]

As national and international concerns grew about the rise of Islamic radicalism in the north, initiatives to contain the phenomenon intensified and became more explicit. In March 2009 a British-based Islamic NGO, suggestively called Radical Middle Way (a group funded in part by the UK government and backed by the Malian government), organized a one-week summit in Timbuktu to which several African sheikhs, imams, and religious scholars were invited (M. Diamoutani, pers. comm., June 2014). The summit resulted in the Timbuktu Declaration, which stresses the organizers' condemnation of all violence and extremism and affirmed their commitment to enhancing peace, economic justice, and gender equality. In its description of the summit, the Radical Middle Way website states, "The suffering of millions through disease, poverty, and poor governance have all played a part in the building [of] support for extremist Islamic movements within Africa—our conference was focused [on] strengthening the alliance to challenge such propaganda."[28]

The choice of Timbuktu for the summit was manifestly symbolic, as Fuad Nahdi, Radical Middle Way's founder, explains: "Africa is a place for Islamic answers. The first Muslim asylum seekers sought refuge here. At least two of the leading schools of thought were developed on the continent."[29] The summit was attended by several Malian religious leaders, including Mahmoud Dicko, president of the Haut conseil islamique du Mali (High Islamic Council of Mali) (HCIM); the imams of Timbuktu's main mosques; state representatives; and scholars. As part of the summit program, all guests were invited to participate in a tour of Timbuktu's historic mosques and saints' mausoleums.

Well before 2012, the state and other statelike entities were exhibiting signs of a growing preoccupation with the rise of Islamist extremist groups (which also intersected with Gaddafi's political ambitions and his support for moderate Islam). This concern led the state and other statelike entities to intervene in support of Sufi Islam and Sufi cultural heritage. Timbuktu was to stand as the symbol of African Islam, which was known for its moderation and tolerance.

## The Destruction of the Saints' Mausoleums

In 2012 all the work of heritage preservation and valorization of the city heritage ground to a halt, due to the occupation of the north by an unstable alliance of Tuareg and armed Islamist groups.[30] The occupation of northern Mali in early April was coordinated by the Mouvement national de libération de l'Azawad (National Movement for the Liberation of Azawad) (MNLA), a Tuareg nationalist movement, and various Islamist extremist groups, such as al-Qaeda in the Islamic Maghreb (AQIM), the Movement for Unity and Jihad in West Africa (MUJAO), and the Tuareg-led Ansar Dine. Dissent soon erupted among these groups, and the MNLA was quickly outnumbered by the other factions and just a few months later "lost control of virtually the entire territory of Mali's three northern regions to a militarily superior alliance of Ansar Dine, AQIM, and MUJAO" (Lecocq et al. 2013). In the distribution of areas of influence among the Islamist groups, Timbuktu came to be controlled by AQIM, with support from the Tuareg-Islamist group Ansar Dine.

The tearing down of most mausoleums occurred intermittently over several months; in most cases, the Islamists did not completely destroy the mausoleums but just reduced their size (figure 16). In other words, they leveled the tombs built upon the saint's grave, in adherence with their more literal version of Islam where unnecessary constructions and decorations should be avoided.[31] The Islamists first destroyed six mausoleums, including some of the most revered ones (e.g., those of Cheick Sidi Mahmoud and Alpha Moya), between Saturday, 30 June, and Sunday, 1 July 2012, which received the greatest media attention. The last demolitions took place on 23 December 2012, shortly before the end of the occupation.

The targets also included the statue of Al Farouk, a tutelary spirit of the city, and the monument dedicated to the memory of the martyrs of the 1991 revolution and celebrating the advent of democracy in Mali. The Islamists also desecrated regular graves in the cemeteries around some of the saints' mausoleums.[32] The mosques were untouched, but their necessary annual replastering was prohibited because the accompanying rituals to ensure the successful completion of the work were deemed un-Islamic by the AQIM and Ansar Dine Islamists, who embrace a more rigorous Islam.[33]

According to the press that covered the events, UNESCO's decision to add Timbuktu to the list of endangered sites had angered the jihadists.[34] Ansar Dine's spokesperson Sanda Ould Boumama announced to the media: "'Ansar Dine will today destroy every mausoleum in the city. All of them, without exception. . . . God is unique. All of this is haram (or forbidden in Islam). We are all Muslims. UNESCO is what?' he said, declaring that Ansar Dine

**FIGURE 16.** Ruins of the mausoleum of eighteenth-century Muslim scholar Cheick Sidi Ahmed Ben Amar Arragadi, Timbuktu, 2013. The mausoleum was destroyed during the Tuareg-Islamist occupation of 2012. Courtesy of MINUSMA/ Sophie Ravier, licensed under CC-BY-NC-SA 2.0.

was acting 'in the name of God'" (Al Jazeera 2012). The destruction of the mausoleums was grounded on religious considerations. Reformist Muslims place great "emphasis on austerity and piety, condemnation of innovations, and insistence on sticking to the letter of the Qur'an" (Becker 2009: 417). The Quran contains very scarce information about burial, and Muslims follow either Fiqh manuals or place-specific ritual traditions (Campo 2014). Islam, generally, prescribes that grave structures be simple and modest in size, not draw attention to the deceased, and express the deceased's complete surrender to Allah—requirements that the Islamist extremists deemed that the Timbuktu mausoleums did not meet. Another spokesperson for Ansar Dine commented, "We are subject to religion and not to international opinion. Building on graves is contrary to Islam. We are destroying the mausoleums because it is ordained by our religion" (Oumar Ould Hamaha, qtd. in Bate 2012). The Islamists destroy sacred sites that to them represent innovation and departure from "the conditions under which Islam was practiced in the 7th century" (O'Dell 2013: 510), and because the Salafists "consider themselves ... the only true Muslims" (Lecocq and Schrijver 2007: 146),[35] they believe they have the authority to carry out such actions. In destroying the saints' mausoleums, Islamist extremists were enforcing their own memories of the past and actualizing their religiously informed vision of the social order.

Claiming to be more egalitarian, the Islamist groups also challenged the learned hierarchies in place—although in Mali in 2012 their egalitarian narrative ultimately failed to convince most of the population. Many Malians accused the Islamists of racism (because of their preferential treatment of people of Arab descent and lighter skin) and opposed the harsh treatment of women under the occupation (Senou Sidi and Niamoye Alidji, pers. comm., 2014). Islamist groups had reportedly made a point of forging alliances with the poor and marginalized segments of the northern populations by marrying women of poor families and investing in charity during the years leading to the occupation. These groups even provided Timbuktu's citizens with a green (toll-free) number to call to report Tuareg exactions during the city's occupation (Bøås and Torheim 2013). Ultimately, however, the Islamists' inconsistencies did not win over most of the Malian population, which welcomed wholeheartedly the Franco-Chadian forces that reasserted most of Mali's territorial integrity in early 2013.[36]

Furthermore, the Islamist extremists' destructive acts were often spontaneous and done in retaliation to Western symbolic actions (e.g., the listing of Timbuktu as an endangered World Heritage Site) or military offensives (e.g., the reconquest of the north). In accounting for the destruction of another important piece of the city's heritage, the famed Timbuktu manuscripts, the president of the Ahmed Baba Institute, Abdel Kadri Maiga, and his adjuncts unanimously observed that manuscripts had been burned only as the Islamists were forced to abandon Timbuktu on 16 June 2014 during the course of Operation Serval. As French and Chadian army forces regained control of the north and restored Mali's national unity, the Islamists burned approximately four thousand manuscripts in a "moment of rage . . . to manifest their anger" as they saw their projects falter (A. K. Maiga, pers. comm., June 2014). Fortunately, representatives of the Timbuktu-based heritage elite foresaw that the manuscripts would be an easy target in the final hours of the occupation and with the help of several Timbuktu residents had secretly transferred most of the Timbuktu manuscripts to Bamako as a preventive measure during the six-month occupation.

## International Responses

The international media (as well as some of the Malian heritage elites) presented the destruction of the mausoleums as criminal or barbaric acts by Islamists allegedly of mostly foreign origins.[37] For instance, the director-general of UNESCO, Irina Bokova, commented on the events by stressing that the Islamists "burned manuscripts, an extraordinary Islamic treasure. I saw barbaric acts of destruction that left nothing but stones of the saints' mausoleums" (SAPA 2013).

Several mausoleums were destroyed two days after the Timbuktu's publicized inscription on the UNESCO list of endangered World Heritage Sites on 28 June 2012. This inscription was prompted by reports of the destruction of a few heritage sites and by the Islamists' threats of further devastation earlier that year. The destructive acts continued irregularly until a French-led military operation (Operation Serval) restored state control over most of Mali's territory in early 2013.

According to UNESCO, its decision to place both Timbuktu and the nearby Tomb of Askia in Gao on its list of World Heritage Sites in Danger "aim[ed] to raise cooperation and support for the sites threatened by the armed conflict in the region" (Agence France Presse 2012). To prevent further destruction to heritage sites in response to a likely UN-sanctioned military operation for the reconquest of the north, UNESCO created a passport-style brochure (*Passeport pour le patrimoine*) and maps (*Cartes*) detailing, among other information, the position and major characteristics of heritage sites in the area.[38] The documents were made available to military personnel and NGOs working in the area to help them avoid further damage to the patrimony of Mali's northern regions.

During the reconquest of Mali's north by French and Chadian army forces, the International Criminal Court (ICC) declared its intention to investigate the destruction of Sufi mausoleums as possible war crimes. Citing the Rome Statute (the 1998 treaty that established the International Criminal Court), ICC prosecutor Fatou Bensouda included "intentionally directing attacks against protected objects" to the list of crimes her organization was going to investigate (Office of the Prosecutor 2013). This international commitment was unprecedented, as O'Dell remarks: "While these attacks on Sufi heritage have been widespread, it is only in Mali that military forces with the blessing of UNESCO protected Sufi heritage" (2013: 507).

Some media outlets' emphasis on heritage loss and the vanishing of traditions represents a further articulation of the tendency to use "cultural framing" to justify military intervention by Western countries, especially when political Islam is concerned (L. Abu-Lughod 2002). In Mali's conflict, "the plight of Afghan women . . . forced wearing the iconic burqa" (a recurring theme in the rhetoric that preceded the 2001 launch of the Western-led war in Afghanistan) was "replaced" by the tearing down of saints' mausoleums and the burning of Islamic manuscripts. The threat of further destruction of heritage of global significance provided a rationale not only for military intervention but also for continuous international involvement in the reconstruction process.

As of 2014, UNESCO was aggressively leading the reconstruction of mausoleums in the postconflict period but struggling to come up with the required funds. A Timbuktu representative of the heritage elite recently lamented, "UNESCO proposes a reconstruction plan over five years. The people of Timbuktu are anxious to rebuild their mausoleums . . . [but] they are not finding favorable responses among the people in power" (Senou Sidi, pers. comm., 2014). Although some of the reports by UNESCO experts take into account citizens' sensibilities and aspirations, the timing and forms of these plans are generating a sense of insecurity and suspicion, particularly at a time when attacks by Islamist extremist and Tuareg groups are once again intensifying in the north.[39]

## National Responses

The reconstruction of Timbuktu's heritage (in particular, the saints' mausoleums) is profoundly affected by broader political and economic transformations that long preceded the postconflict era. The neoliberal democratic turn at the beginning of the 1990s and the unprecedented freedom of expression and association that followed in its wake favored the proliferation and diversification of associations, including religious groups. This associative fervor, coupled with a rapid increase in available funds for the development of the private sector including religious organizations, has been accompanied by a dramatic reduction of state functions. The unrelenting implementation of draconian budget cuts that let go state employees and eliminated state services and state-owned enterprises came at a particularly fragile juncture—the democratic turn—in the life of the Malian state.

The downscaling of state functions has created unprecedented vacancies that other organizations with statelike qualities have been filling. This trend continues unabated into the present: for example, further cuts have directly affected the Ministry of Culture, which was allocated only 0.3 percent of the national budget for 2014 (Njikam 2014). Such cuts have increasingly curtailed the possibility of certain institutions to operate. For instance, in 2014 the Modibo Keita Memorial in Bamako, which has been temporarily closed since 2011, received a fraction of its usual budget. State funding for the Ministry of Culture barely covers the salaries of state employees, thus making the state almost entirely dependent on donors for the development of cultural initiatives.

Remarkably responsive to the changed political context, religious organizations have successfully voiced the concerns of many citizens dissatisfied with the limited results of Malian democracy (Soares 2005b). According to Gilles Holder (e.g., 2014b), the powerful HCIM, founded by the government in 2002 to oversee and coordinate the growing number of Islamic organizations in Mali, increasingly sees its role as taking over several functions of the now-defunct welfare state, particularly, in regard to social-welfare initiatives. The following statement, attributed by Holder and Saint-Lary to HCIM president Mahmoud Dicko,[40] suggests some of the changing relations between secular and religious groups in Mali: "The HCIM sees the state as an airport: it leaves to the state the control of visas and the maintenance of security, and wants to take care of all the rest" (Holder and Saint-Lary 2014: 14).[41] Reflecting an amalgam of global and regional trends that include the increasing relevance of the religious, the Malian neoliberal state is being reduced—rhetorically, in part—to patrolling the borders and (at least in principle) ensuring national security.[42] Other more typical state functions (e.g., those in the domains of health and education) are more and more dependent on the work of very heterogeneous NGOs and on development projects that the state negotiates with a variety of foreign entities.

Many find inappropriate the HCIM leadership's growing involvement in the political concerns of a secular (laic) state. Prior to the 2012 occupation, the HCIM and Dicko, in particular, had played a pivotal role in opposing a new family code that if ratified would have considerably improved women's rights in Malian society.[43] The code that was adopted on 2 December 2011, after a decade of heated debates and confrontations between conservative and liberal groups, reflected the views and aspirations of conservative social and religious groups and actors.[44] Other HCIM leaders criticized some of Dicko's public declarations (e.g., in favor of certain political candidates) on the grounds that the association should maintain a position of neutrality (A. Keita 2012). During the 2012 occupation, the HCIM took on prerogatives typically associated with the state, such as the negotiation of peace agreements with the Islamist groups. For instance, claiming to negotiate a peaceful resolution that would not necessitate foreign intervention, HCIM president Mahmoud Dicko established direct contact with the Islamists (e.g., Groga-Bada 2012). He stated that in order not to alienate the Islamists, he did not issue any public statement in condemnation of the mausoleums' destruction. Ultimately, citing insufficient state backing for his initiative, Dicko abandoned his mediation efforts. Despite this setback, after the conflict, Dicko made judicious use of the media to further emphasize his organization's contribution to the peace process, to which he recursively juxtaposed the state's inaction.

Dicko's reluctance to openly condemn the destructions of saints' mausoleums, his ambiguous public statements, and direct contacts, particularly, with the Ansar Dine's leadership drew him criticism from other religious leaders, in particular from another HCIM representative, the renowned preacher Ousmane Madani Haidara (Schulz 2003; Soares 2004, 2005a). Haidara publicly accused Dicko of not taking a clear stand against the Islamist extremists' destruction of Timbuktu's heritage, suggesting that Dicko shared some of their views. Following such accusations, the national channel Office de Radiodiffusion-Télévision du Mali (Office of Radio and Television of Mali) (ORTM) organized a televised roundtable for the clarification of the religious leaders' positions on Timbuktu's mausoleums' destruction (ORTM 2012). During the debate, Dicko clarified his position regarding their destruction. He argued that the leveling of Muslim tombs was grounded on a misreading of the Quran, and he condemned the Islamists' (whom he defined as rebels) behavior as not conforming to the right path. Furthermore, in talking about the individuals buried in such tombs, Dicko never identified them as saints (*waliw*) but as important persons (*mogobaw*), thus underlining his distance from practices associated with Sufism, such as the veneration of saints.[45] Indeed, media reports and scholarly analyses describe Dicko as a conservative Muslim who is close to those reformist movements that "call for sharia and condemnation of Sufism and saints' tombs as un-Islamic" (Soares 2013). However, the televised roundtable also showed Dicko's attempt to redefine his position in less-contentious terms in response to criticism of his handling of the crisis and for pragmatic considerations (Soares 2013).

Even some of the Sufi representatives with whom I conversed during the summer of 2014 made sure to distinguish their position from what they saw as a vulgar form of Sufism (see Soares 2004). For instance, lawyer Moussa Maiga, a self-professed Sufi, strongly rejected the veneration of saints and the use of intermediaries as characteristics of Sufism.[46] Citing how Cheick Sidi Hamza al-Boutchichi of the Quadriya branch influenced his thought (Chih 2013), Maiga explained that Sufism indicates the forms of a follower's contact with the divine, which Sufi Muslims access through a more hidden and intuitive knowledge, including certain "words" that facilitate their direct access to God (Moussa Maiga, pers. comm., June 2014). Maiga—with whom I conversed in the presence of high-ranking HCIM cadre Mamadou Diamountani—even stated that he had received Dicko's support, thus suggesting that his form of Sufism was fully approved by the highest spheres in the HCIM—information he used to challenge media reports that depicted Dicko as a "*whahhabi*," that is, a representative of a reform movement within Sunni Islam.

During the conversation I had with him and Maiga, Mamadou Diamoutani also distanced himself from the veneration of saints and the whole mauso-

**FIGURE 17.** The reconstructed mausoleum of a saint, Timbuktu, 15 April 2015. Courtesy of MINUSMA/Harandane, licensed under CC-BY-NC-SA 2.0.

leum complex (pers. comm., June 2014).[47] In talking about the destruction of Timbuktu mausoleums, he clarified that he would support their reconstruction only if they were clearly demarcated as historical monuments (things of the past) and not reflections of contemporary practices.

Such debates and repositioning (even within Sufi Islam, as Maiga's example shows)[48] suggest that state and quasi-state incursions into the religious sphere—via the imposition of norms for the preservation and the valorization of religious heritage sites and rituals—may have actually helped tilt the balance further in favor of reformist Islam in Mali. State intervention in the religious has a long history: "In some ways, the current situation in Mali is strikingly similar to the French colonial period when colonial administrators attempted to identify good and bad Muslims and no Muslim cleric ever completely escaped suspicion" (Soares 2013). Dicko's recent reelection to the HCIM leadership (and his defeat of Thierno Hadi Thiam, who once again campaigned as the representative of more moderate forms of Islam) may be further evidence of this shift within Mali's religious sphere (Madiba Keita

2006).[49] Similarly, most representatives of the Timbuktu heritage sector and religious authorities I interviewed distanced themselves somewhat from the devotional practices that surround some of the saints' tombs.[50] Even some of the Timbuktu-based religious authorities who were vocal defenders of the Sufi tradition (and Timbuktu's sacred heritage) prior to the occupation are silent or appear very sparingly (and always with caution) in the national media. As the state and its international partners strive to reconstruct the mausoleums exactly as they were before the conflict (figure 17), past and recent debates about and contestations of Mali's religious heritage are relevant considerations.[51]

## Conclusions

In the promotion of dialogue and sustainable work in cultural-heritage preservation in Mali, clearly, it is critical to take into account the country's changing religious context. I share Soares's and Holder's view that contemporary debates around religious matters indicate the unrelenting expansion (and division) of the religious sphere in Mali at a time when the Malian government and politicians (but also international partners), in general, have lost their credibility among the general population. This process, which began shortly after the democratic turn in the 1990s (and, arguably, has deeper historical roots), continues in the postconflict era.

The Malian state and the international agencies that are endeavoring to provide support for the preservation of Sufi heritage sites may want to consider the changing landscape in which such operations are taking place. The reconstruction of the Sufi mausoleums is not sufficient to secure their preservation—particularly, at a juncture in which the state budget for cultural efforts continues to shrink dramatically, thus making it impossible for the state to develop any coherent cultural policies. Furthermore, the reconstruction of the Islamic patrimony should not be done at the exclusion of other cultural programs. The programmatic document "Politique Culturelle du Mali: Document Cadre" of the Malian Ministry of Culture clearly states that Mali's cultural diversity is central to peace-building efforts and also declares the ministry's intent to support different ways of being Malian today (Ministère de la Culture 2014). Key to ensuring the "sustainability" of heritage work in the long run is the identification of heritage projects that productively include diverse perspectives on the saints' veneration in heritage initiatives, as well as the diversification of heritage initiatives, in general (B. Diakité, pers. comm., June 2014).

# Epilogue
*Further Thoughts on Governmentality and Culture*

**FOLLOWING THE 1991** coup d'état and the 1992 multiparty presidential elections that led to the election of Alpha Oumar Konaré, national culture again became a government priority. The government manifested a new commitment to marking a clear distance from the celebratory tones of the past (e.g., references to Mali's prestigious precolonial period), a rejection of art as a direct servant of power, and an effort to increase culture's autonomy from the immediately political. However, though seemingly freed from the logics of the one-party states, culture and politics were still profoundly interconnected, thus reflecting new or altered logics and practices introduced or intensified by the democratic and neoliberal turn since the early 1990s.

## Heritage and Governmentality

Heritage institutions, such as the museum, are fundamental sites for the articulation and transformation of modern power. Since the late nineteenth century, the museum has been key to the development of a national and then postcolonial identity in Mali. As a site for the experimentation and deployment of specific visual techniques often in the service of nation building, the museum has gradually influenced other areas of social life, thus extending its relevance far beyond the museum's walls (Kratz and Karp 2006). Museological processes, for one, have come to regulate the preservation and management of several heritage sites as well as the range of activities surrounding them, as seen in the analysis of the various efforts to preserve the Sudanese architecture of Djenné and Timbuktu, the construction of the women's museum Muso Kunda, and the creation of the Koulouba monument complex.

The museum itself regulates human conduct in a variety of ways, as in how museum exhibits order, classify, and disclose a certain world order often representative of the postcolonial educated elites as well as representatives of the heterogeneous aid regime.[1] The heritagization of the entire town of Djenné in the context of the town inscription to the World Heritage List by the Malian state and UNESCO, for example, led to the imposition of new aesthetic values and new criteria for the use and management of space. The inhabitants of Djenné had to contend with increased economic inequality (reinforced by the heritage industry), loss of control over the space in which they live, and new forms of visibility in the name of tourism and ever-elusive economic development. The citizens' disenchantment with state-promoted heritage initiatives culminated in a series of riots in the mid-2000s. However, their growing engagement with the heritage field ultimately resulted in more enduring outcomes (including state commitment to greater citizen inclusion and the diversification of initiatives to target more diverse constituencies). Citizens' groups and individual actors contributed to the emergence of a partially independent but still tentative public culture, owing to the continuing insecurity in the north and the lack of tourism. New types of organizations, such as Djenné Patrimoine, and their transnational networks arose to participate in the preservation and valorization of their heritage, although such participation sometimes reflected and further articulated the social hierarchies already in place.[2]

The museum is also a prime example of a heterotopic space (e.g., chapter 3)—that is, a space in which all aspects of a society "are simultaneously represented, contested, and inverted; a kind of places that are outside all places, even though they are actually localizable" (Foucault 2008: 17). As a heterotopic space, the museum can present people with new assemblages and combinations in a not always successful attempt to address profound social tensions (and motivate people to rethink the gendered world order in which they live). In this sense, one paradigmatic heterotopia was the women's museum Muso Kunda. Built with the intent of empowering Malian women's voices, Muso Kunda received very little social and political support, particularly in the post-Konaré period, and throughout most of its existence was questioned by even its own employees, some of whom objected to the general goal of women's emancipation tout court. More successful, overall, was the state's cosmopolitan elites' questioning of limiting dichotomous conceptual frameworks, such as the sharp oppositions between traditions and modernity, and between colonizer and colonized, and the adoption of a historical narrative of hybridity. The colonial experience was thus reclaimed as an episode of the rich history of conquest and subjection of the Malian people and modernity embraced as (one) constitutive root of the Malian nation, a narrative that found visualization in the Koulouba monument complex.

## State Actors, Logics, and Practices

In examining the relationship between culture and power in the neoliberal era in postcolonial Africa, Foucauldian-inspired work on governmentality is particularly useful. It aptly addresses the dispersion of power associated with the neoliberal age, as shown by the proliferation of political entities of various size and shape that have taken on specific state functions. I have analyzed here the role played by a number of heterogeneous entities, such as political parties, religious organizations, supranational entities (e.g., UNESCO), and transnational organizations (e.g., Djenné Patrimoine) in the development of specific heritage projects. I have also discussed some of the ways in which these entities both reinforce and challenge state power. Here I further question the internal homogeneity of the state and the coherence of its operations. It is clear that the state does not act in unison—indeed, different state actors and agencies play significantly different roles in the heritage sector. In particular, despite draconian budget cuts, the executive power managed (with a variety of international entities and quasi-state organizations reinforcing its actions) to play a prominent role in the ideation and orchestration of heritage initiatives at the national level at least until the end of Touré's administration.[3]

While the welfare functions of the state have been curtailed, the executive power—particularly during Konaré's administration—heavily invested in heritage and public culture initiatives in an effort to bring legitimacy to the state and sustain the development of a civil society. The state's substantial investment in heritage initiatives during Konaré's presidency was intended somewhat to compensate for the acceleration of neoliberal changes, donors' top-down approach to development, and the government's inability to address the school crisis (among other problems facing the state). The investment in public culture was made possible by the multiplication of donors and aid entities with the most conflicting programs and objectives.[4] Several of the initiatives that marked Konaré's administration were funded by communist countries, such as China (currently Mali's fourth-largest trading partner) and North Korea, that were invested in supporting initiatives that bolstered the government's legitimacy. This strategic use of non-Western donors continued under Touré, who identified the Aga Khan Trust for Culture, South Africa, and Libya as committed partners in the preservation and valorization of Mali's religious heritage (see chapter 5).[5]

While disclosing new developments and logics, state practices have also reproduced some of the state's autocratic characteristics that arch back to the one-party state and the colonial state and reflect the simultaneous existence of various techniques of governance at any given time. Weakened by years of structural adjustment programs, the state and its representatives can no longer fulfill—or at least not fulfill to the same degree—some of its welfare functions, including its longtime role as Mali's main employer.[6] Redistributive functions had been key to the production of state legitimacy, given both general social expectations pertaining to wealth circulation and consumption but also place-specific mechanisms of mutual aid. Therefore, the end of the welfare state and state withdrawal from areas of former state intervention (e.g., education, public transportation, health) have had significant consequences on state practices, most notably in the rearticulation of some of the state autocratic tendencies.

Donor practices and, particularly, their hierarchical character have strengthened Mali's executive power and bypassed democratic institutions, such as the National Assembly, where crucial matters, including the state budget, are hardly ever discussed (van de Walle 2012). Furthermore, donors have scarcely invested in programs dedicated to the strengthening of the actual workings of democratic institutions (van de Walle 2012).[7] Heritage initiatives offer further insights into the top-down operations of the Malian state. For instance, under Konaré's administration, the unprecedented expansion of public monuments between 1995 and 2002 (twenty-five were inaugurated in Bamako alone)[8] was planned and executed under the direct supervision of the president and a close circle of collaborators, including the late anthropologist Pascal Baba Couloubaly, who was (with the president) one of the chief proponents of the policy of comprehensive remembering. The execution of cultural policies (discussed in chapter 2) further shows the continuation of certain practices of the one-party era: the limited circulation of information (mostly confined to top officials) and the lack of citizens' direct participation in heritage initiatives. Initiatives meant to reinforce democracy were, paradoxically, the outcome of the state's autocratic modalities.[9]

Autocratic tendencies continued under Touré, but he emphasized consensus building over his predecessor's decisive implementation of new policies. Touré reintroduced personalistic techniques of government that had been typical of the one-party era. To this end he cultivated personal connections with some of the most important families and networks in the country. On Touré's leadership style, Malian journalist Amadou Tall commented, "In short, we can say that there is not a family or a 'grin' that ATT cannot access, be welcomed by, and from whom he cannot get what he wants" (2010).[10]

At the state level, the politics of consensus was articulated via the orchestration of public ceremonies in which the reconciliation between political enemies was staged and of which the 2010 celebration of Mali's fiftieth year of independence was the culmination (see chapter 1). Touré managed to co-opt the political opposition by including opposition party leaders and well-networked independent politicians in his governments, thus drawing widespread support for his policies.

Despite some of the autocratic tendencies highlighted here, the state did also encourage the development of rational-critical perspectives among the citizenry, and heritage work became a fundamental medium for the conceptualization and communication of government policies. At least during Konaré's presidency (1992–2002), there was a concerted effort in cultivating what then cultural minister Couloubaly called "a duty of memory" (2001), which entailed not only recovering Mali's precolonial past (as during the one-party era) but also critically reappraising more recent episodes of Mali's history, such as French colonization, the socialist period, and people's pro-democracy struggle. In the state's projects, heritage was to be more inclusive to strengthen national unity on a broader basis, as seen in the Muso Kunda's display of the rich clothing tradition of Mali's major ethnic groups, for example. Culture was to equip Malian citizens—and, particularly, the youth—with the cultural references needed to critically engage with some of the homogenizing effects of globalization. Greater expressive freedom was not to lead to the loss of one's identity but be grounded in a renewed appreciation for Malian history and cultures.[11] National heritage was to suggest new readings of Mali's past, heal old wounds, and bring clarity and perhaps even closure to disputed events in Mali's history.

It is increasingly clear that although Touré did not openly challenge Konaré's heritage work and mostly appeared to follow in Konaré's footsteps, he actually gave very little attention and support to several of Konaré's heritage projects.[12] In a recent interview, Cheick Oumar Sissoko, one of the most influential ministers of culture under Touré, stresses the inadequacy of the state budget for culture (2014). Such a limited budget, he argues, compromises the development of any coherent state-run cultural initiative and increases dependency on the priorities set by international and national donors. Of the three main heritage initiatives that took place under Konaré and are analyzed in this work—the Modibo Keita Memorial (a public institution), the women's museum Muso Kunda (one of the first private institutions), and the Koulouba monument complex (a public monument)—only one was fully functional at the time of my last visit to Mali in June 2014. Muso Kunda has been under construction (for an expansion) at least since 2011 and remains closed until the work is completed. The Modibo Keita Memorial has also been closed since 2011, awaiting sufficient funds to complete renovation and expansion work that includes the opening of a conference center and a cyber café, initiatives intended to transform the memorial into an income-generating institution—the prevailing format that donors wish to see implemented for cultural institutions today. Only the Koulouba monument complex appears to have been unaffected by the recent political turmoil and changes in the country's leadership. Under Touré, the state invested little in public monuments with historical themes but did open a beautiful national park, sponsored by the Aga Khan Trust for Culture, in the heart of Bamako.

During Touré's presidency, the incentivization of the private sector resulted in the creation of numerous partly independent initiatives, such as the organization of various festivals, including the Festival sur le Niger, and cultural centers, such as the Centre Culturel Koré of Ségou. The state increasingly invested in or facilitated heritage initiatives intended to contain the spread of Islamist extremist groups in Mali's northern regions —efforts that had a number of ramifications on Mali's religious sphere (Holder 2014b; chapter 5).[13] A few of Touré's initiatives—in particular, his attempt to rewrite the state narratives of the 1991 revolution to stress his personal contribution and diminish the role of the students and other democratic organizations—elicited some criticism from the little political opposition that remained by the end of his presidential mandate.[14]

## The Ministry of Culture

Although the executive power has successfully navigated uncertain waters, the Ministry of Culture and its representatives have experienced dramatic budget cuts in the neoliberal era (A. C. Touré 2006; Ministère de la Culture du Mali 2014). The devaluing of "soft" disciplines (the social science and, in particular, the humanities) is a worldwide trend and a sentiment that Mali's former prime minister Moussa Mara reiterated in a speech on 6 October 2014, in which he quite openly expressed his contempt for impractical knowledge and encouraged the youth to embrace more scientific subjects in order to help the country improve its economic status (Mara 2014).[15]

Accordingly, the portion of the state budget allocated to the Ministry of Culture, already much reduced in the neoliberal period, has further decreased over time. In 2006 the total budget for the Ministry of Culture amounted to 0.74 percent of the national budget (A. C. Touré 2006: 209); in 2014 this amount was further reduced, reaching the historical low of 0.3 percent of the total state budget (A. Segbedji 2014). Most of the monies allocated to the

Ministry of Culture cover salaries and running expenses, leaving increasingly limited resources (only 25 percent of the ministry's budget in 2006) for the organization and promotion of cultural initiatives. The vast majority (80 percent in 2006) of the Malian budget for cultural initiatives comes from European countries—an indication of the prominent role that foreign entities play in the development of Mali's national heritage (A. C. Touré 2006).

One example from my last visit to Mali, in 2014, illustrates some of these difficult circumstances. A representative of the Ministry of Culture's Ségou branch shared with me the current annual budget for that region. After covering the salaries of the ministry's employees (an expense that used up most of the budget), only 1,750,000 CFA francs (US$3,039.77 in 2014) were left to fund all of its cultural initiatives in the Ségou region for the entire year of 2014. Work-related transportation expenses (e.g., vehicles, fuel) were no longer covered by the budget, and he had had to purchase a small motorbike with his own money in order to be able to conduct his work. Given their small salaries, most state employees were often unable to purchase any transportation—a situation that hampered their abilities to successfully execute their job responsibilities, which included making contacts, coordinating cultural initiatives, and attending cultural performances in the region.

At the time of my visit, the Ségou branch of the Ministry of Culture had just been asked to organize a reception and cultural performance for a July 1, 2014, visit by President Ibrahim Boubacar Keita and Blaise Compaoré, at that time still president of Burkina Faso. But since the Ségou branch had already exhausted its limited budget for the year, Ségouvian performing groups had made it clear that they would not perform for free. This event foregrounds some of the constraints under which the ministry's regional representatives must work. It shows regional administrators as recipients of orders (and delegations) from Bamako, still the site of the centralized power it was in the pre-1991 period (although that power has certainly been reduced). Furthermore, the general lack of funding put regional representatives of the Ministry of Culture in an awkward position vis-à-vis private heritage actors. Indeed, given donors' emphasis on privatization, private entities often have at their disposal much-larger budgets than the Ministry of Culture and its regional branches. Given their minimal budget, state administrators can participate in private cultural activities (such as the Festival sur le Niger) only when invited to do so—and such invitations are often not forthcoming. This marginality in terms of initiatives and funding undermines the ministry's regional branches' mission of facilitating the emergence of a private cultural sector, coordinating cultural initiatives, and preserving and fostering cultural diversity.[16]

## New Political and Religious Actors

Besides the Malian state, other state and quasi-state actors were involved in heritage initiatives during the post-1991 period.[17] For example, foreign entities and supranational organizations, such as UNESCO (see chapters 4 and 5), played substantive roles in the heritage sector. At the same time, however, Malian political parties and religious organizations asserted themselves as the two major players in the heritage field.

The institution of multipartism has had profound repercussions on the management of culture. The play of the political opposition was most evident under Konaré's administration,[18] as public culture and heritage became highly disputed in the ferocious and sometimes seemingly petty party struggles of the democratic-neoliberal period. Opposition parties criticized state-led heritage initiatives and sometimes even boycotted them, for instance, on the occasion of the attempted transfer of the Archinard statue from Ségou to Bamako or the US-RDA party elders' refusal to donate their personal libraries to the Modibo Keita Memorial. The opposition also developed its own heritage projects and organized alternative (to the state) commemorations of historical figures, such as Modibo Keita and Abdoul "Cabral" Karim Camara (see chapters 1 and 2). Not all of these struggles were petty or simply manifestations of individual or corporate interests. Many also critiqued the actual working of Mali's democracy, the intensification of neoliberal policies (in particular, the state's withdrawal from welfare areas), and the growing interference of Western experts in many development initiatives.[19]

The co-optation of political parties under Touré's presidency was accompanied by a reduction in public debate. In this context, religious organizations increasingly asserted themselves as entities capable of conveying individual and collective concerns with neoliberal democracy—which eventually came to include the heritagization promoted by the state and foreign actors in projects that reflected and articulated the new political order.[20] The increase in state investment in the preservation and the valorization of northern Mali's Islamic heritage came to be perceived as interference in religious matters. It was read as a clear sign of state support for certain movements and orders within the Islamic community in an effort to halt the spread of Islamic extremist groups in the north.[21] The preservation of saints' mausoleums became a matter that increasingly divided the Malian religious sphere and elicited opposition to state intervention by segments of the religious community.[22] What were previously primarily local heritage concerns became increasingly national and international in scope, reflecting rapidly globalizing interests and concerns. The state and its representatives were no longer the main actors in the heritage field, and state-promoted projects increasingly had to take into account competing political interests and diverging religious concerns on a scale unprecedented in the one-party era.

## Current State Priorities in Culture and Heritage

One of the Ministry of Culture's current priorities, strongly backed by large segments of the aid regime, is to promote the development of a vibrant private cultural sector while reducing state involvement in cultural programs and initiatives (Ministère de la Culture 2014: 52). Private cultural initiatives, such as the various festivals, cultural centers, and the private libraries (particularly, those based in Timbuktu), are seen as examples of the successful liberalization of state cultural institutions. The liberalization tout court of the heritage sector (coupled by the further reduction of state investment) is a complex issue, especially in a situation characterized by widespread poverty, economic inequality, and unequal access to education.

During my visits to the Ministry of Culture in Bamako, I was introduced to a number of private actors who sought the ministry's support for developing some cultural centers. In particular, I was granted several meetings by a cultural operator from Djenné, Madu Haidara,[23] who shared with me his project for the creation of a library and cultural center in Djenné, which he primarily intended as a space to house the Djenné Islamic manuscripts and possibly even the Timbuktu manuscripts, should their evacuation from Timbuktu be necessary again. He knew that the European Union had recently financed the construction of the Library of Djenné's Manuscripts (Bibliothèque des Manuscripts de Djenné) and the Museum of Djenné, but he downplayed those initiatives, asserting that the citizens of Djenné did not have much trust in state representatives and had already told him that they would certainly deposit their manuscript collections in *his* center when he found funding for it.

This story points to one of the paradoxes of liberalization, that is, the development of a situation in which the state lacks the necessary funds to actually run already existing state cultural institutions (e.g., the Museum of Djenné but also the Modibo Keita Memorial) while private entities are provided with funds to create institutions very similar to the ones already in existence. Citing the malfunctioning of state institutions, such as the Museum of Djenné, completed in 2013 but still closed because of the lack of collections and funds, Haidara (encouraged by some of the owners of libraries in Timbuktu) developed a plan for his own cultural institution, a hybrid between the museum of Djenné and the manuscript library. Haidara's initiative was meant to address citizens' dissatisfaction with state initiatives and their request for greater inclusion, especially when asked to part from their personal holdings or their family's cultural patrimony.[24] Malian citizens' lack of trust in state institutions compromises the very functioning of such institutions. On occasion, libraries and museums stand empty or with insignificant collections because state representatives have been unable or unwilling to productively include the holders of cultural patrimonies in the running of such institutions.

Replicating heritage structures is a risky financial undertaking in the absence of the conditions to ensure private projects' sustainability. The conditions for the sustainability of any cultural project are presently absent, given continuing insecurity in the north (the tourist destination of choice) and the correlated dramatic contraction of the tourism industry in Mali. Despite superficial dichotomies between public and private, certain pervasive logics of corruption and exclusion will not disappear just because an institution is private.[25] Private initiatives involve significant state actors' participation and are heavily subsidized by much of the same international community that drives many of the so-called state initiatives. Inadequate public access to private cultural products is also a problem, as experienced by some of the users of the private libraries of Timbuktu. Finally, privatization may not be the best (or only) way to secure the preservation of cultural diversity, and the state's role in securing such diversity may, indeed, remain crucial, as the following vignette suggests.

Segments of the Muslim community perceive aspects of Mali's "traditional" culture as un-Islamic and have, therefore, discontinued its practice. In this context the action of the state, as guarantor of internal diversity, remains significant. For instance, in my conversations with T. Yattara,[26] I learned that in his village of origin, people had stopped organizing a festival known as the Bariséli. Performed after the harvest, the Bariséli involved music and dance performances and was an occasion for the youth to get to know one another and for marriages to be planned—and for knowledge about a shared past and common "traditions" to circulate across generations. Upon visiting his village around early 2000, Yattara learned that because some residents were under the impression that such performances were forbidden by Islam, the elders and family heads had prohibited them. After extensive work by representatives of the Ministry of Culture and a grassroots organization spontaneously created by some of the ministry's members (and involving Yattara), village inhabitants were encouraged to restart the Bariséli, which was fully restored in 2003 and has since garnered both regional and national attention.[27] This episode illustrates the state's critical role in preserving cultural traditions and in diversifying the collective cultural heritage (a role analyzed in chapter 4, in regard to the Saho youth house of the Bozo). State representatives' work—in association with area residents—was key to the preservation and valorization of the Bariséli.

The differentiation of cultural actors and the privatization of the cultural sector are significant developments of Mali's post-1991 era and reflect profound changes in the nature of modern power. At the same time, however, neoliberal logics and practices have produced new divisions and fractures in the social fabric that need to be addressed. In this context, the role of the state in preserving a diverse cultural heritage remains critical, provided state initiatives can promote greater citizens' inclusion and participation in the heritagization of Mali's past.

# Glossary

**Bamana:** One of Mali's largest ethnic groups and the most widely spoken language in Mali.

**ciwara:** A stylized representation of an antelope; Bamana origin. It symbolizes dedication and hard work and is originally associated with the Bamana ethnic group.

**Islamists:** A heterogeneous group of reform-oriented Muslim actors and organizations, including the Salafis (see Lecocq and Schrijver 2007; Østebø 2008). Some of the groups described here are Islamist extremist groups "engaged in a violent jihad with ideological roots in Salafism" (Lecocq et al. 2013: 1n1).

**jeli:** A semi-endogamous group of people specializing in music, praise giving, and family histories; plural, jeliw; Bamana; also known by the French term "griot."

**Mawlud:** The observance of the birth of the Prophet Muhammad, typically associated with Sufism.

**mogoba:** Important person; plural, mogobaw; Bamana origin.

**Salafism:** A heterogeneous constellation of Islamic reform groups and religious leaders. Salafists support a literal reading of Islamic texts and a return to the devotional practices and simplicity of the first three generations of Muslims. Salafism aims to purify Islam of perceived external cultural and traditional beliefs and practices, such as Sufism (in particular, saint worship). As noted by Thurston and Lebovich, "Salafism in Mali includes both non-violent manifestations and what some analysts call the 'Salafi-Jihadism' of groups like AQIM [Al Qa'ida in the Islamic Maghreb], MUJWA [Movement for Unity and Jihad in West Africa], and Ansar al Din [Ansar Dine]" (2013: 16).

**Sufism:** A mystical and spiritual branch of Islam. Sufism has often resulted in the creation of orders and the formation of religious hierarchies that mediate the worshipper's access to the divine. Many Malian Muslims are not members of specific Sufi orders but still engage in "certain practices closely tied to Sufism, Sufi orders, and their leaders, including the veneration of certain persons with reputations as saints and the use of the Islamic esoteric sciences ('marabouts' and 'maraboutage' in the French colonial lexicon)" (Soares 2007: 79).

**Tuareg:** An internally diverse and stratified nomadic people of Berber origin who live in northern Mali (but also in northern Niger and southern Algeria). Since Mali's independence, the Tuareg have organized periodic rebellions to protest the political hegemony of Mali's southern ethnic groups and their own socioeconomic marginality and endemic poverty. Increasingly (but not exclusively), their political demands are couched in a religious idiom that defines and expands their social change efforts, as seen during the temporary secession of Mali's north in 2012. Despite the legitimacy of some of their demands, the racism the Tuareg display toward the southern populations as well as their internal divisions undermines their social renewal projects.

**Wahhabiyya:** A Salafi reformist movement within Sunni Islam founded by Muhammad Ibn Abd al-Wahhab in Arabia in the eighteenth century. "Wahhabi" is a term used mostly by European speakers. The wahhabis (in Mali as elsewhere) call themselves (the true) Sunnis or Ahl al-Sunna and seek to restore the purity and unity of Islam of the first centuries. The Wahhabiyya was first introduced in Mali in the 1940s by Malian students returning from their studies at al-Azhar University (Cairo, Egypt) and found significant financial backing in wealthy merchants (Levtzion 2008). Its relative influence grew (and spread to the rural areas) in the 1970s partly because of Moussa Traoré's more tolerant regime vis-à-vis Islamic organizations (Niezen 1990: 405).

**wali:** Saint; plural, waliw; Bamana origin.

**zyhara:** A pilgrimage to the resting places of holy people (tombs, kaburuw in Bamana) and mausoleums (dayorow in Bamana) in order to celebrate their pious behavior as well as to request special favors from the holy people. Such visitations intensify during the Mawlud, during which more elaborate celebrations at pious men's tombs take place (as in Timbuktu, for example). Also ziarra, ziarah, or ziara; Arabic, "visit."

# Notes

*Introduction: Malian Cultural Heritage and Governmentality*

1. Democracy cannot be reduced to multipartism and free elections, both of which are limited measures for assessing the democratization of a society. (For a critique of such a simplistic way of looking at democracy, see work by political scientists Michael Chege 1995 and Frederic Schaffer 1997, among others.) By foregrounding actual political practices, anthropologists view democracy as a globally circulating discourse that is locally appropriated and produces alternative democracies (see Paley 2008).

2. On Mali's 2012 political and security crisis, see Whitehouse (2012a, 2012b) and Lecocq et al. (2013).

3. As of the beginning of 2014, there were approximately 244,000 internally displaced people and refugees (Internal Displacement Monitoring Centre, 2014, *IDMC*, www.internal-displacement.org/sub-saharan-africa/mali/).

4. See Arnoldi (2003, 2006, 2007); De Jorio (2003, 2006b).

5. Political anthropologists have increasingly claimed the study of the state and governmentality in the global age as their own domain, a process in which the state as well as the nation have been apprehended and increasingly conceptualized in cultural terms. Although the nation is typically seen as a cultural artifact (particularly in formulations foregrounding the sense of belonging shared by national communities, see Anderson's seminal work 1991), anthropological approaches claim that the state, too, should be examined in cultural terms and not just simply, as has typically been the case, in institutional terms (Sharma and Gupta 2006: 8). Anthropologists see both the study of everyday practices by which the state is experienced and the study of representations by which the state is known as areas of anthropological interest.

6. See also De Cesari (2010, 2012); Bendix, Eggert, and Peselmann (2012); O'Dell (2013).

7. On the public sphere, see Jürgen Habermas's seminal work (1989). See also

Fraser's constructive critique of it, which emphasizes how gender dynamics come to inhibit women's (as well as other marginalized groups') full participation in the public sphere (1992, 2007).

8. On the anthropology of the state from a Marxist perspective, see also Trouillot (1995, 2001). For Foucault, power is relational and "a constitutive element of social relationships" (Scott 1999: 42; see also Bayart 2014).

9. Foucault focused on a particular category of space that he called heterotopias, or "other spaces," that is, heterogeneous spaces that present some of the contradictions, ambiguities, and disjuncture of contemporary societies (2008; see also Dehaene and De Cauter 2008).

10. For example, see Death (2011: 8, 2013); Bayart (2009, 2014); Mbembe (2001, 2003).

11. Examples of extensive reports on Malian cultural heritage include *Carte culturelle du Mali: Esquisse d'un inventaire du patrimoine culturel* and *Carte culturelle des fêtes et festivals organisés au Mali* produced by Ministère de Culture du Mali in 2005. Several other reports are available on the UNESCO website. Evidence of the continuing preoccupation with reporting and assessing can be seen in A. Koné (2011).

12. The annual Festival in the Desert, for example, is made possible by the coordination of numerous entities: the grassroots organization that plans and runs the festival, international foundations (e.g., the Dutch DOEN foundation and the Italian Fabbrica Europa per l'Arte), foreign governmental entities (e.g., the Norwegian embassy), supranational organizations (e.g., UNESCO), and national enterprises (e.g., the Banque Malienne de Solidarite). For information on this festival, see www.festival-au-desert.org/.

13. For other entities that play statelike functions, see Ferguson and Gupta (2002); Ferguson (2006); Sharma and Gupta (2006); Collier and Ong (2005); De Cesari (2010, 2012).

14. Structural adjustment programs (SAPs) are a set of conditionalities developing countries must meet in order to qualify for loans from the World Bank and the International Monetary Fund. Imposed since the mid-1980s, such conditionalities include the liberalization of the economy, the privatization of state-owned enterprises, the reduction of state infrastructure, and the devaluation of local currencies.

15. Critics of SAPs immediately predicted some of the negative effects of SAPs in developing countries, such as increased poverty and increased socioeconomic disparity. Recent studies underline the emergence of additional pitfalls, such as the growing tendency for aid to be dispensed in a top-down manner. Another problem is the reinforcement of executive power (something also evident in cultural-heritage initiatives, as seen in chapters 1 and 5), given that most decisions pertaining to aid are negotiated by donors with the executive, thus increasing the president's power and undermining the influence of democratic institutions, such as the national assembly (see van de Walle 2012). Recent shifts in aid programs, aimed to counter developing countries' dependency on donors and their agendas (and in particular the rise of "country ownership"), have had limited results in Mali so far (Bergamaschi 2011). The

Malian government's investment in "design[ing] and implement[ing] development polity" has been limited (van de Walle 2012: 2; Bergamaschi 2011: 136). Bergamaschi reports a change in style more than substance: while still calling the shots, aid organizations have moved from "straight coercion . . . to [exerting] influence and persuasion" (2011: 137). Similar processes and, in particular, the reinforcement of the executive power have been linked to advanced neoliberalism (see work on U.S. politics by Greenhouse 2008).

16. See Ferguson 2006; Soares 2005b; Holder 2014a, 2014b; Holder and Sow 2014; Holder and Saint-Laury 2013; and De Cesari (2010).

17. Appadurai's concept of public culture builds on Foucault's theory of governmentality but highlights other more agentic aspects of Foucault's theory of subjectivation (Foucault 1982; see Cole 2001 and Bayart 2014).

18. For discussion of the religious sphere, see Launay and Soares (1999); Soares (2005a, 2005b); and De Jorio (2009).

19. The literatures on heritage and, particularly, memory are vast; the following section covers only some of the approaches most relevant to this work.

20. See, for instance, Kögler (2007). The situatedness of knowledge—key to the postmodern perspective—is developed within the subfield of psychological anthropology by Holland (e.g., 1992) and Holland and Leander (2004), among others.

21. On forgetting, see Küchler and Forty (1999) and Morris (2011).

22. Furthermore, memory often carries important implications—not just for political projects but for moral ones, too (e.g., Antze and Lambek 1996).

23. The TRC and its underlining narrative of redemptive memory are a trope of global circulation. See also Huyssen (2003).

24. See also Lowenthal (1998).

25. See also Lambek and Antze (1996: xiii).

26. This tendency continued unmodified during the next twenty-three years, under Moussa Traoré's regime.

27. Furthermore, not all "traditions" (in particular, those traditions that were reappropriated and redefined within the oppressive context of colonial domination) were retained, and indeed at independence, among the removed "traditions" are some "traditional" titles, for example, the *chef de canton*, a customary authority who worked as intermediary for the colonial administration; territorial units, such as *chefferies coutumiers* ("traditional" chieftaincies); and ethnic-based census categories (which reflect the colonial obsession with classifying people into ethnic groups), that is, those aspects of "traditions" that were more closely tied to the system of colonial domination. For a discussion of similar processes in postindependence Ghana, see Schramm (2004: 161). On the topic of "invented traditions" in Mali and the US-RDA's efforts to dismantle the vestiges of French colonial administration and build a new independent African nation, see historian Gregory Mann's (2015) work. Due to the timing of our respective publications, I cannot fully engage with his book here.

28. Mali was one of the great African empires that flourished in this region from the thirteenth to the sixteenth centuries.

29. General information on Mali's party system can be found at "The Party System and Conditions of Candidacy: Mali," 2 Feb. 2014, http://sahelresearch.africa.ufl.edu/tsep/themesissues/the-party-system-and-conditions-of-candidacy/mali/.

30. Chapter 1 provides an overview of several state-run heritage initiatives during the democratic period.

31. I refer here to the women's museum Muso Kunda, in principle a private institution but in actuality not so neatly distinguishable from a public institution, a topic I discuss in chapter 3.

32. Under Konaré, the Biennale was initially restarted in 2001 under a modified name, La Semaine nationale des arts et de la culture (The National Week of Arts and Culture). In 2003, under Touré, the festival was renamed La Biennale artistique et culturelle (The Artistic and Cultural Biennale), but sports competitions continued to be omitted, as under Konaré.

33. The representatives of the artistic group representing Malians in the diaspora (read Malians in France) were allowed to participate only as performers, not as competitors.

34. For instance, the 2012 Semaine nationale du patrimoine culturel centered on "cultural heritage, factor of dialogue, peace and social cohesion for the consolidation of national unity" (Diaouré 2012; see also Ministère de la Culture 2014).

35. UNICEF, 2013, "Statistics," UNICEF, www.unicef.org/infobycountry/mali_statistics.html.

36. See also Arnoldi (2003, 2007).

37. It is uncertain if the museum will be reopened any time soon, above all because the government and donors are currently preoccupied with restoring the cultural heritage that was destroyed during the Tuareg-Islamist occupation of the northern regions in 2012.

38. "Pre-Islamic tradition" lies within quotation marks because traditions, of course, change over time and because even those traditions that were once deemed as pre-Islamic show evidence of the continuing Islamic influence in the region.

## 1. *Commemorating the Nation's Heroes in Mali's Neoliberal Democracy*

1. See Bagayogo (1992); Arnoldi (2006); Schulz (2007).

2. Multipartism, at least during Konaré's administration, created greater internal differentiation than the opposition between state official memory (and its objectification in specific heritage projects) and popular memory can adequately express.

3. De Jorio (2003) expands this discussion considerably.

4. Though still present, the opposition was already less active during Konaré's second mandate because it was preparing for the upcoming presidential election, widely perceived to be a game changer because it would usher in a new president (per the 1991 constitution, Konaré could not fill a third term in office). The arrests of opposition leaders around the 1997 presidential elections, which resulted in the reelection of Konaré, may also have discouraged the opposition from further action.

(For more information, see Amnesty International 1997.) I thank Alioune Sow for suggesting this clarification.

5. On violence in postcolonial Mali as a colonial legacy, see, for instance, Mann (2007) and Schulz (2012).

6. L'Union soudanaise–Rassemblement démocratique africain (Sudanese Union–African Democratic Rally) (US-RDA) was one of the first parties created in French Sudan, today's Mali, in 1946. After Mali's independence in 1960, the US-RDA was established as the only legal party, and its leadership governed the country. The US-RDA was dissolved in 1968 following Traoré's military coup and reconstituted after the democratic turn of 1991. It recently joined other parties to form L'Union malienne du rassemblement démocratique africain/faso jigi (Malian Union of the African Democratic Rally) (UM-RDA), thus sanctioning the overcoming of some old party splits and their fusion into a larger entity (although some of the old members of the US-RDA have decided to withdraw from the political scene and do not identify with this new political formation) (A. S. Traoré, pers. comm., Bamako, June 2014).

The UDS party originally arose from the struggle for the leadership of a state organism, La Société mutuelle de développement rural (Mutual Society for Rural Development), between Dramane Coulibaly, the highest-ranking representative of the US-RDA in Ségou, and Moussa Diarra, the future founder of the UDS party. The struggle is also to be interpreted as a particularly painful episode in the ongoing history of rivalries among some of the most powerful families in Ségou.

7. See also Diop (1999).

8. Sissoko and Dicko were leaders of the Parti soudanais progressiste (Sudanese Progressive Party) (PSP), one of Mali's first parties and long-time US-RDA rival. The PSP was the party of neotraditional chiefs who acted as French intermediaries at the local level and who sought to maintain their privileges. When the US-RDA won the elections and the separation from France was decided, PSP members dissolved their party and joined the ranks of the US-RDA in 1959. Despite the constitution of a common front, divisions remained and resurfaced as in the case discussed in these pages.

9. Indeed, some of the most despised US-RDA policies, such as the creation of collective fields at the village level to fund community projects, were dismantled in the aftermath of the 1968 military coup.

10. I thank Alioune Sow for clarifying the significance of 1977 and, particularly, the events surrounding Modibo Keita's death and in the national rehabilitation of Keita.

11. Mali's relative political stability lasted until 2012. In March 2012 a military coup d'état, which was soon followed by the establishment of an interim government to prepare the country for its next elections, as well as the secession of the north by a shaky alliance of Tuareg and Islamists, brought Mali to the verge of state collapse. The crisis was formally ended by the reconquest of the north by French and Chadian forces and by the democratic elections of a new president, Ibrahim Boubacar Keita, in the summer of 2013. Insecurity and episodes of violence remain a recurring problem in the north, however. Investments in the field of culture have been dramatically reduced. The Ministry of Culture is currently predominantly concerned

with the reconstruction of the World Heritage Sites in the north, which is seen as an international priority (see chapter 5).

12. On Mali's school crisis and its political ramifications, see Gérard (1997) and Bagayogo (2007), among others.

13. In the 1991 interview with Pivin for *Revue Noire*, Konaré also recognized that some Malian artists had greatly contributed to the development of Mali's democratic movement. He mentioned theater groups and writers, in particular.

14. Some of the values (e.g., hospitality) were already celebrated during Les Biennales (see introduction).

15. In South Africa, memory discourse similarly "implement[s] inclusiveness at all levels in an attempt to redress the exclusiveness and elitism of the previous era" (Marschall 2006: 179–80).

16. Several scholars have commented on the minimization or erasure of socialism from representations of the fathers of African independence in the democratic neoliberal era. On Tanzania, see Fouéré (2009); on Mozambique, see Pitcher (2006).

17. ADEMA's autocratic face was also reinforced by the aid regime, which actually strengthened the executive's power and bypassed democratic institutions, such as the National Assembly (see van de Walle 2012).

18. Critiques of "Alpha's monuments" were also informed by religious, economic, and aesthetic concerns (see Barry 2004 for an in-depth presentation of the different viewpoints).

19. Retrospectively, however, such confrontations had some unexpected consequences as individuals and groups began to take on the organization of independent heritage projects, a trend in dramatic expansion.

20. Le Mouvement citoyen, the alliance of parties and civil society organizations that brought Touré to power, was transformed into a political party, Le Parti pour le développement economique et social (Party for Economic and Social Development) (PDES), in preparation for the 2012 presidential election (Camara 2010).

21. Very few monuments were built under Touré. For instance, the only one built in Bamako was one dedicated to General Abdoulaye Soumaré (2011), the architect of the professionalization of the Malian Army immediately after independence. The state-of-the-art National Park of Mali (a large space within a protected forest reserve, with a rich variety of plants, walking paths, coffee shops, and restaurants) sponsored by the AKTC, was opened in 2010 in Bamako on the fiftieth anniversary of Mali's independence.

22. The statements by which Touré presented himself as Keita's heir did not materialize in any effort to sustain the Modibo Keita Memorial, a state-owned cultural institution dedicated to the study of the First Republic (Modibo Diallo, pers. comm., June 2014). As of 2015 the memorial remains closed, although some wedding photo shoots and some occasional conferences still take place on its premises.

23. The new PSP claims to be the heir of Fily Dabo Sissoko's old PSP; indeed, Dicko is the son of a leader of the former PSP (Hamadoun Dicko).

24. Amselle (2006); Bagayogo (1987, 1992); Hoffman (2000); Schulz (1997, 2001).

25. In 2009 the Manden Charter of Kurukan Fuga was added to UNESCO's Representative List of the Intangible Cultural Heritage of Humanity.

26. The original in Bamana is: "Amadu Tumani, k' i tɛ sunɔgɔ Mali kɔnɔ i tɛ sunɔgɔ surɔ I tɛ sunɔgɔ tile kɔnɔ. I ya sunɔgɔ baliya k'a kun bɛrɛ don Mali kɔnɔ, ko k'o yirila" (ORTM 2010). I express here my deepest appreciation to Amadou Beidy Sow for his transcription, translation, and discussion of this complex state ceremony.

27. One of the griots in attendance at the 2010 state-promoted commemoration of the Charter of Kurukan Fuga in the Kangaba region commented, "*Janjo fɔra cɛ kuluw ye fɔlɔ fɔlɔ, an bɛ janjo fɔ Manju Ture ye*" (They [griots] played *janjo* for many people, and we play *janjo* for Manju Ture [referring to Touré]) (ORTM 2010). Manju is one of the praise-names given to Samori Touré, the founder of a theocratic state in present-day Guinea and one of the leaders of the resistance against French colonization in the late nineteenth century (Johnson, Hale, and Belcher 1997). Manju is also used to praise members of the Touré family (by suggesting association with such a great ancestor and his exceptional accomplishments). I thank Amadou Beidy Sow for his transcription and translation of this passage.

28. Richard Werbner (1998) talks about anti-memory, a form of popular memory as opposed to elite memory. I use countermemory to refer to the memory of the political opposition (among others) and to stress some of the ramifications of party politics on the management of Mali's cultural heritage.

29. On the tropes of rationality and modernity of the South African elites, see Marschall (2006: 184).

30. In 2010 and 2011, Moussa Traoré was invited by the defense to testify in the defamation trial against Amadou Seydou Traoré. The latter was accused by the heirs of the late Faran Samaké of vilifying their father's memory in a speech given during one of the many fiftieth anniversary celebrations of Mali's independence. In that speech, A. S. Traoré accused Samaké of being responsible for Modibo Keita's death, which was a widely held belief. Moussa Traoré refused to testify in court. Although the court ultimately acquitted A. S. Traoré, the trial once more revealed Moussa Traoré's unwillingness to testify and bring clarity to some of the most horrifying events of his regime (B. Dembelé 2011).

## 2. Remembering the Colonial Past

1. For civil servants, *la descente* (the end of the workday) is around 4 P.M.

2. Mali was formerly known as French Soudan. In the aftermath of independence (1960), the name was changed to Mali to indicate Malian leaders' commitment to the ideals of the short-lived Mali Federation with Senegal (1959–60) and as a reference to one of the great empires that had blossomed in this area during medieval times.

3. Historical reports conflict on the year when the statue was actually removed: Some sources claim it was removed shortly after independence (1960), when the most evident signs of colonial presence were removed; others claim that the statue was removed during the Active Revolution 1967–68 (that is, in the last effort to save

Modibo Keita's rule). The descriptions of the ways in which the statue was removed (the toppling, dragging, etc.) are, on the other hand, very consistent.

4. The year is a typo by the journal, as the correct publication date is 2000.

5. I do not wish to suggest that such narratives are necessarily coherent or well received. They manifest people's multiple engagements with the past, including interrogations of the past motivated by the search for alternative paths to modernity and development.

6. See Bhabha (1994); Canclini (1995); Morton (1998, 2000); De Jorio (2006b); de Jong (2009).

7. On the history of postcolonial education in Mali, see, for instance, Zolberg (1976) and Bagayogo (2007).

8. On the ciwara, see Wooten (2000).

9. For a detailed description of the complex, see the exhaustive work by Malian scholar Harouna Barry (2004).

10. In the entire monument complex, this is the only monument that honors Malian women's role in politics.

11. See also Grosz-Ngaté analysis of the representation of Mande societies and cultures in the work of European explorers and French colonial administrators such as Mungo Park, René Caillié, Charles Monteil, and Maurice Delafosse (1988).

12. The square appears to have been inspired by an existing room of the National Archives, the scarcely known Salle d'informatique et de photos (Room of Electronic Data and Photos), which contains portraits of several French governors and Mali's presidents.

13. The statue to the memory of Moussa Traoré (1968–91) was also criticized as a suggestion that he be acquitted of responsibility for his crimes and (prematurely) rehabilitated (Barry 2004: 39–41).

14. Such cultural and political impasses are evident when certain ways of thinking and acting are dismissed as supposedly Western imports. For example, these impasses have dramatically hampered the women's cause in Mali (Soares 2009; De Jorio 2009).

15. For the significance of the trope of debt, see Mann (2007), whose historical analysis of colonial monuments diverges from mine, as he interprets them to an anticolonial stance or, at best, a narrative emphasizing France's continuing responsibility vis-à-vis Mali. Here, I detail the public debates and confrontations triggered by Konaré's heritage initiatives, taking into account the diversity of views on this topic held by different Malian individuals and groups (and their political underpinnings).

16. The information discussed here was collected on 11 July 2003.

17. Author's meetings with representatives of the Diarra family in Ségou, June 2001 and July 2014.

18. In 2014 the Diarra were also fighting against their marginalization from the now relatively established Ségou-based heritage elite.

19. A similar position—that is, of rejection of oversimplifying and limiting dichotomies—is developed by postcolonial authors, such as Canclini (1995) and Bhabha (1990, 1994).

## 3. The Women's Museum Muso Kunda: Citizenship, Gender, and Social Memory

1. The last reported activity taking place at Muso Kunda dates back to Sunday 6 March 2011 (see Diaspora Action 2011). News of the temporary closing of the institution and renovation plans was already posted on the museum's website—www.museedelafemme.com—in 2006 and 2007 (no longer available, last accessed 4 October 2013).

2. My discussion and analysis locate the museum in the time prior to its temporary closure.

3. Touré's administration also redirected its priorities by placing greater emphasis on strengthening state infrastructures to attract investments (e.g., roads and new housing projects). While a systematic assessment of the infrastructure built under Touré remains to be done, the work I was able to observe directly was mostly unfinished, with the exclusion of the successful completion of Bamako's third bridge. The road between Bamako and Ségou, for example, was widened but remained unfinished as of June 2014.

4. On the new family code, the Nouveau Code des personnes et de la famille, see Soares (2009); De Jorio (2009); Ramadan (2012).

5. The 2014 programmatic document "Politique culturelle du Mali: Document-cadre" by the Ministry of Culture contains no reference to the women's museum Muso Kunda. Its few references to women's participation in cultural initiatives are generally unspecific and insignificant.

6. Even though the museum remains closed and has been under renovation, its permanent closure has not been officially announced. I consider it a current (albeit, hibernating) institution and use the present tense to describe its exhibits and programs. Moreover, Adame Ba Konaré continues to this date to be introduced in formal settings as (among her many titles) Muso Kunda's founder and director.

7. Under Konaré's presidency, women's political participation increased. In 2000 seven out of twenty-one ministers (33.3 percent) were women, the highest in Mali's postcolonial history (US Department of State 2001). The percentage participation of women decreased under President Touré. In 2007, five out of twenty-seven cabinet members (18.51 percent) were women (Freedom House 2011). Despite a decline in women's participation, Touré did nominate the first woman prime minister in Mali's history, Cissé Mariam Kaidama Sidibé, as his presidential mandate was coming to an end (22 March 2011). Cissé's appointment was regarded as a highly political move (to please donors' expectations). It lasted less than a year and was further cut short by the coup d'état of 22 March 2012. The decline in women's political participation continues in the post-2012 period. As of 2015 there are three women (9 percent) only in President Ibrahim Boubacar Keita's cabinet of thirty-three ministers. The number of women seated at the National Assembly also experienced a slight decline; from 12.24 percent in 1997 to 9.52 percent in 2013. Data on Mali's parliamentary elections are available at http://www.ipu.org/parline-e/reports/2201_A.htm.

8. See Ba Konare's (1993) *Dictionnaire des femmes célèbres du Mali*, a work that details the many contributions of Malian women to the arts, politics, sports, culture, economy, and so on.

9. Literature on Muso Kunda includes Ba Konare's writings (1998a, 1998b, 1999b), articles published in the museum's magazine, *Faro*, and De Jorio (2002b).

10. See, for instance, Aoua Keita's (1975) autobiography.

11. See De Jorio (2009).

12. Many of the so-called pre-Islamic practices are in reality heavily influenced by Islam (given Islam's presence in the region since at least the ninth century) but are perceived as "closely identified with the un-Islamic" (Soares 2005b: 91). Such practices are still called "animistic" in bureaucratic documents, reports, and part of the media and thus reflect the enduring influence of colonial paradigms (grounded in nineteenth-century cultural evolutionism) on contemporary thought. Although fully aware that these "pre-Islamic practices" are constantly morphing and that they syncretically integrate elements from Islam, I still use them here to reflect the terms of contemporary debates in Mali today.

13. Faro is a dual supernatural spirit with a female (water) and male (earth) form. The earthly version of Faro is often described as an androgynous being, but the director reinterpreted this myth to emphasize the feminine contribution in the Bamana creation myth, thus countering more androcentric readings (Dieterlen 1955; de Heusch 2001).

14. This Fanta Damba is called "number 1" to differentiate her from another famous singer by the same name.

15. In particular, legislation from 1939, 1951, 1962, and 1992 that improved women's rights is mentioned.

16. On the concept of tradition as a social construction—and, as such, constantly renegotiated—see Terence Ranger's seminal work (e.g., 1983). Critiques of Ranger's work, however, point out his failure to include the meanings and feelings people attach to their traditions (see Briggs 1996; Bellagamba and Paini 2000). I have endeavored to overcome such limitations in my own work by including the views about women's heritage from museum representatives and visitors.

17. At Muso Kunda these costumes are worn by female mannequins—which suggests that women could wear them—whereas traditionally only men could wear masks in the Bamana popular theater. Here, as elsewhere, the museum offers a female-centric interpretation of ethnic and regional traditions.

18. The mannequin of the urban woman displays a more recent variant of the boubou with loosely shaped sleeves; the classic boubou has undefined sleeves and some embroidery in the front. On the cultural history of women's clothing in Francophone West Africa see work by Mustafa (1997, 2002, 2006) and Rovine (2011).

19. In addition, there is no mention of style variation within an ethnic group or acknowledgment of the fact that such ethnic classifications are, indeed, the result of a historical process in which French colonization played a significant role (Bazin 1985; Amselle 1990). Each model embodies a distinct and apparently immutable ethnicity.

20. I use "traditional" to indicate weddings that are defined by regional and ethnic particularities. The other two forms of marriage available to Malians are religious weddings and civil weddings (see De Jorio 2002a).

21. Readings of the boubou vary, even in the museum literature, and include more critical interpretations, such as in the work by Oumou Ahmar Traoré. She sees in the boubou's restrictions on movement a sign of how, shortly after independence, "religious and social barriers were erected and were successful in wrapping the woman in a prison of cloth" (1999: 9). The adoption of the boubou did not terminate women's creative experimentation with fashion. The transformation of the Islamic head covering into a beautiful and versatile head scarf signals for Traoré a partial victory of Malian women vis-à-vis conservative attempts to regulate women's dress.

22. The use of explanatory texts is very limited in the exhibit with the exception of some parts of the newest section, which highlights work tools and kitchen utensils.

23. See Agnès Lambert de Frondeville (1987).

24. The museum and world's fair were also the platforms for the display of a certain world order, expressed by the organization of artifacts in lineal progressions, and helped to justify Europeans' colonial agenda (see seminal work by Errington 1998).

25. See also Fath Davis Ruffins (2006).

26. Radio France Internationale, 2010, "Après-coup de Adame Ba Konaré," 22 Sept., http://deuxamours.blogs.rfi.fr/article/2010/09/22/apres-coup-de-adame-ba-konare.

27. For further information about the Wahhabiyya in Mali, see, for instance, Lansiné Kaba (1974); Jean-Loup Amselle (1985); R. W. Niezen (1990); David Gutelius (2007).

28. These antagonistic views of women's social and historical roles have a long history in Mali, as suggested by a debate in the 1950s between writer and US-RDA party leader Mamadou El Béchir Gologo and Sister Jean-Bernard (see De Jorio 1997).

## 4. The Heritagization of Islamic and Secular Architecture: Djenné

In this chapter I build and expand on my previous work (2006a, 2009) on the heritagization of Djenné. This chapter is based on a close analysis of an online bulletin published biannually by the cultural organization Djenné Patrimoine from 1996 to 2015, Malian newspaper articles, blogs by Djenné residents, email lists, and my fieldwork in Mali. During June 2014 I interviewed representatives from the Djenné and Timbuktu heritage sectors (including architects and ministry of culture officials), the Aga Khan Trust for Culture, and UNESCO. I thank Charlotte Joy for her comments and suggestions on an earlier version of this chapter.

1. For instance, with a few exceptions, only Muslims are allowed to enter the Great Mosque of Djenné.

2. On tourism in Djenné, see Joy (2007b, 2010). Among others, her publications foreground the participatory and culturally sensitive (and typically unacknowledged) perspective embraced by some of Djenné's tourists who, following their visit, expressed a concern "about what is being asked of the town: to remain materially the same in order to retain World Heritage status" (Joy 2010: 61–62).

3. Already in 1967 Cruise O'Brien brought attention to the construct of l'Islam noir as a strategy of colonial domination. For recent developments in (Malian) state practices of religious "containment," see Brenner (2001) and Soares (2005b, 2013).

4. The Aguibou Tall Palace was reconstructed under the French in recognition of Aguibou Tall's support of French colonial interests. On the history of the Aguibou Tall Palace, see Centre Edmon Fortier, n.d., "Mali 1905: Le fils d' El Hadj Oumar Tall," 21 December 2015, http://home.planet.nl/~kreke003/Aguibou.htm.

5. This quote and the next were taken from www.tourisme.gov.ml/fr/cgi-bin/view_article.pl?id=189 (no longer available, accessed 12 August 2010).

6. Prussin traces the "influence of French engineers trained in the Ecole Polytechnique and coached in the rationalism of Viollet-le-Duc" on Sudanese architecture (1977: 73).

7. See also Clericuzio 2009.

8. See also Betts (1985).

9. Wright examines the complexities of French colonial intervention in the domain of North African architecture (with an emphasis on Morocco). The colonies represented laboratories for the experimentation of solutions that could potentially be applied to the resolution of social and urban problems back in France. See also Maussen (2007: 988).

10. See also Newcomb (2006).

11. For a discussion of French Islamic policies and their legacies in contemporary Mali see, for instance, Brenner 2001 and Soares 2013.

12. The Great Mosque of Djenné was originally built in 1280, when Koi Konboro became the first king of Djenné to convert to Islam (Bourgeois 1987: 54).

Sekou Amadou founded the Peul Empire of Masina and ruled from 1818 to 1843 (Bourgeois 1987: 55).

13. Prussin also adduces the Great Depression as a cause for the end of colonial expositions (1985: 225).

14. The neo-Sudanese style was replaced by the International Style, characterized by "that rectangular, vertical look identified with Los Angeles, Miami, and Casablanca" (Betts 1985: 200).

15. At that time the minister of culture position was called the minister of youth, sports, arts, and culture.

The revaluation and protection of Mali's tangible heritage is strongly tied to the work of archaeologist Konaré, first as minister of culture (1978–80) and as president of the country (1992–2002). As minister of culture, Konaré spearheaded legislative changes to develop a coherent plan for the protection of Mali's monuments, until then a remarkable but somewhat neglected dimension of Malian national patrimony (see also Konaré 1983). As president he worked to further develop programs for the preservation and valorization of Mali's tangible heritage, which he also expanded considerably through the construction of a remarkable number of new monuments and cultural institutions both in Bamako and in the surrounding regions.

16. The ICOMOS is a nongovernmental international organization for the preservation of cultural heritage.

17. For example, Mali's exhibit at the 2010 World Expo in Shanghai included "a simulated Malian mosque, [where] the production processes of Malian food and the culinary culture [were] exhibited" (World Expo 2010 Shanghai, 2010, "Mali Pavilion at Expo 2010 Shanghai China," http://worldexpo2010shanghai.blogspot.com/2010/05/mali-pavilion-at-expo-2010-shanghai.html.

18. It also does not sufficiently acknowledge individuals' rights to make choices pertaining to the management and preservation of their culture (Eriksen 2001).

19. Rowlands 2007; De Jorio 2006a, 2009; Joy 2007a, 2007b, 2012.

20. *Djenné Patrimoine Informations* (1999, 6: 3).

21. Here as elsewhere in Mali, household heads regulate the organization and distribution of the household space, and many household heads were unwilling to delegate their power, even in light of obvious economic returns for their participation (Rowlands 2003).

22. Joseph Brunet-Jailly and Djenné Patrimoine have criticized the restoration of Djenné precisely because it resulted in too many compromises by permitting the use of modern materials and construction techniques and the revision of house plans. In their opinion, the restoration of Djenné should have been limited to fewer houses and more accurately reflected the guidelines the Venice Charter established in order to preserve "authentic know-hows" (Brunet-Jailly 2002: 179).

23. These events show some continuity in state-society relations under Konaré's and Touré's governments. See chapter 2 for similar state-society confrontations under Konaré.

24. On the 2006 popular revolt in Djenné, see De Jorio 2006a, 2009; Joy 2012; Rowlands 2007.

25. Interview with Aga Khan Trust for Culture representatives in Bamako, June 2014.

26. *Banco* is a mix of mud, vegetable fibers of various origins, and other organic waste.

27. See also *Djenné Patrimoine Informations* 31, 2015, http://www.acroterre.org/wp-content/uploads/2015/11/Bulletin-de-DJENNE-PATRIMOINE1.pdf. The last issue (31) of the online newsletter *Djenné Patrimoine Informations* was published in the summer of 2015 after a four-year interruption; past issues (up to number 28) are archived on the organization's website, http://djenne-patrimoine.org. Issue 31 (2015) can be found at http://www.acroterre.org/wp-content/uploads/2015/11/Bulletin-de-DJENNE-PATRIMOINE1.pdf.

28. State inability to implement UNESCO guidelines rests on a number of factors, including the lack of funds, the size of the world heritage site to be preserved (the old towns of Djenné), and the extractive practices of Mali's political elites.

29. See also *Djenné Patrimoine Informations* 31, 2015, http://www.acroterre.org/wp-content/uploads/2015/11/Bulletin-de-DJENNE-PATRIMOINE1.pdf.

30. UNESCO's predominantly museological approach resembles what Renato

Rosaldo (1989) has described as imperialist nostalgia, the longing for a past prior to the ravages of colonization and made possible only by the modernization of the present and its devastating effects and temporal distance.

31. These initiatives were also seen, in principle, as key to the development of the region's tourist industry and its economy. At least, this was the case prior to the 2012 crisis, from which Mali is slowly recovering.

32. See also *Djenné Patrimoine Informations* 22, 2007, http://djenne-patrimoine.org/dp22.htm.

33. I thank Charlotte Joy, one of the main organizers of the ornithology exhibit in Djenné, for sharing this information.

34. The decision to open the mosque dates to 16 June 1998 (Djenné Patrimoine 1998b). Despite this decision, the mosque remains "still more or less closed" to non-Muslims. People who are "close to the administration of the mosque" can, for a price, provide admission (Sarin 2011).

35. Cissé's choice of words is revealing of the top-down nature of heritage preservation in Djenné so often criticized in the pages of *Djenné Patrimoine Informations*. Cissé first describes the refusal of the city elites as motivated by "mysterious beliefs," showing no great effort to understand the position of segments of the local population. He then cryptically summarizes their response to his intermediations with "they have understood" and offers no further qualification (qtd. in Touré and Sissoko 2005).

36. Gatti suggests that the state's incursion into the domain of the religious has resulted in the "appropriation and nationalization of religion by the state" (2001: 8). Brenner (1993) points out that the separation between the state and religion is questionable and discusses some of the ways in which the state has exerted control over Muslim religious authorities throughout Mali's history.

37. French colonial policies toward Islam reflected the underling belief that "Enclosed within communities infused with 'fetishism,' 'Black Islam' would lose by this all its power of causing harm. It would be ethnicized and tribalized. It would cease to be a historic agent while waiting for its final assimilation to civilization" (Triaud 2000).

38. A new project for the dam was then developed in response to citizens' complaints, and the new dam was opened in 2007.

39. For changes in Ousmane Madani Haidara's public image (he is now seen as a much more moderate preacher than other Muslim leaders and scholars within the High Islamic Council), see chapter 5. See also Holder (2012); Schulz (2003); Soares (2005a, 2005b, 2013).

40. Touré mentions the U.S. embassy's gift of fans for the Great Mosque as one example of foreign intervention. See also Joy (2012).

41. See *Djenné Patrimoine Informations* 17, 2004, and 22, 2007, http://djenne-patrimoine.org/lejournal.htm; Brunet-Jailly (2002).

42. Marchand (2009) points also to the inflation of masons' fees caused by the various restoration projects (and the accompanying injection of foreign capital), making repairs increasingly out of reach for most inhabitants of Djenné (see, for instance, Marchand 2009: 20).

43. Joy (2007b, 2010) estimates that the revenues from tourism in Djenné are still very limited and concentrated in a few months of the year. The main beneficiary of tourism remains the Malian state, which receives funds for the promotion and preservation of Djenné's cultural heritage (see also Brunet-Jailly 2002).

44. The social groups behind the construction of La Maison du Patrimoine are the barey ton (or masons' association), the Malian cultural organization Djenné Patrimoine, and Acroterre (a French organization specializing in earth architecture).

## 5. The Fate of Timbuktu's Sufi Heritage: Controversies around Past Traces and Current Practices

I thank Talatou A. Maiga (University of Utah), Sane Chirphi Alpha (Timbuktu), Issa Fofana (Point Sud), and Mamadou Diamountani (Haut conseil islamique) for sharing their knowledge of Timbuktu, its mausoleums, and Mali's recent troubled history. Earlier versions of this chapter were presented as a talk in three distinct institutional settings: "Heritage and the Arab Spring," an international symposium and roundtable at the Freer Gallery of Art of the Smithsonian Institution, Washington, DC (28 February 2014); the Fifty-Seventh Annual Meeting of the African Studies Association, Indianapolis, Indiana (20 November 2014); and the Islam in Africa Working Group, Center for African Studies, University of Florida (9 December 2014). In particular, I thank the organizer of the symposium at the Smithsonian, Nancy Um, for soliciting my contribution, which ultimately resulted in this chapter. I also thank Maria Grosz-Ngaté, Mary Jo Arnoldi, Andrew Hernann, Leonardo Villalon, Fiona McLaughlin, Terje Østebø, Alioune Sow, Renata Serra, Aboulaye Kane, and Steven Brandt for their generous comments on earlier versions of this chapter. I also thank Benjamin Soares for his insightful comments and critiques of this chapter.

1. The term "Islamists" (which includes the Salafis) refers to a heterogeneous group of actors and organizations (see Lecocq and Schrijver 2007; Østebø 2008). The groups I describe here are Islamist extremist groups and are "engaged in a violent jihad with ideological roots in Salafism" (Lecocq et al. 2013: 1n1). The term "saint" is an English approximation of the Arabic *wali* (friend of God) (Soares 1997). While aware of the limitations in the English translation of this term, I continue to use it here because it is most commonly used in the literature on the mausoleums.

2. According to Becker, "place-specific" suggests exchanges, travels, and fluxes. This term points to the transregional quality of places (2009: 417).

3. "Scape" is a concept Appadurai (1990) introduced to describe global cultural flows. Scapes are imagined worlds, with irregular shapes and fluid boundaries. They are perspectival constructs that reflect the viewpoint of the socially positioned actor or groups.

4. On the religious economy, see Soares (2004, 2005a, 2005b).

5. Their exact resting place, however, is known only to the city's elders (Senou Sidi, pers. comm., 2014).

6. See Triaud (2009) on the ever-growing number of Timbuktu manuscripts and the role of media in the process.

7. Ten more mausoleums and graves were recently identified, however, possibly leading to the expansion in the number of mausoleums listed on the UNESCO World Heritage Site list (Ghetti 2014: 19).

8. Ghetti states, "The term mausoleum was established in the literature and local parlance to designate the main tombs of saints, to stress their spiritual importance" (2014: 19).

9. The Timbuktu-based tombs and mausoleums were not necessarily of Sufi saints. According to Brenner (1988), Sufism came late to Timbuktu, probably in the eighteenth century. However, in much of the contemporary literature, these mausoleums and surrounding practices have been reapprehended in a narrative emphasizing their connections to Sufism (e.g., O'Dell 2013). I thank B. Soares for his generous insights on this topic.

10. "Senou Sidi" is a pseudonym to protect the identity of this individual.

11. See Soares (2004, 2005a, 2005b, 2007: 81).

12. See also Scheele (2013) on the nexus of status and knowledge in the region.

13. Disagreements, exchanges, and mutual accommodations between Salafi reform movements and Sufi orders figure prominently in the history of Islam (see, for instance, Soares 2005a; Howell and van Bruinessen 2007; Becker 2009).

14. On heritage work during Konaré's presidency, see Arnoldi (2003, 2006, 2007); De Jorio (2003, 2006b). The democratic government has put much greater emphasis on the development and valorization of regional cultures, recognized as a vehicle for a more even development of Mali's regions. This trend was spearheaded under Konaré's presidency with the creation of Missions culturelles; located through Mali, these offices were tasked with overseeing the management of the country's World Heritage Sites, most of which are located in Mali's northern towns (e.g., Djenné, Timbuktu, and Gao). During Konaré's presidency, the privatization of heritage also began to take off. One notable example of this is the successful work for the preservation and valorization of the Timbuktu manuscripts by L'association pour la sauvegarde et la valorisation des manuscrits pour la défense de la culture islamique (SAVAMA-DCI). This NGO was funded in 1996 by its main representative, Abdel Kader Haidara, and brought together the owners of several private libraries in Timbuktu. The transfer of manuscripts was made possible by Haidara's dedication. Haidara is a writer, an expert on the Timbuktu manuscripts, the owner of a private library (the Mamma Haidara Memorial Library), and the founder of SAVAMA-DCI. The transfer was coordinated with the support of several other city residents.

15. Mali's partnership with South Africa also built on Konaré's groundwork during South African president Thabo Mbeki's 2001 visit to Timbuktu.

16. See Holder (2014b) for a detailed analysis of the 2006 Mawlud.

17. The 2006 Mawlud saw the participation of a number of African political and religious leaders. These leaders included the presidents of Senegal, Abdoulaye Wade; Niger, Mamadou Tanja; and Mauritania, Ely Ould Mohamed Vall. Also present were important Islamic leaders from Africa and abroad, including the Modou Kara Mbaké, Senegalese Muride preacher, and Louis Farrakhan, the North American leader of the Nation of Islam.

18. For instance, in March 2007 Gaddafi was in Agadez, Niger, for the celebration of the Prophet's birthday; in 2008 in Kampala, Uganda (to support the minority Muslim population there); and in 2009 in Nouakchott, Mauritania (see Holder 2014b). For further information on Gaddafi's many investments in Mali, see D. Dembele 2011.

19. Gaddafi's speech is available at "El Gathafi—dirige à Tombouctou . . . les musulmans . . . et prononce son discours," 29 December 2011, www.youtube.com/watch?v=2M2gc6Iu_YQ.

20. "El Gathafi—dirige à Tombouctou . . . les musulmans . . . et prononce son discours," 29 December 2011, www.youtube.com/watch?v=2M2gc6Iu_YQ. At the 2006 Mawlud, Gaddafi presented the Timbuktu Chart, a plan to develop further ties and cooperation among the people of the desert (see Holder 2014b).

21. Holder clarifies that the 2006 Mawlud was preceded by the ten-year anniversary celebration of the Flamme de la Paix, which on 27 March 1996 marked the settlement of ethnic rivalries and the pacification of the north via the state's adoption of a national pact. The 2006 commemoration of the pact was intended to renew the state's commitment to it during a time when ethnic and economic unrest was on the rise in the north (Holder 2014b).

22. The presence of radical Islamic groups in the region was already well known in 2006. In 2003 it had garnered international media attention when thirty-two European tourists were kidnapped in the south of Algeria; some were freed in Mali due to Touré's intervention (which revealed the government's knowledge of and ability to negotiate with related groups in Mali). On Salafist groups in Mali, see also Bøås and Utas (2013); Gaasholt (2013); Lecocq and Schrijver (2007); Lecocq et al. (2013).

The 2006 Mawlud served as the stage not only for the expression of regional political ambitions coated in a religious idiom (and also indirect references to growing instability in the north) but also for the confrontation between Malian religious authorities for the leadership of the powerful umbrella organization the Haut conseil islamique du Mali (High Islamic Council of Mali) (HCIM) and, more broadly, the Malian religious sphere. Thierno Hadi Thiam, a representative of Sufi Islam and a rival of Mahmoud Dicko (a Muslim reformist) for the leadership of the HCIM, used the occasion to reiterate his links to moderate Islam and seek greater visibility through the media. Dicko was also present but remained silent in the media (M. Kéita 2006). I thank Leonardo Villalon for his insights on Thiam's position and rationales at the 2006 Mawlud.

23. Prior to the 2012 occupation, a number of initiatives were in support of "moderate Islam" in the region. In his examination of US Agency for International Development's (USAID) investment in "soft security" in Mali since 2005, Daniel P. Aldrich (2014) analyzes the impact of radio programming in support of peace and civic engagement in Timbuktu as countermeasures to stop the development of political Islam in the region.

24. For similar debates in East Africa, see Becker (2009).

25. "Le Sphinx" is the collective name for a group of active or retired members of the security service who claim to act in the interest of their country and inform

the citizenry of ATT's responsibilities in Mali's bad governance (Afribone 2006; see also Holder 2014b: 495n37).

26. See Holder (2014b: 488–89n3). The mawlud (*maulidi*) is a highly contested practice in East Africa; for coverage of this discussion, see Becker (2009). "Bid'ah" refers to all "ritual practices that were not directly traceable to the Qur'an or hadith (sayings of the Prophet)" (Becker 2009: 416), and as such these practices are rejected by Reformist Muslims.

27. See Maliweb Forum, 2007, "La Célébration du Mahouloud Est-elle Bid'a (Innovation)," www.maliweb.net/services/forums/showthread.php?661-La-Celebration -Du-Mahouloud-Est-il-Bid-a%28innovation%29.

28. Radical Middle Way, ca. 2010, http://issuu.com/radmw/docs/5year. In a summary of the meeting, Fuad Nahdi, the founder of Radical Middle Way, further elaborated: "It is time for Africa to be heard with a lion's roar in the Islamic world." Radical Middle Way, ca. 2009, "Making Things Happen: Gathered for Change," http://issuu .com/radicalmiddleway/docs/timbuktu.

29. Fuad Nahdi, ca. 2009, foreword, "Making Things Happen: Gathered for Change," www.radicalmiddleway.org/uploads/editor/files/Timbuktu_online.pdf.

30. The armed Islamist groups in question represent a more extreme form of Salafism. Salafism is a heterogeneous Islamic reform movement, which includes nonviolent forms.

31. The two mausoleums adjacent to the Djingarey Ber Mosque were more seriously damaged. All the others were just partially demolished, which will greatly facilitate the reconstruction work (Direction Nationale 2014: 20).

The dates of the destruction of the mausoleums and other monuments vary from publication to publication. The dates cited here are from the thorough 2014 report by the Malian Ministère de la Culture (Direction Nationale 2014).

32. Chirfi Moulaye Haidara reports that the tomb of his mother, who died in 1974, was also destroyed by the Islamist extremists when they destroyed the mausoleum of saint Cheick Sidi Mahmoud (C. M. Haidara 2013: 69).

33. See Bourgeois (1987) for historical antecedents.

34. Agence France Press (2012) reports: "The Ansar Dine spokesman suggested Saturday's action [30 June 2012] was in retaliation for the UNESCO decision to put the world heritage site, a cradle of Islamic learning founded in the fifth century, on its endangered list on Thursday."

35. As Lecocq and Schrijver point out, the name of this group "refers to *al-salaf al salih* (the pious forefathers), the first three generations of Muslims" (2007: 146).

36. This warm welcome proved to be short-lived. Southern Malians became increasingly unhappy with the French for giving the Tuareg of the northern region of Kidal too much autonomy and credit, and anti-French sentiments resurfaced. See Lefébure (2014).

37. The representation of AQIM's and MUJAO's members as foreign elements is an oversimplification that is unsupported by the available data. Several of their fighters are Malian citizens or individuals with multiple nationalities, Malian citizenship included (Lebovich 2013).

38. UNESCO acted in partnership with the National Directorate of Cultural Heritage in Mali and the International Centre for Earthen Architecture (CRAterre).

39. See Bruce Whitehouse (2014).

40. On Mahmoud Dicko, see Soares (2013).

41. See also Thurston and Lebovich (2013).

42. See Agamben (2005); Stratton (2009).

43. See Soares (2009); De Jorio (2010).

44. The new family code deeply disappointed many women's groups and their international sponsors; indeed, "far from increasing protection [it] eliminates rights and perpetuates discrimination" (Worldwide Movement 2011).

45. I am grateful to Beidy Sow for his help with the translation of the roundtable video.

46. "Moussa Maiga" is a pseudonym to protect the identity of this individual.

47. Mamadou Diamoutani, an influential representative of the High Islamic Council, was also appointed as head of the CENI, the organization in charge of monitoring Malian elections. Holder (2014b) rightly presents Diamoutani's appointment as CENI head, a position he retained as of October 2015, as a further sign of the increasing influence of the religious in the political domain (and of the redefinition of boundaries between the sacred and the profane in Mali today).

48. See, for instance, Soares (2005a).

49. Holder (2012) rightly identifies a conservative shift in Mali's religious sphere already in the course of the ten-year debate surrounding the family code.

50. While some controversy surrounds the preservation of the saints' mausoleums, that is not the case for the manuscripts: the support for Timbuktu's manuscript libraries is not in question. In fact, at least one of Ansar Dine's initial videos contained footage of Timbuktu's manuscripts, presenting them as symbols of Islam's long history of influence in the region while calling all Muslims to join forces together.

51. Several mausoleums have been reconstructed since the completion of this manuscript. No high-quality image of a mausoleum prior to reconstruction was available, hence the inclusion of this image from 2015.

## *Epilogue: Further Thoughts on Governmentality and Culture*

1. This is not, however, the whole story, as Clifford's (1997) concept of the contact zone suggests. The museum is, indeed, also a site for unpredictable exchanges and frictions.

2. As discussed in previous chapters, museological processes were at work not only in the creation of specific public monuments but also in the management of already existing heritage sites, as with the monuments and sites inscribed on the UNESCO World Heritage List. On social hierarchies and heritage work, see, for instance, Herzfeld (2003).

3. On the cooperation of the Ministry of Culture and the Ministry of Crafts and Tourism in Mali, see Doquet (2008).

4. The only existing detailed analysis of the funding behind state heritage initiatives is by A. C. Touré (2006), who concentrates on the initiatives sponsored by the European Union, France, Switzerland, and Belgium (the largest Western donors for heritage)

and leaves out other Western donors (including the United States, whose funding primarily supported programs in nonheritage areas) and all non-Western donors.

5. My analysis is limited to cultural heritage here; that is, it does not include other dimensions of Mali's development initiatives carried out in partnership with the AKCT, Libya, and South Africa.

6. Until the late 1980s and the beginning of the 1990s, many Malians found employment in the state administration and in state-owned enterprises.

7. The multiplicity and lack of coordination among donor entities (who often hold very conflicting goals) also afford greater freedom of action to the institution of the presidency.

8. See Arnoldi (2006).

9. See also Arnoldi (2003). Such paradoxes are not uncommon: the events in Mali follow patterns observed elsewhere. See Greenhouse's (2008) seminal article on the shrinking of the public sphere in the United States under the George W. Bush administration.

10. See also Schulz (1997, 2001).

11. Similar processes of cultural revival were going on in South Africa; see, for instance, Marschall (2006) and Coombes (2003).

12. Touré maintained some of Konaré's engagement projects, such as Mali's 2003 participation in the Thirty-Seventh Annual Smithsonian Folklife Festival on the National Mall, Washington, DC; see Arnoldi (2012).

13. Some of the state's work in the heritage sector of the northern regions was also the result of Gaddafi's initiatives (and funding) in support of moderate forms of Islam and his political ambitions in Africa (Ronen 2002, 2011; Otayek and Soares 2007; chapter 5).

14. This narrative minimizing students' historical contribution to the 1991 revolution persists today under current president Ibrahim Boubacar Keita.

15. Moussa Mara, 2014, "Les interventions du Premier Ministre Moussa Mara à la réunion organisée à la salle Colbert de l'Assemblée Nationale, à Paris, par Emmanuel Dupuy (IPSE) et David Gakunzi (IREA)," 6 Oct, www.youtube.com/watch?v=Y5RTRBfRf10&feature=youtu.be.

16. Even the Ministry of Culture in Bamako has scaled down its initiatives considerably and organizes more circumscribed events (e.g., regional workshops on specific themes). Larger-scale events, such as festivals and exhibits, are organized in cooperation with, and mostly funded by, a number of heterogeneous partners; see A. C. Touré (2006).

17. I am grateful to Robert Launay for his comments on the role of religious organizations in Mali's public sphere; they were key to the clarification of my thoughts here.

18. During Konaré's second mandate, however, the political opposition was already in decline as parties geared up for the presidential election in 2002, which was anticipated to be a game changer.

19. Some of the political and cultural struggles between the state and opposition parties were resolved via intraparty negotiations and accommodations; others

continue to this day and are often articulated through alternative narratives and commemorations of the past.

20. See Soares (2005a, 2005b, 2013); Holder (2014a, 2014b); Holder and Sow (2014); and Schulz (2003).

21. Ousmane Madani Haidara and the imam of the great mosque of Timbuktu are prime examples of Muslim leaders who support the preservation of the Sufi heritage as both a living tradition and a trace of the past.

22. This is seen elsewhere; see Becker (2009).

23. Madu Haidara is a pseudonym.

24. Ashforth (2002) makes a similar point in his analysis of witchcraft and democracy in South Africa. Noting that democracy is ultimately an unrealistic objective in the absence of trust, he urges the South African state to take witchcraft very seriously and address the social and political problems that have led to its drastic increase in recent decades.

25. On the pervasiveness of corruption and state exclusionary practices, see Fay (1995) and Blundo and de Sardan (2001), among others.

In chapter 3, about Muso Kunda, I suggest that some of the private initiatives in the heritage field have little local support but are widely liked abroad, thus creating further internal divisions. Private institutions often replicate many of the shortcomings of the public sector but are subject to far less oversight over their initiatives, personnel training, type of activity promoted, and public access.

26. T. Yattara is a pseudonym.

27. Similarly, the organizers of the Festival sur le Niger in Ségou have had to work with local groups and agree to the formation of a youth brigade charged with making sure that tourists exhibit proper behavior, for example, appropriate dress and no open displays of affection in public.

# References

Abu-Lughod, Janet. 1981. *Rabat, Urban Apartheid in Morocco*. Princeton: Princeton University Press.
Abu-Lughod, Lila. 2002. "Do Muslim Women Really Need Saving? Anthropological Reflections on Cultural Relativism and Its Others." *American Anthropologist* 104, no. 3: 783–90.
Afribone. 2006. "ATT-cratie: La promotion d'un homme et de son clan, un livre qui crée beaucoup de remous dans notre pays." *Afribone*, 23–27 October. http://www.afribone.com/spip.php?article4760.
Agamben, Giorgio. 2005. *State of Exception*. Chicago: University of Chicago Press.
Agence France Presse. 2012. "Islamists Destroy Timbuktu Treasures." *ABC News Online*, 30 June. www.abc.net.au/news/2012-06-30/islamists-destroy-timbuktu-religious-treasures/4102688.
Aldrich, Daniel P. 2014. "First Steps towards Hearts and Minds? USAID's Countering Violent Extremism Policies in Africa." *Terrorism and Political Violence* 26, no. 3: 523–46.
Al Jazeera. 2012. "Ansar Dine Fighters Destroy Timbuktu Shrines," 1 July. www.aljazeera.com/news/africa/2012/06/201263010174879506.html.
Amnesty International. 1997. "Mali: Des libertés essentielles remises en cause." *Amnesty International*. https://www.amnesty.org/en/documents/afr37/001/1997/fr/.
Amselle, Jean-Loup. 1985. "Le Wahabisme à Bamako (1945–1985)." *Journal of African Studies* 19, no. 2: 345–57.
———. 1990. *Logiques métisses: Anthropologie de l'identité en Afrique et ailleurs*. Paris: Payot.
———. 2006. "Les usages politiques du passé. Le N'ko et la décentralisation administrative du Mali." In *Décentralisations et pouvoirs en Afrique: En contrepoint, modèles territoriaux français*, edited by Claude Fay, Yaouaga Félix Koné, and Catherine Quiminal, 33–67. Paris: Éd. IRD.

Antze, Paul, and Michael Lambek. 1996. *Tense Past: Cultural Essays in Trauma and Memory.* New York: Routledge.

Anderson, Benedict. 1991. *Imagined Communities.* London: Verso.

Appadurai, Arjun. 1988. "Why Public Culture?" *Public Culture* 1, no. 1: 5–9.

———. 1990. "Disjuncture and Difference in the Global Cultural Economy." *Theory, Culture and Society* 7, no. 2: 295–310.

———. 1996. *Modernity at Large: Cultural Dimensions of Globalization.* Minneapolis: University of Minnesota Press.

———. 2002. "Deep Democracy." *Public Culture* 14, no. 1: 21–47.

———. 2003. "Archive and Aspiration." In *Information Is Alive*, edited by J. Brouwer and A. Mulder, 14–25. Rotterdam: V2.

———. 2008. "The Globalization of Archaeology and Heritage: A Discussion with Arjun Appadurai." In *The Heritage Reader*, edited by Graham Fairclough, Rodney Harrison, John H Jameson, and John Schofield, 209–18. New York: Routledge.

Appadurai, Arjun, and Carol A. Breckenridge. 2004. "Museums Are Good to Think: Heritage on View in India." In *Representing the Nation: A Reader: Histories, Heritage and Museums*, edited by Jessica Evans and David Boswell, 404–699. London: Routledge.

Arnoldi, Mary Jo. 1999. "Overcoming a Colonial Legacy: The New National Museum in Mali: 1976 to the Present." *Museum Anthropology* 22, no. 3: 28–40.

———. 2003. "Symbolically Inscribing the City: Public Monuments in Mali, 1995–2002." *African Arts* 36, no. 2: 56–65, 95–96.

———. 2006. "Youth Festivals and Museums: The Cultural Politics of Public Memory in Postcolonial Mali." *Africa Today* 52, no. 4: 55–78.

———. 2007. "Bamako, Mali: Monuments and Modernity in the Urban Imagination." *Africa Today* 54, no. 2: 3–24.

———. 2012. "'From Timbuktu to Washington': Reflections on the 2003 Mali Program at the Smithsonian Folklife Festival." *Africa Today* 59, no. 1: 3–24.

Ashforth, Adam. 2002. "An Epidemic of Witchcraft? The Implications of AIDS for the Post-Apartheid State." *African Studies* 61, no. 1: 121–43.

Bagayogo, Shaka. 1987. "L'état au Mali: représentation, autonomie et mode de fonctionnement." In *L'État contemporain en Afrique*, edited by Emmanuel Terray, 91–122. Paris: L'Harmattan.

———. 1989. "Lieux et théorie du pouvoir dans le monde mandé: passé et présent." *Cahiers des sciences humaines* (ORSTOM) 25, no. 4: 445–60.

———. 1992. "Littérature orale et légitimation politique au Mali (1960–1990)." In *Constructions identitaires: questionnements théoriques et études de cas*, edited by Bogumil Jewsiewicki and Jocelyn Létourneau. Quebec: Actes du Célat.

———. 2007. "La crise de l'enseignement supérieur au Mali." In *Challenges of Education Financing and Planning in Africa*, edited by Adebayo Olukoshi and Mohamed Chérif Diarra, 18–32. Dakar: ADEA; CODESRIA.

Ba Konaré, Adame. 1991. "Rôle et image de la femme dans l'histoire politique du Mali (1960–1991): Perspectives pour une meilleure participation de la femme au processus démocratique." Paper presented at CODESRIA's Workshop on Gender Analysis and African Social Science, Dakar, Senegal.

———. 1993. *Dictionnaire des femmes célèbres du Mali*. Bamako: Éditions Jamana.

———. 1998a. "Ouverture musée de la femme, Muso Kunda et vernissage de l'exposition: image de la femme. Discours inaugural, Bamako, 8 Mars 1998." In *Ces mots que je partage: Discours d'une première dame d'Afrique*, 267–81. Bamako: Éditions Jamana.

———. 1998b. "Discours de Madame Adame Ba Konaré." Paper presented at the International Museum Conference Museum without Walls, Swedish African Museum Programme and ICOM Sweden, Skansen Open Air Museum, Stockholm, Sweden (no longer available; last accessed 11 June 2011.) http://www.natmus.cul.na/samp/mwwtheme/mkonare.html.

———. 1999a. Preface to *Les Associations Feminines au Mali*, edited by Sira Diop, 17–28. Bamako, Mali: Éditions Jamana.

———. 1999b. "L'éditorial d'Adame Ba Konaré: aux sources de la vie." *Faro* 00: 3–4.

———. 2000. "Perspectives on History and Culture: The Case of Mali." In *Democracy and Development in Mali*, edited by R. James Bingen, David Robinson, and John M. Staatz, 15-22. East Lansing: Michigan State University Press.

Barry, Harouna. 2004. *Les charmes discrets de Bamako*. Bamako: Association Développement et Culture.

Bate, Felix. 2012. "Mali Islamists Destroy More Holy Timbuktu Sites," 1 July. www.reuters.com/article/2012/07/01/us-mali-crisis-idUSBRE86008Z20120701.

Baudais, Virginie, and Grégory Chauzal. 2006. "Les partis politiques et l'indépendance partisane d'Amadou Toumani Touré." *Politique Africaine* 104: 61–80.

Bayart, Jean-François. 2009. *The State in Africa: The Politics of the Belly*. 2nd ed. Cambridge: Polity.

———. 2014. "Foucault nous aide-t-il à mieux comprendre la globalization?" Blog entry. 25 Septembre. https://blogs.mediapart.fr/jean-francois-bayart/blog/050914/foucault-nous-aide-t-il-mieux-comprendre-la-globalisation.

Bazin, Jean. 1985. "A chacun son Bambara." In *Au coeur de l'ethnie*, edited by Jean-Loup Amselle and Elikia M'Bokolo, 87–126. Paris: Éditions La Découverte.

Beaudet, Pierre 2006. "Le néolibéralisme à l'assaut du Mali." *Alternatives International*, 2 January. http://www.alterinter.org/article88.html?debut_articles_rubrique=105.

Becker, Felicitas. 2009. "Islamic Reform and Historical Change in the Care of the Dead: Conflicts over Funerary Practice among Tanzanian Muslims." *Africa* 79, no. 3: 416–34.

Bedaux, Rogier M. A., Boubacar H. Diaby, and Pierre Maas, eds. 2003. *L'architecture de Djenné, Mali: La Pérennité d'un Patrimonie Mondial*. Gant: Snoeck.

Bellagamba, Alice, and Anna Paini. 2000. *Costruire il passato: il dibattito sulle tradizioni in Africa e Oceania*. Torino: Paravia.

Bendix, Regina F., Aditya Eggert, and Arnika Peselmann, eds. 2012. *Heritage Regimes and the State*. Göttingen Studies in Cultural Property 6. Universitätsverlag Göttingen. http://webdoc.sub.gwdg.de/univerlag/2012/GSCP6_Bendix.pdf.

Bennett, Tony. 1988. "The Exhibitionary Complex." *New Formations* 4, no. 1: 73–102.
———. 1990. "The Political Rationality of the Museum." *Continuum: The Australian Journal of Media and Cultural Studies* 3, no. 1: 35–55.
———. 1995. *The Birth of the Museum: History, Theory, Politics*. New York: Routledge.
———. 1998. "Regulated Restlessness: Museums, Liberal Government and the Historical Sciences." In *Culture: A Reformer's Science*, 135–64. London: Sage.
———. 2006. "Exhibition, Difference, and the Logic of Culture." In *Museum Frictions: Public Cultures/Global Transformations*, edited by Ivan Karp, Corinne A. Kratz, Lynn Szwaja, and Tomas Ybarra-Frausto, 46–69. Durham: Duke University Press.
Bergamaschi, Isaline. 2011. "'Appropriation' et 'lutte contre la pauvreté' au Mali: Interprétations, pratiques et discours concurrents." *Revue Tiers Monde* 205, no. 1: 135–50.
Bernal, Victoria. 2005. "Eritrea On-line: Diaspora, Cyberspace, and the Public Sphere." *American Ethnologist* 32, no. 4: 660–75.
———. 2014. *Nation as Network: Diaspora, Cyberspace, and Citizenship*. Chicago: University of Chicago Press.
Berthé, Aboubacar. 2014. "Culture: impatience autour des Musées de Bandiagara et de Djenné." *Canard Déchaîné*, 10 September. http://www.maliweb.net/art-culture/culture-impatience-autour-musees-bandiagara-djenne-518092.html.
Betts, Raymond F. 1985. "Imperial Designs: French Colonial Architecture and Urban Planning in Sub-Saharan Africa." In *Double Impact: France and Africa in the Age of Imperialism*, edited by G. Wesley Johnson, 191–207. Westport: Greenwood.
Bhabha, Homi. 1990. *Nation and Narration*. London: Routledge.
———. 1994. *Location of Culture*. London: Routledge.
Blundo, Giorgio, and Olivier de Sardan Jean-Pierre. 2001. "La corruption quotidienne en Afrique de l'Ouest." *Politique africaine* 83, no. 3: 8–37.
Bøås, Morten, and Liv Elin Torheim. 2013. "The Trouble in Mali—Corruption, Collusion, Resistance." *Third World Quarterly* 34, no. 7: 1279–92.
Bøås, Morten, and Mats Utas. 2013. "Introduction: Post-Gaddafi Repercussions in the Sahel and West Africa." *Strategic Review for Southern Africa* 35, no. 2: 3–15.
Bourgeois, Jean-Louis. 1987. "The History of the Great Mosques of Djenné." *African Arts* 20, no. 3: 54–63, 90–92.
Brasseur, Gérard. 1968. *Les établissements humains au Mali*. Dakar: Ifan.
Brenner, Louis. 1988. "Concepts of Tariqa in West Africa. The Case of the Qadiriyya." In *Charisma and Brotherhood in African Islam*, edited by Donal B. Cruise O'Brien and Christian Coulon, 33–52. Oxford: Clarendon.
———. 1993. "Constructing Muslim Identities in Mali." In *Muslim Identity and Social Change in Sub-Saharan Africa*, edited by Louis Brenner, 59–78. Bloomington: Indiana University Press.
———. 2001. *Controlling Knowledge: Religion, Power, and Schooling in a West African Muslim Society*. Bloomington: Indiana University Press.
Briggs, Charles L. 1996. "The Politics of Discursive Authority in Research on the 'Invention of Tradition.'" *Cultural Anthropology* 11: 435–69.

Brunet-Jailly, Joseph. 2001. "Crépissage de la mosque." *Djenné Patrimoine Informations* 11. http://djenne-patrimoine.org/dp11.htm.

———. 2002. *Djenné d'hier à demain*. Bamako: Éditions Donniya.

Bussi, Michel, Stéphanie Lima, and David Vigneron. 2009. "L'État-nation africain à l'épreuve de la démocratie, entre présidentialisation et décentralisation: l'exemple du Mali." *L'Espace Politique*. http://espacepolitique.revues.org/1270.

Camara, Mamadou. 2010. "L'après-ATT a déjà commencé." *Jeune Afrique*, 14 July. http://www.jeuneafrique.com/Articleimp_ARTJAJA2582p032-034.xmlo_l-apres-att-a-deja-commence.html.

Campo, Juan Eduardo. 2014. "Burial." *Encyclopedia of the Qur'ān*. General editor Jane Dammen McAuliffe. Washington, DC: Brill Online.

Canclini, Nestor Garcia. 1995. *Hybrid Cultures*. Minneapolis: University of Minnesota Press.

Ceuppens, Bambi, and Peter Geschiere. 2005. "Autochthony: Local or Global? New Modes in the Struggle over Citizenship and Belonging in Africa and Europe." *Annual Review of Anthropology* 34: 385–407.

Chauzal, Grégory. 2011. "Les règles de l'exception: la régulation (du) politique au Mali et au Niger: Political science." *Institut d'études politiques de Bordeaux*. https://tel.archives-ouvertes.fr/tel-00604128.

Chege, Michael. 1995. "Between Africa's Extremes." *Journal of Democracy* 6, no. 1: 44–51.

Chih, Rachida. 2013. "*Shurafâ* and Sufis: The Qâdiriyya Bûdshîshiyya in Contemporary Morocco." In *Family Portraits with Saints. Hagiography, Sanctity and Family in the Muslim World*, edited by Catherine Mayeur-Jaouen and Alexandre Papas, 198–218. Berlin: Klaus Schwarz-Ehess.

Cissé, Amadou "Papa." 2006. *Letter of 23 September*.

Cissé, Baba Alpha. 1998. "Tuguna national sur le patrimoine." *Djenné Patrimoine Information* 5. http://djenne-patrimoine.org/dp5.htm.

Clericuzio, Peter. 2009. "Shifting Natures of Representation with the Great Mosques of Djenné." Paper presented at the Annual Meeting of the Society of Architectural Historians, Pasadena, California, April.

Clifford, James. 1997. *Routes*. Cambridge: Harvard University Press.

Cole, Jennifer. 2001. *Forget Colonialism? Sacrifice and the Art of Memory in Madagascar*. Berkeley: University of California Press.

———. 2003. "Narratives and Moral Projects: Generational Memories of the Malagasy 1947 Rebellion." *Ethos* 31, no. 1: 95–126.

Collier, Stephen, and Aihwa Ong. 2005. "Global Assemblages, Anthropological Problems." In *Global Assemblages: Technology, Politics, and Ethics as Anthropological Problems*, edited by Aihwa Ong and Stephen Collier, 3–21. Oxford: Blackwell.

Comaroff, Jean, and John L. Comaroff. 2004. "Policing Culture, Cultural Policing: Law and Social Order in Postcolonial South Africa." *Law and Social Inquiry* 29, no. 3: 513–46.

Connerton, Paul. 1989. *How Societies Remember*. Cambridge: Cambridge University Press.

Coombes, Annie E. 2003. *History after Apartheid: Visual Culture and Public Memory in a Democratic South Africa.* Durham: Duke University Press.
Cooper, Frederick. 1994. "Conflict and Connection: Rethinking Colonial African History." *American Historical Review* 99, no. 5: 1516–45.
Coulibaly, Daouda, Modibo Oumar Coulibaly, and Denis Koné. 2000. "Statue d'Archinard à Ségou: où la placer?" (press archives of the Cefib, no longer available, last accessed 12 March 2014). http://www.cefib.com/presse/Archives/12-02-2000/mali-profond.
Coulibaly, Falé. 2010. "Les présidents Modibo Kéïta et Amadou Toumani Touré: Deux leaders pour un destin panafricaniste partagé." 7 June. http://ml.telediaspora.net/fr/texte.asp?idinfo=37847.
Coulibaly, Modibo O. 1999. "Vestiges de la colonization à Ségou: convoitises autour de la statue d'Archinard." *Yeko* 162, no. 1: 6.
Coulibaly, Yamoussa. 2001. "Aperçu sur l'histoire de la ville de Ségou." Ministère de la Culture et Direction Regionale de la Jeunesse de Sports et de la Culture, Ségou.
Couloubaly, Pascal Baba. 1993. "Rebâtir la mémoire cassée d'un peuple." *Jamana* 33: 10–11.
———. 2001. "Discours d'ouverture du ministre de la culture." In *Tradition et modernité dans l'oeuvre littéraire de Fily Dabo Sissoko: colloque international organisé par le Ministère de la culture du Mali du 13 au 14 mai 2000 à Bamako.* Ministère de la culture du Mali. Bamako: Éditions Jamana.
———. 2004. *Le Mali d'Alpha Oumar Konaré.* Paris: L'Harmattan.
Cruise O'Brien, D. 1967. "Toward an 'Islamic Policy' in French West Africa, 1854–1914." *Journal of African History* 26: 33–49.
Cutter, Charles. 1968. "The Politics of Music in Mali." *African Arts* 1, no. 3: 38–39, 74–77.
Davis Ruffins, Fath. 2006. "Revisiting the Old Plantation: Reparations, Reconciliation, and Museumizing American Slavery." In *Museum Frictions: Public Cultures/Global Transformations*, edited by Ivan Karp, Corinne A. Kratz, Lynn Szwaja, and Tomas Ybarra-Frausto, 394–434. Durham: Duke University Press.
Davison, Graeme. 2008. "Heritage: From Patrimony to Pastiche." In *The Heritage Reader*, edited by Graham Fairclough, Rodney Harrison, John H. Jameson, and John Schofiel, 31–41. New York: Routledge.
Death, Carl. 2011. "Foucault and Africa: Governmentality, IR theory, and the Limits of Advanced Liberalism." http://www.open.ac.uk/socialsciences/bisa-africa/files/bisa-2011-death.pdf.
———. 2013. "Governmentality at the Limits of the International: African Politics and Foucauldian Theory." *Review of International Studies* 39, no. 3: 763–87.
de Benoist, Joseph Roger. 1989. *Le Mali.* Paris: L'Harmattan.
De Cesari, Chiara. 2010. "Creative Heritage: Palestinian Heritage NGOs and Defiant Arts of Government." *American Anthropologist* 112, no. 4: 625–37.
———. 2012. "Thinking through Heritage Regimes: Heritage Regimes and the State." In *Heritage Regimes and the State*, edited by Regina F. Bendix, Aditya Eggert, and Arnika Peselmann, 399–413. Göttingen Studies in Cultural Property 6. Univer-

sitätsverlag Göttingen. http://webdoc.sub.gwdg.de/univerlag/2012/GSCP6_Bendix
.pdf.
Dehaene, Michiel, and Lieven De Cauter. 2008. "Heterotopia in a Postcivil Society." In *Heterotopia and the City: Public Space in a Postcivil Society*, edited by Michiel Dehaene and Lieven De Cauter, 3–9. New York: Routledge.
de Heusch, Luc. 2001. "Ma dette de reconnaissance envers Germaine Dieterlen." *Journal des africanistes* 71, no. 1: 69–75.
de Jong, Ferdinand. 2007. "A Masterpiece of Masquerating: Contradictions of Conservation in Intangible Heritage." In *Reclaiming Heritage: Alternative Imaginaries of Memory in West Africa*, edited by Ferdinand de Jong and Michael Rowlands, 161–84. Walnut Creek: Left Coast.
———. 2009. "First Word: Hybrid Heritage." *African Arts* 42, no. 4: 4–5.
De Jorio, Rosa. 1997. "Female Elites, Women's Formal Associations, and Political Practices in Mali (West Africa)." PhD diss., University of Illinois at Urbana-Champaign.
———. 2001. "Women's Organization, the Ideology of Kinship, and the State in Postindependence Mali." In *New Directions in Anthropological Kinship*, edited by Linda Stone, 322–40. Lanham: Rowman.
———. 2002a. "When Is 'Married' Married? Multiple Marriage Avenues in Urban Mali." *Mande Studies* 4: 31–44.
———. 2002b. "Gendered Museum, Guided He(tour)topias: Women and Social Memory in Mali." *Polar: Political and Legal Anthropology Review* 25, no. 2: 50–72.
———. 2003. "Narratives of the Nation and Democracy in Mali: A View from the Modibo Keita Memorial." *Cahiers d'études africaines* 172: 827–55.
———. 2006a. "On the Secularization of Sacred Spaces: The Case of Djenné." Paper presented at the Annual Meeting of the American Anthropological Association, San Jose, California, 17 November.
———. 2006b. "Politics of Remembering and Forgetting: The Struggle over Colonial Monuments in Mali." *Africa Today* 52, no. 4: 79–106.
———. 2009. "Da Siti Sacri a Patrimonio Pubblico: Il Caso di Djenné Mali." In *Afriche: Scritti in Onore di Bernardo Bernardi*, edited by Paola Bacchetti and Vanni Beltrami, 207–20. Rome: Istituto Italiano per l'Africa e l'Oriente.
———. 2010. "Between Dialogue and Contestation: Gender, Islam, and the Challenges of a Malian Public Sphere." In *Islam, Politics, Anthropology*, edited by Filippo Osella and Benjamin Soares, 91–106. Malden: Wiley-Blackwell.
———. 2013. "Public Debate under Amadou Toumani Touré." Fieldsights—Hot Spots. *Cultural Anthropology*, 10 June. http://www.culanth.org/fieldsights/310-public-debate-under-amadou-toumani-toure.
Dembelé, Baba. 2011. "Mort de Modibo Kéita: Amadou Djicoroni non coupable." *Le Republicain*, 1 June. http://www.maliweb.net/category.php?NID=76305.
Dembelé, David. 2011. "Bamako marche pour Khaddafi!" 25 March. www.journaldumali.com/article.php?aid=2930.
De Noray, Marie Laure, and Oumar Maiga. 2002. *Bamako génération vingt ans*. Bamako: Éditions Donniya.

Diakité, Abdoulaye. 2010. "Réconciliation d'acteurs politiques: L'US-RDA et le PSP tournent la page sombre de leur histoire." *L'indicateur Renouveau*, 1 April. http://www.maliweb.net/category.php?NID=58673.

Diallo, Aly. 1993. *Die Rolle des kulturgeschichtlichen Museums in Afrika am Beispiel Mali*. Frankfurt: Lang.

Diallo, Modibo. 1997. "Proposition de schéma d'organisation pour le mémorial Modibo Keita." Unpublished manuscript. Bamako, Mali.

Diaouré, Ramata. 2012. "Semaine Nationale du Patrimoine culturel 2012: L'actualité malienne impose cette année le theme." 22 Septembre, 19 Jun. http://www.maliweb.net/art-culture/semaine-nationale-du-patrimoine-culturel-2012-lactualite-malienne-impose-cette-annee-le-theme-80888.html.

Diarrah, Cheick Oumar. 1996. *Le défi démocratique au Mali*. Paris: Harmattan.

———. 2000. "The Malian Democracy: A Continuing Process for the Quest of Perfection." In *Democracy and Development in Mali*, edited by R. James Bingen, David Robinson, and John M. Staatz, 369–76. East Lansing: Michigan State University Press.

Diaspora Action. 2011. "Muso Kunda: Institution d'une journée communion du couple." *Le Républicain*, 8 March. http://www.maliweb.net/societe/muso-kunda-institution-d%E2%80%99une-journee-communion-du-couple-16815.html.

Dieterlen, Germaine. 1955. "Mythe et organization sociale au Soudan français." *Journal de la Société des Africanistes* 25: 39–76.

Diop, Sira. 1999. *Les associations feminines au Mali*. Bamako: Éditions Jamana.

Direction Nationale du Patrimoine Culturel. Ministère de la Culture République du Mali. 2014. "Stratégie de reconstruction des Biens du Patrimoine Mondial du nord du Mali: Tombouctou, Tombeau des Askia, et autre biens culturels affectés." Internal document.

Djebbari, Elina. 2013. "La Biennale Artistique et Culturelle du Mali: la mise en scène d'une culture nationale, de l'indépendance à aujourd'hui." In *Une histoire des festivals, XXème–XXIème siècles*, edited by Anaïs Fléchet, Pascale Goetschel, Sophie Jacotot, Patricia Hidiroglou, Caroline Moine, and Julie Verlaine, 291–302. Paris: Sorbonne.

Djenné Patrimoine. n.d. "Crépissage de la mosquée." http://djenne-patrimoine.org/crepissage.html.

———. 1998a. "Nouvelles du Patrimoine de Djenné: La question de la reconstruction de l'école en dur." *Djenné Patrimoine Informations* 4. http://djenne-patrimoine.org/dp4.htm.

———. 1998b. "Réunion du bureau." *Djenné Patrimoine Informations* 5. http://djenne-patrimoine.org/dp5.htm.

———. 1998c. "Pose de la première pierre du futur Musée de Djenné." *Djenné Patrimoine Informations* 5. http://djenne-patrimoine.org/dp5.htm.

———. 1999. "Réception provisoire des 12 classes en dur." *Djenné Patrimoine Informations* 6. http://djenne-patrimoine.org/dp6.htm.

———. 2001. "La fête du Maouloud à Djenné." *Djenné Patrimoine Informations* 11. http://djenne-patrimoine.org/dp11.htm.

———. 2006. "Nouvelles du Patrimoine de Djenné: Musée de Djenné: DANGER!!!" *Djenné Patrimoine Informations* 21. http://djenne-patrimoine.org/dp21.htm.

Domian, Sergio. 1989. *Architecture soudanaise: vitalité d'une tradition urbaine et monumentale: Mali, Côte-d'Ivoire, Burkina Faso, Ghana*. Paris: Harmattan.

Doquet, Anne. 2008. "Festivals touristiques et expressions identitaires au Mali." *Africultures* 73: 60–67.

Doumbi-Fakoli. 2002. *Le Mali sous Alpha Oumar Konaré*. Ivry: Silex.

Drabo, Gaoussou. 1999. "L'avenir politique au Mali: le sens de l'histoire." *L'Essor*, 1 juin (press archives of the Cefib, last accessed 2 March 2014, no longer available).

Eriksen, Thomas Hylland. 2001. "Between Universalism and Relativism: A Critique of the UNESCO Concept of Culture." In *Culture and Rights: Anthropological Perspectives*, edited by Jane K. Cowan, Marie-Bénédicte Dembour, and Richard A. Wilson, 127–48. Cambridge: Cambridge University Press.

Errington, Shelley. 1998. *The Death of Authentic Primitive Art and Other Tales of Progress*. Berkeley: University of California Press.

Fané, Yamoussa. 2011. "Expérience de conservation d'un patrimoine bâti: cas des saho de Kouakourou." http://www.bk.tudelft.nl/fileadmin/Faculteit/BK/Actueel/Symposia_en_congressen/African_Perpectives/Programme/Built_Heritage/doc/APD_wp_5_fane_paper.pdf.

Fay, Claude. 1995. "La Démocratie au Mali, ou le pouvoir en pâture." *Cahiers d'Études africaines* 137: 19-53.

Ferguson, James. 2006. *Global Shadows: Africa in the Neoliberal World Order*. Durham: Duke University Press.

Ferguson, James, and Akhil Gupta. 2002. "Spatializing States: Toward an Ethnography of Neoliberal Governmentality." *American Ethnologist* 29, no. 4: 981–1002.

Fofana, Mamadou. 2010. "Cinquantenaire de l'indépendance: Pour ne pas avoir à serrer la main de l'ex-dictateur Moussa Traoré: Alpha Oumar Konaré boycotte le défilé militaire du Cinquantenaire." *L'Indépendant*, 24 September. http://www.maliweb.net/politique/cinquantenaire-de-lindependance/pour-ne-pas-avoir-a-serrer-la-main-de-l%E2%80%99ex-dictateur-moussa-traore-alpha-oumar-konare-boycotte-le-defile-militaire-du-cinquantenaire-1817.html.

Fofana, Modibo. 2010. "ATT et Modibo Keita: une même vision, un même combat panafricain." *Journal du Mali.com*, 6 June. http://www.journaldumali.com/article.php?aid=1540.

Foucault, Michel. 1982. "The Subject and the Power." In *Michel Foucault: Beyond Structuralism and Hermeneutics*, edited by H. Dreyfus and P. Rabinow, 208–26. Brighton: Harvester.

———. 1991. "Governmentality." In *The Foucault Effect: Studies in Governmentality*, edited by G. Burchell, C. Gordon, and P. Miller, 87–104. Hemel Hempstead: Harvester Wheatsheaf.

———. 2008. "Of Other Spaces (1967)." In *Heterotopia and the City: Public Space in a Postcivil Society*, edited by Michiel Dehaene and Lieven De Cauter, 13–30. New York: Routledge.

Fouéré, Marie-Aude. 2009. "J. K. Nyerere entre mythe et histoire: analyse de la production d'une mémoire publique officielle en Tanzanie post-socialiste." *Les Cahiers d'Afrique de l'Est* 41: 197–224.

François, Pierre. 1982. "Class Struggles in Mali." *Review of African Political Economy* 24: 22–38.

Fraser, Nancy. 1992. "Rethinking the Public Sphere: A Contribution to the Critique of Actually Existing Democracy." In *Habermas and the Public Sphere*, edited by Craig Calhoun, 109–42. Cambridge, MA: MIT Press.

———. 2007. "Transnationalizing the Public Sphere: On the Legitimacy and Efficacy of Public Opinion in a Post-Westphalian World." *Theory, Culture, and Society* 24, no. 4: 7–30.

Freedom House. 2011. "Mali Country Report." https://freedomhouse.org/report/freedom-world/2011/mali.

Gaasholt, Ole Martin. 2013. "Northern Mali 2012: The Triumph of Irredentism." *Strategic Review for Southern Africa* 35, no. 2: 68–91.

Gardi, Bernard. 2000. *Le boubou c'est chic*. Basel: Museum der Kulturen.

Gatti, Roberto Christian. 2001. "Ecoles coraniques au sud du Sahara face à la 'patrimonialisation' de l'UNESCO: problème ou ressource? L'exemple de Djenné (Mali)." 3 February 2013. http://www.unifr.ch/ipg/aric/assets/files/ARICManifestations/2001Actes8eCongres/GattiRCh.pdf.

———. 2006. "Genesis and Structure of Djenné as a Work of Art." *Museum International* 229–30: 104–12.

Gérard, Etienne. 1997. *La tentation du savoir en Afrique: politiques, mythes et stratégies d'éducation au Mali*. Paris: Karthala.

Geschiere, Peter. 2009. *The Perils of Belonging: Autochthony, Citizenship, and Exclusion in Africa and Europe*. Chicago: University of Chicago Press.

Ghetti, Pietro M. Apollonj. 2014. *Etude sur les mausolées de Tombouctou*. Paris: UNESCO.

Ghetti, Pietro M. Apollonj, Mauro Bertagnin, and Giovanni Fontana Antonelli. 2002. "Les sites du patrimoine mondial au Mali: Rapport de Mission du 11 au 26 Juillet 2002." UNESCO. http://whc.unesco.org/archive/2003/mis-mali-2002.pdf.

Ghetti, Pietro M. Apollonj, Mauro Bertagnin, Klessigué Sanogo, and Ali Ould Sidi. 2011. "Protection et Sauvegarde des Mausolées des 'Saints dans la Ville de Tombouctou et Leur Place dans le Contexte Culturel Saharien." In *Terra 2008: Proceedings of the 10th International Conference on the Study and Conservation of Earthen Architectural Heritage, Bamako, Mali, February 1–5, 2008*, edited by Leslie Rainer, Angelyn Bass Rivera, and Davis Gandreau, 18–22. Los Angeles: Getty Conservation Institute.

Greenhouse, Carol J. 2008. "Fractured Discourse: Rethinking the Discursivity of States." In *Democracy: Anthropological Approaches*, edited by Julia Paley, 193–218. Santa Fe: School for Advanced Research Press.

Groga-Bada, Malika. 2012. "Mali: Mahmoud Dicko, imam médiateur." *Jeune Afrique*, 23 August. http://www.jeuneafrique.com/140316/politique/mali-mahmoud-dicko-imam-m-diateur/.

Grosz-Ngaté, Maria. 1988. "Power and Knowledge. The Representation of the Mande World in the Works of Park, Caillié, Monteil, and Delafosse." *Cahiers d'études africaines* 111–12: 485–511.

Gupta, Akhil, and Aradhana Sharma. 2006. "Globalization and Postcolonial States." *Current Anthropology* 47, no. 2: 277–93.

Gutelius, David. 2007. "Islam in Northern Mali and the War on Terror." *Journal of Contemporary African Studies* 25, no. 1: 59–76.

Habermas, Jurgen 1989. *Structural Transformation of the Public Sphere*. Cambridge, MA: MIT Press.

Haidara, Chirfi Moulaye. 2012. *Réplique de Chirfi Moulaye Haïdara. Réplique, de Salem Ould Elhadje, Chirfi Moulaye Haïdara, Mahmoud Zouber et Zeidan Ag Sidalamine*, Edited by Salem Ould Elhadje, Chirfi Moulaye Haïdara, Mahmoud Zouber, and Zeidan Ag Sidalamine. Bamako: La Sahélienne.

———. 2013. *Tombouctou Meurtrie: Regard sur les Stigmates de l'Occupation du Nord du Mali*. Bamako: Éditions Jamana.

Halbwachs, Maurice. 1992. *On Collective Memory*. Chicago: University of Chicago Press.

Hall, Stuart. 1999. "Un-settling 'the Heritage,' Re-imagining the Post-Nation: Whose Heritage?" *Third Text* 13, no. 49: 3–13.

Henry, Joseph. 1910. *L'âme d'un peuple Africain: Les Bambara: Leur Vie Psychique, Éthique, Sociale, Religieuse*. Paris: Picard.

Herzfeld, Michael. 2003. "A Place in History: Social and Monumental Time in a Cretan Town." In *Anthropology of Space and Place: Locating Culture*, edited by Setha M. Low and Denise Lawrence-Zuñiga, 363–69. Malden: Wiley-Blackwell.

Hoffman, Barbara G. 2000. *Griots at War: Conflict, Conciliation, and Caste in Mande*. Bloomington: Indiana University Press.

Holder, Gilles. 2014a "Introduction. Vers un espace public religieux: pour une lecture contemporaine des enjeux politiques de l'islam en Afrique" In *L'Islam, nouvel espace public en Afrique*, edited by Gilles Holder, 9–33. Paris: Karthala. iBooks e-book.

———. 2014b. "'Maouloud 2006,' de Bamako à Tombouctou: Entre réislamisation de la nation et laïcité de l'État: la construction d'un espace public religieux au Mali." In *L'Islam, nouvel espace public en Afrique*, edited by Gilles Holder, 414–508. Paris: Karthala. iBooks e-book.

———. 2012. "Chérif Ousmane Madani Haïdara et l'association islamique Ançar Dine." *Cahiers d'études africaines* 206–7: 389–425.

Holder, Gilles, and Maud Saint-Lary. 2014. "Enjeux démocratiques et reconquête du politique en Afrique: De l'espace public religieux à l'émergence d'une sphère islamique oppositionnelle." *Sens public* (Revue Web): 1–17. http://www.sens-public.org/IMG/pdf/SensPublic_Gilles_Maud.pdf.

Holder, Gilles, and Moussa Sow. 2014. *L'Afrique des laïcités État, religion et pouvoirs au sud du Sahara*. Éditions Tombouctou. Paris: Institut de recherche pour le développement.

Holland, Dorothy. 1992. "The Woman Who Climbed Up the House: Some Limitations of Schema Theory." In *New Directions in Psychological Anthropology*, edited by Theodore Schwartz, Geoffrey M. White, and Catherine Lutz, 68–79. Cambridge: Cambridge University Press.

Holland, Dorothy, and Kevin Leander. 2004. "Ethnographic Studies of Positioning and Subjectivity: An Introduction." *Ethos* 32, no. 2: 127–39.

Howell, Julia Day, and Martin van Bruinessen. 2007. Introduction to *Sufism and the "Modern" in Islam*, edited by Julia Day Howell and Martin van Bruinessen, 3-18. London: Tauris.

Hull, Matthew S. 2012. "Documents and Bureaucracy." *Annual Review of Anthropology* 41: 251–67.

Huyssen, Andreas. 2003. *Present Pasts: Urban Palimpsests and the Politics of Memory*. Stanford: Stanford University Press.

Imperato, Pascal James. 1996. *Historical Dictionary of Mali*. 3rd ed. Lanham: Scarecrow.

Johnson, John William, Thomas A. Hale, and Stephen Belcher, eds. 1997. *Oral Epics from Africa: Vibrant Voices from a Vast Continent*. Bloomington: Indiana University Press.

Joseph, Jonathan. 2010. "The Limits of Governmentality: Social Theory and the International." *European Journal of International Relations* 16, no. 2: 223–46.

Joy, Charlotte. 2007a. "'Enchanting Town of Mud': Djenné, a World Heritage Site in Mali." In *Reclaiming Heritage: Alternative Imaginaries of Memory in West Africa*, edited by Ferdinand de Jong and Michael Rowlands, 145–59. Walnut Creek: Left Coast.

———. 2007b. "Heritage and Tourism: Contested Discourses in Djenné, a World Heritage Site in Mali." Paper presented at the Annual Meeting of the African Studies Association, New York. http://www.nomadit.co.uk/asa/asa07/panels.php5?PanelID=196.

———. 2010. "Heritage and Tourism: Contested Discourses in Djenné, a World Heritage Site in Mali." In *Tourism, Power, and Culture: Anthropological Insights*, edited by Donald V. L. Macleod and James G. Carrier, 47–63. Bristol: Channel View.

———. 2012. *The Politics of Heritage Management in Mali: From UNESCO to Djenné*. Walnut Creek: Left Coast.

Kaba, Lansiné. 1974. *The Wahhabiyya: Islamic Reform and Politics in French West Africa, 1945–1960*. Evanston: Northwestern University Press.

Kamian, Bakari. 2001. *Des tranchées de Verdun à l'église Saint-Bernard*. Paris: Karthala.

Karp, Ivan, Corinne A. Kratz, Lynn Szwaja, and Tomas Ybarra-Frausto, eds. 2006. *Museum Frictions: Public Cultures/Global Transformations*. Durham: Duke University Press.

Kébé, Boubacar Hamadoun. 2013. Preface. *Saho: Joyaux de l'architecture Malienne*. Edited by Anette Schmidt and Geert Mommersteeg, 5. Amsterdam: KIT.

Keita, A. 2012. "Haut Conseil islamique du Mali: La division est consommé." *Aurore*, 23 October. http://www.maliweb.net/societe/haut-conseil-islamique-du-mali-la-division-est-consommee-101009.html.

Keita, Aoua. 1975. *Femme d'Afrique: La vie d'Aoua Kéita racontée par elle-même*. Paris: Présence Africaine.

Keita, Madiba. 2006. "Célébration du Maouloud 2006 à Tombouctou," *Le Reflet Hebdo*, 20 April. www.afribone.com/spip.php?article3436.

Keita, Mamadou B. n.d. "Étude sur les sites, monuments et vestiges de la commune de Ségou et des arrondissements de Ségou central et Markala." Ségou: Association Libre pour la Promotion de l'Habitat et du Logement.

Kiabou, Bamba. 1998. "Tuguna Week in Djenné." *UNESCO Courier* 51, no. 7–8: 70.

Kirshenblatt-Gimblett, Barbara. 2004. "Intangible Heritage as Metacultural Production." *Museum International* 56, no. 1–2: 52–65.

———. 2006a. "Exhibitionary Complexes." In *Museum Frictions: Public Cultures/ Global Transformations*, edited by Ivan Karp, Corinne A. Kratz, Lynn Szwaja, and Tomas Ybarra-Frausto, 34–45. Durham: Duke University Press.

———. 2006b. "World Heritage and Cultural Economics." In *Museum Frictions: Public Cultures/Global Transformations*, edited by Ivan Karp, Corinne A. Kratz, Lynn Szwaja, and Tomas Ybarra-Frausto, 161–202. Durham: Duke University Press.

Klein, Martin. 1998. *Slavery and Colonial Rule in French West Africa*. Cambridge: Cambridge University Press.

Klimkeit, Dirk. 1997. "La construction d'une culture nationale par l'état au Mali. Résumé de mémoire remis à la faculté des arts et des lettres de l'Université de Cologne." Cologne.

Klute, George. 1995. "Hostilités et alliances: Archéologie de la dissidence des Touaregs au Mali." *Cahiers d'études africaines* 137: 55–71.

Kögler, Hans-Herbert. 2007. "The Ethics of Interpretation after Postmodernism." In *The Future of Religion: Towards a Reconciled Society*, edited by Michael Ott, 333–42. Leiden: Brill.

Konaré, Alpha Oumar. 1983. "Pour d'autres musées 'ethnographiques' en Afrique." *Museum* 35, no. 3: 146–49.

———. 1992. *Discours d'investiture d' Alpha Oumar Konaré*. 8 June. http://www.bamanet.net/index.php/actualite/les-echos/11106-8-juin-1992discours-dinvestiture-dalpha-oumar-konare.html (no longer available; last accessed 12 June 2011).

———. 1995. *Hommage au Président Modibo Keita, Premier Président de la République du Mali de 1960 á 1968*, 16 May. http://www.anaisbko.org.ml/koulouba/hommodibo.html (no longer available; last accessed 9 June 2011).

———. 1999. "Discours de son Excellence Monsieur Alpha Oumar Konaré, Président de la République, Chef de l'État a l'occasion du Symposium Modibo Keita, Premier Président de la République du Mali. Palais des Congrès, le 06 juin 1999." http://modibokeita.free.fr/Discours%20Alpha%20Oumar%20Konare.htm.

———. 2010. "Figure de l'indépendance malienne: Modibo Keita." www.youtube.com/watch?v=pltitiLuVfI.

Koné, Assane. 2009. "Dr Oumar Mariko dit tout ! (suite): Le code de la famille, le cinquantenaire, Moussa Dadis Camara, l'or du Mali." *Le Republicain*, 22 October.

http://malijet.com/a_la_une_du_mali/18759-docteur_oumar_mariko_dit_tout_suite_et_fin.html.

———. 2011. "Patrimoine culturel du Mali: c'est parti pour l'inventaire." *Le Républicain*, 31 May. http://www.maliweb.net/non-classe/patrimoine-culturel-du-mali-cest-parti-pour-linventaire-23609.html.

Koné, Denis. 2011. "ATT au Monument des Martyrs: 'Le 26-Mars est un patrimoine national.'" *Les Echos*, 28 March. http://www.afribone.com/spip.php?article32388.

Kratz, Corinne A., and Ivan Karp. 2006. Introduction to *Museum Frictions: Public Cultures/Global Transformations*, edited by Ivan Karp, Corinne A. Kratz, Lynn Szwaja, and Tomas Ybarra-Frausto, 1–31. Durham: Duke University Press.

Küchler, Susanne, and A. Forty. 1999. *The Art of Forgetting*. Oxford: Berg.

Lambek, Michael, and Paul Antze. 1996. "Introduction: Forecasting Memory" to *Tense Past: Cultural Essays in Trauma and Memory*, edited by Paul Antze and Michael Lambek, xi–xxxviii. New York: Routledge.

Lambert de Frondeville, Agnès. 1987. "Une alliance tumultueuse: les commerçantes maliennes du Dakar-Niger et les agents de l'Etat." *Cahiers des sciences humaines* 23, no. 1: 89–103.

Lang, Peter. 2008. "Stalker Unbounded: Urban Activism and the Terrain Vague as Heterotopia by Default." In *Heterotopia and the City: Public Space in a Postcivil Society*, edited by Michiel Dehaene and Lieven De Cauter, 215–24. New York: Routledge.

Lange, Marie France. 1999. "Insoumission civile et défaillance étatique: Les contradictions du processus démocratique malien." *Autrepart* 10: 117–34.

Larkin, Brian. 1997. "Indian Films and Nigerian Lovers: Media and the Creation of Parallel Modernities." *Africa: Journal of the International African Institute* 67, no. 3: 406–40.

Launay, Robert, and Benjamin F. Soares. 1999. "The Formation of an 'Islamic Sphere' in French Colonial West Africa." *Economy and Society* 28, no. 4: 497–519.

Lebovich, Andrew. 2013. "The Local Face of Jihadism in Northern Mali." *Combating Terrorism Sentinel* 6, no. 6: 4–10.

Lecocq, Baz, Gregory Mann, Bruce Whitehouse, Dida Badi, Lotte Pelckmans, Nadia Belalimat, Bruce Hall, and Wolfram Lacher. 2013. *One Hippopotamus and Eight Blind Analysts: A Multivocal Analysis of the 2012 Political Crisis in the Divided Republic of Mali: Extended Editors Cut*. http://media.leidenuniv.nl/legacy/lecocq-mann-et-al---one-hippo-8-blind-analysts-editors-cut.pdf.

Lecocq, Baz, and Paul Schrijver. 2007. "The War on Terror in a Haze of Dust: Potholes and Pitfalls on the Saharan Front." *Journal of Contemporary African Studies* 25, no. 1: 141–66.

Lefébure, Anaïs. 2014. "Combats au nord du Mali: La France a sa part de responsabilité." *JOL Press*, 22 May. www.jolpress.com/nord-mali-armee-mnla-minusma-serval-france-jihadistes-article-826156.html.

Le Sphinx. 2006. *ATT-cratie: la promotion d'un homme et de son clan*. Book 1. Paris: L'Harmattan.

———. 2007. *ATT-cratie: la promotion d'un homme et de son clan*. Book 2. Paris: L'Harmattan.

Levtzion, Nehemia. 2008. "Resurgent Islamic Fundamentalism as an Integrative Factor in the Politics of Africa and the Middle East." *Canadian Journal of African Studies* 42, no. 2–3: 546–59.

Liebmann, Matthew. 2008. "Postcolonial Cultural Affiliation: Essentialism, Hybridity, and NAGPRA." In *Archaeology and the Postcolonial Critique*, edited by Matthew Liebmann and Uzma Z. Rizvi, 73–90. Lanham: Altamira.

Low, Setha M. 2004. "The Memorialization of September 11: Dominant and Local Discourses on the Rebuilding of the World Trade Center Site." *American Ethnologist* 31, no. 1: 326–40.

———. 2008. "The Gated Community as Heterotopia." In *Heterotopia and the City: Public Space in a Postcivil Society*, edited by Michiel Dehaene and Lieven De Cauter, 153–63. New York: Routledge.

Lowenthal, David. 1998. *The Heritage Crusade and the Spoils of History*. Cambridge: Cambridge University Press.

Ly, Hassimiyou. 2000. "Le culte des monuments et la citoyenneté." (no longer available; last accessed 8 June 2011). www.culture.gov.ml/monuments/index.html.

Maas, Pierre. 2011. *The Restoration of Djenné, Mali: African Aesthetics and Western Paradigms*. http://www.bk.tudelft.nl/fileadmin/Faculteit/BK/Actueel/Symposia _en_congressen/African_Perpectives/Programme/Built_Heritage/doc/APD _wp_5_maas_paper.pdf.

Maas, Pierre, and G. Mommersteeg. 1993. "L'architecture dite Soudanaise: Le modèle de Djenné." In *Vallées du Niger*, edited by Jean Devisse, 478–92. Paris: Réunion des musées nationaux.

Macdonald, Sharon J. 2003. "Museums, National, Postnational and Transcultural Identities." *Museum and Society* 1, no. 1: 1–16.

Maliweb. 2012. "Spéciale: Destruction des mausolées à Tombouctou: qu'en pense le Haut conseil islamique?" 6 July. www.maliweb.net/video/emission-speciale -destruction-des-mausolees-a-tombouctou-quen-pense-le-haut-conseil -islamique-78210.html.

Mann, Gregory. 2005. "Locating Colonial Histories: Between France and West Africa." *American Historical Review* 110, no. 22: 409–34.

———. 2007. "Colonialism Now: Contemporary Anti-colonialism and the *facture coloniale*." *Politique Africaine* 105: 181–200.

———. 2015. *From Empires to NGOs in the West African Sahel: The Road to Nongovernmentality*. Cambridge: Cambridge University Press.

Marchand, Trevor H. J. 2009. *The Masons of Djenné*. Bloomington: Indiana University Press.

Mariko, Oumar. 2010. "Déclaration du Dr Oumar Mariko sur le cinquantenaire (21 septembre 2010)." (no longer available; last accessed 3 February 2014) http:// infomali.net/LeMali/index.php/permalink/3485.html.

———. 2011. "Témoignage sur le 26 mars 1991." *YouTube*, 30 March. https://www.youtube.com/watch?v=ervD2ngTGfE.
Marschall, Sabine. 2006. "Commemorating 'Struggle Heroes': Constructing a Genealogy for the New South Africa." *International Journal of Heritage Studies* 12, no. 2: 176–93.
Maussen, Marcel. 2007. "Islamic Presence and Mosque Establishment in France: Colonialism, Arrangements for Guestworkers and Citizenship." *Journal of Ethnic and Migration Studies* 33, no. 6: 981–1002.
Mbembe, Achille. 2001. *On the Postcolony*. Berkeley: University of California Press.
———. 2003. "Necropolitics." *Public Culture* 15, no. 11: 11–40.
McLaughlin, Fiona. n.d. "The Governor and the Marabout: Contesting the Place Faidherbe in Saint-Louis du Sénégal." Unpublished manuscript.
Meillassoux, Claude. 1970. "A Class Analysis of the Bureaucratic Process in Mali." *Journal of Development Studies* 6, no. 2: 97–110.
Ministère de la Culture du Mali. 2005a. "Carte culturelle du Mali: Esquisse d'un inventaire du patrimoine culturel." *Ministère de la Culture*. http://www.malikunnafoni.com/bibliostat/docs/050216003_mc_2005.pdf.
———. 2005b. "Carte culturelle des fêtes et festivals organisés au Mali." http://www.malikunnafoni.com/bibliostat/index.php?tema=981.
———. 2014. "Politique culturelle du Mali: Document-cadre." Internal document.
Molins Lliteras, Susana. 2013. "From Toledo to Timbuktu." *South African Historical Journal* 65, no. 1: 105–24.
Mommersteeg, Geert, and Sebastiano Pedrocco. 2013. "Les maisons communes des jeunes dans le delta intérieur du Niger: histoire et continuité." In *Saho: Joyaux de l'architecture Malienne*, edited by Anette Schmidt and Geert Mommersteeg, 19–31. Amsterdam: KIT.
Monteil, Charles. 1903. *Soudan français. Monographie de Djenné, cercle et ville*. Tulle: Mazeirie.
Morris, Benjamin. 2011. "Forgetting an Overview." In *Heritage, Memory and Identity*, edited by Helmut K. Anheier and Yudhishthir Raj Isar, 27–28. London: Sage.
Morton, Pat. 1998. "A Study in Hybridity: Madagascar and Morocco at the 1931 Colonial Exposition." *Journal of Architectural Education* 52, no. 2: 76–86.
———. 2000. *Hybrid Modernities: Architecture and Representation at the 1931 International Colonial Exposition in Paris*. Cambridge, MA: MIT Press.
Mustafa, Hudita Nura. 1997. "Sartorial Ecumenes: African Styles in a Social and Economic Context." In *The Art of the African Fashion*, edited by Els van der Plas and Marlous Willemsen, 13–45. Prince Claus Fund, Netherlands. Eritrea: African World.
———. 2002. "Portraits of Modernity: Fashioning Selves in Dakarois Popular Photography." In *Images and Empires: Visuality in Colonial and Postcolonial Africa*, edited by Paul Landau and Deborah Kaspin, 172–92. Berkeley: University of California Press.
———. 2006. "La mode Dakaroise: Elegance, Transnationalism, and an African

Fashion Capital." In *Fashion's World Cities*, edited by C. Breward and D. Gilbert, 177–200. Oxford: Berg.

Nagy, Rosemary. 2004. "After the TRC: Citizenship, Memory, and Reconciliation." *Canadian Journal of African Studies* 38, no. 3: 638–53.

Newcomb, Rachel. 2006. "Gendering the Nation: Contesting Urban Space in Fes, Morocco." *City and Society* 18, no. 2: 288–311.

Niezen, R. W. 1990. "The 'Community of Helpers of the Sunna': Islamic Reform among the Songhay of Gao (Mali)." *Africa: Journal of the International African Institute* 60, no. 3: 399–424.

Njikam, Clarisse. 2014. "Le ministre Rama Diallo à propos de l'organisation d'un véritable évènement culturel au Mali." *L'Indépendant*, 23 June. http://maliactu.net/le-ministre-rama-diallo-a-propos-de-lorganisation-dun-veritable-evenement-culturel-au-mali-le-festival-international-de-bamako-feinba-une-initiative-de-salif-keita-aura-t/.

Nora, Pierre. 1989. "Between Memory and History: Les lieux de mémoire." *Representation* 26: 7–24.

O'Dell, Emily Jane. 2013. "Waging War on the Dead: The Necropolitics of Sufi Shrine Destruction in Mali." *Archaeologies* 9, no. 3: 506–25.

Office de Radiodiffusion-Télévision du Mali (ORTM). 2010. "Kurukan Fuga." https://www.youtube.com/watch?v=usmc9XWDx2s.

———. 2012. "Emission Spéciale: Destruction des mausolées à Tombouctou: qu'en pense le Haut conseil islamique?" 6 July. www.maliweb.net/videoemission-speciale-destruction-des-mausolees-a-tombouctou-quen-pense-le-haut-conseil-islamique-78210.html.

Office of the Prosecutor. 2013. "ICC Prosecutor Opens Investigation into War Crimes in Mali: 'The legal requirements have been met. We will investigate.'" 16 January. https://www.icc-cpi.int/en_menus/icc/press%20and%20media/press%20releases/news%20and%20highlights/Pages/pr869.aspx.

Østebø, Terje. 2008. "The Question of Becoming: Islamic Reform Movements in Contemporary Ethiopia." *Journal of Religion in Africa* 38, no. 4: 416–46.

Ouallet, Anne. 2002. "Patrimoine mondial et pauvreté locale: Tombouctou et Djenné au Mali." *Annales de la Recherche Urbaine: Recherches et Débats: Revue Trimestrielle* 92: 87–94.

Ouologuem, Ogopémo. 2010. "Reconciliation nationale." *Les Echos*, 12 November. http://www.jamana.org/lesechos/articles/2010/novembre/ec_12novembre.html.

Paley, Julia. 2008. *Democracy: Anthropological Approaches*. Santa Fe: School for Advanced Research Press.

Pedrocco, Sebastiano. 2003. "Il Saho: La Casa Comune dei Giovani Bozo." *Africa: Rivista trimestrale di studi e documentazione dell' istituto italiano per l' Africa e l' Oriente* 58, no. 2: 158–78.

Philippe, Sébastien. 2013. *Ségou une Région d'Histoire*. Bamako: Éditions Memoria.

Pitcher, M. Anne. 2006. "Forgetting from Above and Memory from Below: Strategies of Legitimation and Struggle in Postsocialist Mozambique." *Africa* 76, no. 1: 88–112.

Pivin, Jean Loup. 1991. "La mémoire en marche entretien avec Alpha Oumar Konaré." *Revue Noire*. http://www.revuenoire.com/index.php?option=com_content&view=article&id=3569%3Aqla-memoire-en-marcheq-entretien-avec-alpha-oumar-konare&catid=11%3Aarticles&Itemid=13&lang=fr.
Prussin, Labelle. 1977. "Pillars, Projections, and Paradigms." *Architectura* 7, no. 1: 65–71.
———. 1985. "The Image of African Architecture in France." In *Double Impact: France and Africa in the Age of Imperialism*, edited by G. Wesley Johnson, 209–35. Westport: Greenwood.
———. 1986. *Hatumere: Islamic Design in West Africa*. Berkeley: University of California Press.
———. 2007. "Architecting a Life, a Building, a Nation, a Conference." (no longer available; last accessed 5 January 2014) http://www.mudonline.org/aat/programme.html.
Radio France Internationale (RFI). 2012. "La chute d'Amadou Toumani Touré au Mali ou la défaite d'une politique de consensus." *RFI*, 24 March. www.rfi.fr/afrique/20120323-chute-amadou-toumani-toure-mali-defaite-une-politique-consensus.
Ralph, Michael. 2005. "Oppressive Impressions, Architectural Expressions: The Poetics of French Colonial (Ad)Vantage, regarding Africa." In *African Urban Spaces in Historical Perspective*, edited by Steve Salm and Toyin Falola, 22–48. Rochester: University of Rochester Press.
Ramadan, Maryam. 2012. "The Malian Family Code and the Different Ideological Sources for Its Reform." Master's thesis, School of Oriental and African Studies, University of London.
Ranger, Terence O. 1983. "The Invention of Tradition in Colonial Africa." In *The Invention of Tradition*, edited by Eric J. Hobsbawm and Terence O. Ranger, 211–62. Cambridge: Cambridge University Press.
Rassool, Ciraj. 2000. "The Rise of Heritage and the Reconstitution of History in South Africa." *Kronos* 26: 1–21.
———. 2006. "Community Museums, Memory Politics, and Social Transformation in South Africa: Histories, Possibilities, and Limits." In *Museum Frictions: Public Cultures/Global Transformations*, edited by Ivan Karp, Corinne A. Kratz, Lynn Szwaja, and Tomas Ybarra-Frausto, 286–321. Durham: Duke University Press.
Reed, Adam. 2005. "My Blog Is Me: Texts and Persons in UK Online Journal Culture (and Anthropology)." *Ethnos* 70, no. 2: 220–42.
Ronen, Yehudit. 2002. "Qadhafi and Militant Islamism: Unprecedented Conflict." *Middle Eastern Studies* 38, no. 4: 1–16.
———. 2011. "Between Africanism and Arabism: Libya's Involvement in Sudan." *Journal of the Middle East and Africa* 2, no. 1: 1–14.
Rosaldo, Renato. 1989. *Culture and Truth: The Remaking of Social Analysis*. Boston: Beacon.
Rose, Nikolas. 1996. "Governing 'Advanced' Liberal Democracies." In *Foucault and Political Reason. Liberalism, Neo-liberalism, and Rationalities of Government*, edited

by Andrew Barry, Thomas Osborne, and Nikolas Rose, 37–64. Chicago: University of Chicago Press.

Rose, Nikolas, Pat O'Malley, and Mariana Valverde. 2009. "Governmentality." *Annual Review of Law and Social Science* 2: 83–104.

Rovine, Victoria L. 2011. "Continuity, Innovation, Fashion: Three Genres of Malian Embroidery." *African Arts* 44, no. 3: 58–67.

Rowlands, Michael. 2003. "Patrimoine et modernite a Djenné: identites locale et nationale." In *L'architecture de Djenné, Mali: La pérennité d'un Patrimoine Mondial*, edited by Rogier M. A. Bedaux, Boubacar H. Diaby, and Pierre Maas, 78–84. Gant: Snoeck.

———. 2007. "Entangled Memories and Parallel Heritages." In *Reclaiming Heritage: Alternative Imaginaries of Memory in West Africa*, edited by Ferdinand de Jong and Michael Rowlands, 127–45. Walnut Creek: Left Coast.

Rowlands, Michael, and Beverley Butler. 2007. "Conflict and Heritage Care." *Anthropology Today* 23, no. 1: 1–2.

Rowlands, Michael, and Charlotte Joy. 2011. "Can Djenné Remain a World Cultural Heritage Site? A Rhetorical Question." Delft University of Technology, Delft, Netherlands. http://www.bk.tudelft.nl/fileadmin/Faculteit/BK/Actueel/Symposia_en_congressen/African_Perpectives/Programme/Built_Heritage/doc/APD_wp_5_rowlands_paper.pdf.

Rowlands, Michael, and Ferdinand de Jong. 2007. "Reconsidering Heritage and Memory." In *Heritage: Alternative Imaginaries of Memory in West Africa*, edited by Ferdinand de Jong and Michael Rowlands, 13–29. Walnut Creek: Left Coast.

Russell, Nicolas. 2006. "Collective Memory before and after Halbwachs." *French Review* 79, no. 4: 792–804.

Saad, Elias N. 1983. *Social History of Timbuktu: The Role of Muslim Scholars and Notables 1400–1900*. Cambridge: Cambridge University Press.

SAinfo Reporter. 2009. "New Home for Ancient Texts in Timbuktu." *South Africa Info*, 26 January. http://www.southafrica.info/africa/timbuktu-project.htm#.VIPAy2SgnHM#ixzz3LB1GlDT4.

Sanankoua, Bintou. 1990. *La chute de Modibo Keïta*. Paris: Éditions Chaka.

SAPA. 2013, "UNESCO Pledges Help for Timbuktu." 14 February. http://sbeta.iol.co.za/news/africa/unesco-pledges-help-for-timbuktu-1470643.

Sarin, Sophie. 2011. "Djenne djenno." *Blogspot*. 23 January. djennedjenno.blogspot.com/2011/01/five-years-after-my-first-arrival-in.html.

Sassen, Saskia. 2000. "Spatialities and Temporalities of the Global: Elements for a Theorization." *Public Culture* 12, no. 1: 215–32.

Schaffer, Frederic. 1997. "Political Concepts and the Study of Democracy: The Case of Demokaraasi in Senegal." *Polar: Political and Legal Anthropology Review* 20, no. 1: 40–50.

Scheele, Judith. 2013. "A Pilgrimage to Arawān: Religious Legitimacy, Status, and Ownership in Timbuktu." *American Ethnologist* 40, no. 1: 165–81.

Scherrer, Olivier. 2009. "Ce que devient Djenné, hélas!" *Djenné Patrimoine Informations* 27. http://djenne-patrimoine.org/dp27.htm.

Schmidt, Anette, and Yamoussa Fané. 2013. "Heritage architectural: la gestion du patrimoine culturelle." In *Saho. Joyaux de l'architecture Malienne*, edited by Anette Schmidt and Geert Mommersteeg, 7–18. Amsterdam: KIT.

Schramm, Katharina. 2004. "Senses of Authenticity: Chieftaincy and the Politics of Heritage." *Etnofoor* 17, no. 1–2: 156–77.

Schulz, Dorothea E. 1997. "Praise without Enchantment: Griots, Broadcast Media, and the Politics of Tradition in Mali." *Africa Today* 44: 443–64.

———. 2001. *Perpetuating the Politics of Praise: Jeli Singers, Radios, and Political Mediation in Mali*. Cologne: Koppe.

———. 2003. "Charisma and Brotherhood Revisited: Mass-Mediated Forms of Spirituality in Urban Mali." *Journal of Religion in Africa* 33, no. 2: 146–71.

———. 2007. "From a Glorious Past to the Lands of Origin: Media Consumption and Changing Narratives of Cultural Belonging in Mali." In *Reclaiming Heritage: Alternative Imaginaries of Memory in West Africa*, edited by Ferdinand de Jong and Michael Rowlands, 185–213. Walnut Creek: Left Coast.

———. 2012. *Culture and Customs of Mali*. Santa Barbara: Greenwood.

Scott, Joan Wallach. 1999. *Gender and the Politics of History*. New York: Columbia University Press.

Segbedji, André. 2014. "Le ministre de la culture à la rencontre des acteurs culturels du Mali." 16 June. http://news.abamako.com/h/48547.html.

Segbedji, Bruno D. 2010. "Oumar Mariko au 3ème Congrès ordinaire du parti SADI à Ségou: 'Non à l'assaut des multinationales sur l'économie malienne!'" *L'Indépendant*, 8 December. http://www.maliweb.net/category.php?NID=68090.

Séméga, Hawa. 2012. "Tombouctou: L'imam Essayouti parle de la grande mosquée de Djingarey-Ber." http://www.tamoudre.org/tombouctou-limam-essayouti-parle-de-la-grande-mosquee-de-djingarey-ber/touaregs/territoire/.

Sharma, Aradhana, and Akhil Gupta. 2006. "Introduction: Rethinking Theories of the State in an Age of Globalization." In *The Anthropology of the State: A Reader*, edited by Aradhana Sharma and Akhil Gupta, 1–41. Malden: Blackwell.

Shaw, Rosalind. 2002. *Memories of the Slave Trade: Ritual and the Historical Imagination in Sierra Leone*. Chicago: University of Chicago Press.

———. 2007. "Memory Frictions: Localizing the Truth and Reconciliation Commission in Sierra Leone." *International Journal of Transitional Justice* 1, no. 2: 183–207.

Simonis, Francis. 1994. "La Colonization Française." In *Pays du Sahel: du Tchad au Sénégal, du Mali au Niger*, edited by Vernet Joël. Paris: Éditions Autrements.

———. 1995. "Le drame de Sakoïba." *Droit et Cultures* 30: 231–41.

Sissoko, Cheick Oumar. 2010. "Discours du Président Cheick Oumar Sissoko au 3ème Congres Ordinaire du Parti Sadi à Ségou les 04–05 decembre 2010." http://www.sadi.wahost.org/discours/Discours-du-President-lu-par-le-secretaire-generale-au-troisieme-congres-ordinaire-les-4-et-5-decembre-2011-a-Segou (no longer available; last accessed 5 January 2014).

———. 2014. "Visite d'écoute Mme N'Diaye Ramatoulaye Diallo à l'écoute du Cinéaste Cheick Oumar Sissoko." *Mali Buzz TV*. www.youtube.com/watch?v=Dcoh_oHrlls.
Sissoko, Issa Fakaba. 2010. "Pyramide du souvenir: Le directeur dans le collimateur du Mouvement 'Alternatives Mariko 2012.'" *L'indicateur Renouveau*, 6 October. http://www.maliweb.net/category.php?NID=65679.
Sissoko, Sada. 1995. *Le Kòtèba et l'évolution du théâtre moderne au Mali*. Bamako: Jamana.
Smith, Etienne. 2007. "The Mande Charter: Reply. H-Africa." 23 May. http://h-net.msu.edu/cgi-bin/logbrowse.pl?trx=vx&list=h-africa&month=0705&week=d&msg=IlIfqapG/LQWpt3yiw4nbg&user=&pw=.
———. 2009. "'L'Esprit des Lois' de Soundiata Keita." *Nonfiction.fr*. http://www.nonfiction.fr/article-2532-p1-lesprit_des_lois_de_soundiata_keita.htm.
Snyder Francis G. 1967. "The Political Thought of Modibo Keita." *Journal of Modern African Studies* 5, no. 1: 79–106.
Soares, Benjamin. F. 1997. "The Fulbe 'shaykh' and the Bambara 'pagans': Contemporary Campaigns to Spread Islam in Mali." In *Peuls et Mandingues: dialectiques des constructions identitaires*, edited by Mirjam de Bruijn and Han van Dijk, 267–80. Paris: Karthala.
———. 2004. "Muslim Saints in the Age of Neoliberalism." In *Producing African Futures: Ritual and Reproduction in a Neoliberal Age*, edited by B. Weiss, 79–105. Leiden: Brill.
———. 2005a. *Islam and the Prayer Economy: History and Authority in a Malian Town*. Ann Arbor: University of Michigan Press.
———. 2005b. "Islam in Mali in the Neoliberal Era." *African Affairs* 105: 77–95.
———. 2007. *Saint and Sufi in Contemporary Mali. Sufism and the "Modern" in Islam*. Edited by Julia Day Howell and Martin van Bruinessen, 76–91. London: Tauris.
———. 2009. "The Attempt to Reform Family Law in Mali." *Die Welt des Islams* 49, no. 3–4: 398–428.
———. 2012. "On the Recent Mess in Mali." *Anthropology Today* 28, no. 5:1–2.
———. 2013. "Islam in Mali since the 2012 Coup." Fieldsights—Hot Spots. *Cultural Anthropology* Online. American Anthropological Association. http://www.culanth.org/fieldsights/321-islam-in-mali-since-the-2012-coup.
Sow, Alioune. 2010. "Nervous Confessions: Military Memoirs and National Reconciliation in Mali." *Cahiers d'études africaines* 197: 69–93.
Sow, Samba. 2009. "Érection du monument Archinard à Ségou: L'acte inqualifiable du gouverneur Abou Sow." *L'Indépendant*, 26 February. malijet.com/les_faits_divers_au_mali/lettres_ouvertes_mali/10904-rection_du_monument_archinard_s_gou_l_acte_inqualifiable_du_gouv.html.
Sow, Soumaila. 2004. "Elections communales: Quelques observations." *Djenné Patrimoine Informations* 17. http://djenne-patrimoine.org/dp17.html.
Steiner, Christopher B. 1995. "Museums and the Politics of Nationalism." *Museum Anthropology* 19, no. 2: 3–6.
Stoller, Paul. 1995. *Embodying Colonial Memories: Spirit Possession, Power, and the Hauka in West Africa*. New York: Routledge.

Straker, Jay. 2008. "Performing the Predicaments of National Belonging: The Art and Politics of the Tuareg Ensemble Tartit at the 2003 Folklife Festival." *Journal of American Folklore* 121, no. 479: 80–96.

Stratton, Jon 2009. "Uncertain Lives: Migration, the Border, and Neoliberalism in Australia." *Social Identities: Journal for the Study of Race, Nation and Culture* 15, no. 5: 677–92.

Sy, Alpha Amadou. 2012. "Festival sure le Niger. Forum de la 8e édition 'Création et changement social.'" *Présence Africaine* 185–86: 311–25.

Tall, Amadou. 2010. "Réconciliation national: Si ATT le veut vraiment, elle se fera." *Le Matin* (Bamako, Mali), 30 December. http://www.maliweb.net/category.php?NID=69096.

Thurston, Alexander, and Andrew Lebovich. 2013. "A Handbook on Mali's 2012–2013." Working Paper No. 13-001, Institute for the Study of Islamic Thought in Africa (ISITA). http://buffett.northwestern.edu/documents/working-papers/ISITA-13-001-Thurston-Lebovich.pdf.

Touré, Abdoulaye. 2008. "Le musée de Djenné présenté par son architecte." *Djenné Patrimoine Informations* 25. http://djenne-patrimoine.org/dp25.htm.

Touré, Amadou Chab. 2006. "L'argent de la culture au Mali." *Africultures* 69: 209–13.

Touré, Amadou Toumani. 1994. "Comment j'ai pris le pouvoir, pourquoi je l'ai quitté." *Jeune Afrique* 24 November.

———. 2011. "ATT et nous: Interview sur Africa 24—Face a Nous." 24 September. https://www.youtube.com/watch?v=fKkivpmZNoY.

Touré, B., and A. Sissoko. 2005. "Festival Djennery: Djenné déploie ses charmes." *L'Essor*, 24 February. http://www.afribone.com/spip.php?article2309.

Touré, Boureima, 2004. "L'identité *Djennenké* et les réformes politiques: démocratie et decentralization." *Djenné Patrimoine Informations* 17. http://djenne-patrimoine.org/lejournal.htm.

Touré, Younoussa. 1996. "La biennale artistique et culturelle du Mali (1962–1988): Socio-anthropologie d'une action de politique culturelle africaine." Doctorat Nouveau Régime, Ecole des Hautes Etudes en Sciences Sociales, Marseille.

Traoré, Oumou Ahmar. 1999. "La mode des années 60: rêves, art et liberté." *Faro* 3: 8–9.

Triaud, Jean-Louis. 2000. "Islam in Africa under French Colonial Rule." In *The History of Islam in Africa*, edited by Nehemia Levtzion and Randall L. Pouwels, 169–88. Athens: Ohio University Press.

———. 2009. "Tombouctou ou le retour du mythe. L'exposition médiatique des manuscrits de Tombouctou." In *La fabrique des savoirs en Afrique subsaharienne*, edited by Daouda Gary-Tounkara and Didier Nativel, 201–22. Paris: Karthala.

Trouillot, Michel-Rolph. 1995. *Silencing the Past: Power and the Production of History*. Boston: Beacon.

———. 2001. "The Anthropology of the State in the Age of Globalization: Close Encounters of the Deceptive Kind." *Current Anthropology* 42, no. 1: 125–39.

U.S. Department of State. 2001. "Country Reports on Human Rights Practices

2000: Mali." 23 February. http://www.state.gov/j/drl/rls/hrrpt/2000/af/853.htm.
van de Walle, Nicolas. 2012. "Foreign Aid in Dangerous Places: The Donors and Mali's Democracy." Helsinki: United Nations University World Institute for Development Economics Research (UNU-WIDER). http://www.wider.unu.edu/publications/working-papers/2012/en_GB/wp2012-061/.
Villalon, Leonardo A., and Abdourahmane Idrissa. 2005. "The Tribulations of a Successful Transition: Institutional Dynamics and Elite Rivalry in Mali." In *The Fate of Africa's Democratic Experiments: Elites and Institutions*, edited by Leonardo A. Villalon and Peter VonDoepp, 49–74. Bloomington: Indiana University Press.
Villesuzanne, Marie-Laure. 2002. "Quel avenir pour l'architecture de Djenné?" *Djenné Patrimoine Informations* 12. http://djenne-patrimoine.org/dp12.htm.
Werbner, Richard. 1998. "Smoke from the Barrel of a Gun: Postwars of the Dead, Memory, and Reinscription in Zimbabwe." In *Memory and the Postcolony: African Anthropology and the Critique of Power*, edited by Richard Werbner, 71–102. London: Zed.
Wertsch, James V. 2008. "The Narrative Organization of Collective Memory." *Ethos* 36, no. 1: 120–35.
Wertsch, James V., and Doc M. Billingsley. 2011. "The Role of Narratives in Commemoration: Remembering as Mediated Action." In *Heritage, Memory, and Identity*, edited by Helmut Anheier and Yudhishthir Raj Isar, 25–38. London: Sage.
White, Geoffrey. 2006. "Epilogue: Memory Moments." *Ethos* 34, no. 2: 325–41.
Whitehouse, Bruce. 2012a. "What Went Wrong in Mali?" *London Review of Books* 34, no. 16: 17–18.
———. 2012b. "The Force of Action: Legitimizing the Coup in Bamako, Mali." *Africa Spectrum* 47, no. 2–3: 93–110.
———. 2014. "A Hard Look at Mali's Problems." *Bridges from Bamako*, 10 November. http://bridgesfrombamako.com/2014/11/10/a-hard-look-at-malis-problems/.
———. 2015. "How to Get Filthy Rich in Sinking Africa." *Bridges from Bamako*, 19 October. http://bridgesfrombamako.com/2015/10/19/how-to-get-filthy-rich-in-sinking-africa/.
Wing, Susanna. 2013. "Mali: Politics of a Crisis." *African Affairs* 112, no. 448: 476–85.
Wooten, Stephen R. 2000. "Antelope Headdresses and Champion Farmers: Negotiating Meaning and Identity through the Bamana: Ciwara Complex." *African Arts* 33, no. 2: 19–34.
Wright, Gwendolyn. 1991. *The Politics of Design in French Colonial Urbanism*. Chicago: University of Chicago Press.
———. 1997. "Tradition in the Service of Modernity: Architecture and Urbanism in French Colonial Policy, 1900–1930." In *Tensions of Empire: Colonial Cultures in a Bourgeois World*, edited by Frederick Cooper and Ann Laura Stoler, 322–45. Berkeley: University of California Press.
Zolberg, Vera L. 1976. "National Goals, Social Mobility, and Personal Aspirations: Students in Mali." *Canadian Association of African Studies* 10, no. 1: 125–42.

# Index

Page numbers in *italics* refer to illustrations.

ADEMA (Alliance pour la démocratie au Mali): Archinard statue relocation and, 67, 73; Konaré-era hegemony of, 10, 21, 31–32, 38–40; top-down state power and, 10, 40, 67, 154n17; US-RDA relationship, 37–40. *See also* democracy
ADID (Association pour le Développement de l'Islam à Djenné), 113
Aguibou Tall Palace, 98–99, 159n4
Ahmed Baba Institute of Higher Islamic Studies, 122
AKTC (Aga Khan Trust for Culture), 19, 95, 106, 121, 137, 140, 154n21
Amadou, Sekou, 101, 107, 112
Amselle, Jean-Loup, 45
AMUPI (L'Association Malienne pour l'Unité et le Progrès de l'Islam), 111
Ansar Dine, 114, 125–26, 130–31, 167n50
Antze, Paul, 25
Appadurai, Arjun, 6–9, 20, 151n17
AQIM (al-Qaeda in the Islamic Maghreb), 125
Archinard, Louis (statue), 21, 53–55, *54*, 65, 67–75, 142, 155n3
architecture: Beaux Arts style, 99; democratization, 34; Djenné heritage in, 22, 95, 97–98; Konaré preservation of, 17; neo-Sudanese, 160n14; postcolonial, 22; Sudanese, 22, 58, 97–101, 160n6, 160n9; Timbuktu heritage in, 116–21, 125–33, 135

Arnoldi, Mary Jo, 15–16, 62
Arragadi, Cheick Sidi Ahmed Ben Amar, 126
ATT-cratie ("Le Sphinx"), 123

Bagayogo, Shaka, 74
Ba Konaré, Adame, 22, 33–34, 78, 81, 84, 89–90, 157n6
Bamako: Biennale decentralization and, 17, 152n32; Camara memorial, *48*; as center of power, 8; First Republic festivals, 16; heritage initiatives in, 168n16; Konaré-era monuments, 138; neoliberal transformation, 10; Place des Martyrs de Thiaroye, 66. *See also* Koulouba monument complex; Modibo Keita Memorial; Muso Kunda
Bamana, 15, 27, 71–72, 81, 85–86, 123, 147
*bara* (dance of the Ségou region), 16
Bariséli Festival, 144–45
Becker, Felicitas, 119, 126, 163n2, 166n26
Bennett, Tony, 2–3, 5, 7, 22–23, 88–89, 95–96
Betts, R. F., 101
Bibliothèque des Manuscripts de Djenné, 143
Biennale artistique, culturelle, et sportive, 16–18, 152n32
Bokova, Irina, 127–28
Borgnis-Desbordes, Gustave, 62–63, *63*
Bourgeois, Jean-Louis, 99
Boutchichi, Cheick Sidi Hamza al-, 131
Bozo, 82, 108–11

Breckenridge, Carol A., 6–7, 20
Brenner, Louis, 164n9
Brunet-Jailly, Joseph, 111, 161n22

Caillé, René, 62
Camara, Abdoul "Cabral" Karim, 21, 27, 29–30, 48–50, *48*, 142, 152n4
Centre Culturel Koré, 140
China, 39, 137
class and social inequality: colonization and, 58–67, 73, 136; Djenné, 136; memory and, 11; museums and, 88–89; neoliberal tourism and, 116; political class, 15, 37, 40–42, 44, 52, 58, 67; Tuareg-Islamist occupation and, 127; women and, 22, 77, 80, 84–88, 91–92, 94
CNID (Congrès national d'initiative démocratique), 67
Cole, Jennifer, 12, 55
colonial/colonization: cosmopolitan elite views of, 58–67, 73, 136; debt trope in, 156n15; historical accident narrative, 57; hybridity narrative, 33–36, 56, 58–59, 62, 64–67, 73–75, 136–37, 156n14; Islamic policy, 100–101; and nostalgia, 21, 58–59, 74, 161–62n30; politique des races policy, 100; and precolonial history, 15; resistance, 55, 57, 59, 61–62; women's stereotypes, 84–87, 158n19. *See also* French Sudan colonial era; postcolonial period; precolonial era
Connerton, Paul, 12, 25–26
consensus, democracy of, 40–45, 50–52, 138–39, 149n1
Coulibaly, Dramane, 153n6
Couloubaly, Pascal Baba, 58, 65–66, 67, 138
countermemory, 11, 27, 46–47, 155n28
culture, public. *See* public culture

Death, Carl, 4–5
De Cesari, Chiara, 2, 6, 8, 14
de Jong, Ferdinand, 3, 14, 65, 70
democracy: citizenship and, 5, 7, 34–35, 50–51, 88–89, 136, 138–39; cosmopolitan elites and, 22, 37, 40, 44, 58–67, 73–74, 77, 80, 94, 136; culture of, 7, 9, 17, 26–27, 31, 35, 37, 51, 154n16, 164n14; duty of memory in, 20, 72–73, 139; elections in, 30–31, 32–33, 38, 41, 152n4, 153n11; as fluid social construct, 149n1; heritage and, 7, 20, 25–26, 33, 35, 51, 56, 89, 94, 164n14; modernity and, 25–26, 49, 110, 155n29, 156n5; neoliberal, 1–4, 7, 9, 26, 37, 73, 96, 114, 129, 140, 142; public

sphere and, 9, 20, 26, 74, 88, 97, 149n7, 168n9, 168n17; role of history in, 20, 26, 33, 35, 37, 154n16; Touré, of consensus, 40–42, 44–45, 50–52, 138–39, 149n1. *See also* ADEMA; governmentality; multiparty democracy; nation-state; neoliberalism; public culture; public sphere
Diallo, Modibo, 36
Diamoutani, Mamadou, 131–32, 167n47
Diarra family, 71–73
diaspora (Malian), 17–19, 89, 122, 152n33
Dicko, Hamadoun, 28, 36, 153n8
Dicko, Mahmoud, 124, 130–31
Djebbari, Elina, 17
Djenné: colonial heritage in, 97–101; exhibitionary complex and, 22–23, 95–97, 111–14; Great Mosque of, 22, 97–102, *98*, 111, 115, 162n34; heritagization of living spaces in, 103–7, 114–15, 160n2, 161n22; neoliberalism and, 96, 102, 114, 143; postcolonial heritage in, 101–3; saho preservation in, 23, 108–11; UNESCO World Heritage recognition of, 22, 95, 97, 101–2, 115, 136
Djenné Museum, 108, *109*, 143
Djenné Patrimoine, 10, 19, 95, 99, 106, 111, 115, 136, 161n22
Djenné Patrimoine Informations, 106, 108, 110, 112–13
Djennery, 111–12
Djingarey Ber Mosque, 118–20, *119*
Doumbi-Fakoly, 63
Dubois, Félix, 97

economy: fashion and, 84–88; heritage-triggered inflation, 162n42; international currency and, 31; Keita legacy, 51–52; Malian youth crisis and, 89; neoliberal, 7, 32, 50, 150n14; postindependence, 2, 50, 52, 137–38; privatization initiatives and, 32; religious, 120; SAPs, 7–8, 150–51nn14–15; state extractive practices and, 28; tourism and, 6, 107, 111, 115, 116, 120, 136, 144, 162n43
education: heritage, 6–7; Islamic schools, 101, 107, 111–12; Konaré spending cuts to, 32; Koulouba literacy statue, 59; post-1991 school crisis, 7, 68–69; women as educators, 78, 80–81, 83. *See also* students
ethnography, 20, 85–87
exhibitionary complex (Bennett), 5, 7, 22–23, 95–97, 111, 114
expositions and world's fairs, 99, 161n17

Faidherbe, Louis, 62
FAMA (Le Front africain pour la mobilisation et l'alternance), 44
family: heritage, 71–72, 75, 156n18; in Malian society, 80; opposition to Keita commemoration, 37, 42; Touré-era code, 76, 83, 130
Fané, Yamoussa, 109–10
Fanga Fing, 69
Faro, 81, 92, 158n13
Farouk, Al-, 125
fashion, 84–88, 91–92, 94, 158–59nn17–22
Ferguson, James, 3, 5
Festival au désert, 17, 150n12
Festival sur le Niger, 17, 53, 140–41, 169n27
forgetting, 13, 151n21
Foucault, Michel, 4–5, 78, 80, 93–94, 136, 137, 150n9
French Sudan colonial era (1880–1960): Archinard statue relocation, 55–56, 65, 67–75, 142, 155n3; class status symbols, 87–88; colonial monuments, 57, 62–64, 63; cosmopolitan elite view of, 73–74; ethnic politics, 100, 151n27; Islam and, 100–101, 112–14; Konaré hybridity narrative and, 58–59, 65–67, 73–75, 136–37; memorialization of, 21; Modibo Keita heritagization of, 56–57; Ségou patrimony and, 72–73; Sudanese architecture preservation, 22, 58, 97–101; women's stereotypes, 84–87, 158n19. *See also* colonial/colonization
Fresques Murales de Koulouba, Les, 62

Gaddafi, Muammar, 117, 122–24, 168n13
Gallieni Monument, 57
Gardi, Bernhard, 84
Gatti, Roberto Christian, 162n36
Ghetti, Pietro M., 116
Goundiam, Diarra Marie, 80, 81, 92
governmentality: citizenship and, 6–7, 34–35; exhibitionary complex and, 95–97; and fields of government, 8; Konaré liberalization/decentralization, 17, 56; neoliberal power and, 4–5; transnationalism and, 7–8. *See also* democracy; multiparty democracy; nation-state; neoliberalism
Governors' Square, 63–64, 64
Great Mosque of Djenné, 22, 97–102, 98, 111, 115, 162n34
griots (*jeliw*), 33–34, 45, 73, 147, 155n27
Gupta, Akhil, 3, 8, 55

Haidara, Ousmane Madani, 114, 131
Halbwachs, Maurice, 11
Hall, Stuart, 6
HCIM (Haut conseil islamique du Mali), 124, 130–32, 165n22
Henry, Joseph, 86
heritage (cultural): alternative, 21; collective identity and, 2–3; contested commemoration, 36–40; Creole character of, 97, 103; as cultural production, 72; diversification, 9, 19, 22–23, 26, 36, 42, 96, 108–11, 133, 144–45; failed heritagization, 14–15; heritagization defined, 25; imperialist nostalgia, 161–62n30; institutions, 135–36; Konaré-era inclusive, 33–40, 139, 160n15, 164n14; local economy and, 115, 162nn42–43; Mande political hegemony, 15–16; neoliberal budget cuts, 129; patrimonialization and, 5–6; protection laws, 102; public culture and, 2, 9, 111; public memory and, 13–15; resistance to state heritagization, 103–7, 136; social control and, 5; Touré-era, 139–40, 168n12; tradition and, 158n16. *See also* memory; museums; private heritage; tourism
heritage elites: anticolonial resistance, 15; colonial heritage and, 56, 73; contestation of heritage and, 9; fieldwork with, 18–19; Keita socialism and, 37; Koulouba monument complex and, 73–74; religious patrimony and, 106, 108, 111–12; Sufi mausoleums destruction and, 23; Timbuktu manuscripts rescue, 127, 143, 164n14; Touré reconciliation and, 44; Traoré engagement with, 29; women and, 22, 77, 80, 94. *See also* Konaré era
hero narratives, 27, 43–44. *See also* survivor narratives
heterotopias, 5, 78, 80, 93–94, 136, 150n9
Holder, Gilles, 121, 130, 132, 164n21
hybridity narrative. *See under* colonial/colonization

ICOMOS (International Council on Monuments and Sites), 102
Idrissa, Abdourahmane, 30, 32
IMF (International Monetary Fund), 31, 150n14
Imperato, Pascal James, 29
inequality. *See* class and social inequality
intangible cultural heritage, 6
International Monetary Fund, 31, 150n14

*Index* 197

Islam: Djenné heritage, 95; French colonial views of, 100–101; funerary rituals, 126; Gaddafi support for, 122–24, 168n13; investment in moderate, 23, 115, 121, 123–24, 132, 162n39, 165n22, 168n13; Islamist extremists, 1, 117, 121–29, 130–31, 140, 147, 164n22; Konaré architectural preservation, 17; *marabouts* as heritage figures, 33–34, 119; Mawlud national holiday, 122–24, 147, 164n17, 164nn21–22; noir, 101, 112, 162n37; opposition to Christian symbolism, 82; opposition to heritage initiatives, 123–24, 142; pre-Islamic tradition and, 23, 81–82, 110–11, 144–45, 152n38, 158n12; public heritage and, 111; saho preservation and, 23, 108–11; Salafism, 126, 147; secular state and, 112–14, 123–24, 130; Sufi mausoleum destruction and, 125–28, 131–33; Timbuktu importance for, 116–24; Wahhabiyya, 90, 148, 165n22; women's fashion, 85, 159n21; *zyhara* (pilgrimage), 116, 148. See also Sufism; Tuareg-Islamist 2012 occupation

*jeliw*, 33–34, 45, 147. See also griots
Joy, Charlotte, 97, 102–3, 115, 160n2

Kamian, Bakary, 66
Karp, Ivan, 5, 10, 26
Kassonké, 87, 90–91
Kayes, 17, 87, 90–91
Kébé, Boubacar Hamadoun, 109–10
Keita, Aoua, 62, 83, 156n10
Keita, Ibrahim Boubacar, 2, 3, 76–77, 141, 153n11, 157n7
Keita, Mamadou B., 70–71
Keita, Modibo: commemoration of, 14–15, 30, 35–40, 42, 50, 62, 142; death of, 155n30; heritage festivals, 15–16; precolonial history emphasis of, 15; socialist legacy and, 46–49; Touré hero narratives and, 43–44, 50. See also Keita era; Modibo Keita Memorial
Keita, Sunjata, 45
Keita era (1960–68): colonial heritage in, 56–57; economic independence initiatives, 50, 52; festivals of national identity, 15–16; historical treatment of, 21, 26–27, 35–40; naming of Mali, 156n2; notable women, 83; as one-party state, 9; socialism and, 46–49; suppression of opposition, 28, 36–37. See also Keita, Modibo

Kirshenblatt-Gimblett, Barbara, 72
Koi Konboro mosque, 101, 112
Konaré, Alpha Oumar: address of 1991, 51; heritage initiatives, 10, 34, 43, 160n15; as historian, 65–66; as Traoré Minister of Culture, 29, 101. See also Konaré era
Konaré era (1992–2002): ADEMA hegemony in, 18, 21, 31–32, 38–40; Archinard statue relocation, 21, 53–55, 54, 65, 67–75, 142; cultural narratives in, 20–21, 40; decentralization of culture, 16–17, 56, 135, 164n14; disputed 1997 election, 38, 152n4; Djenné heritagization, 101–2; election of 1992, 30–31, 41, 135; *griots* critique of, 33–34, 45; heritage and national identity, 57–58, 139; hybrid heritage narrative, 33–36, 58–59, 62, 64–67, 73–75, 136–37; Keita-era heritage in, 26–27, 35–40; monument expansion, 17, 34–35, 138; neoliberal reforms, 31–32, 137; political stability of, 31; socialist critique of, 46–47; women's issues and, 77–78, 157n7. See also Konaré, Alpha Oumar; multiparty democracy
Koulouba monument complex, 60–61; colonial emphasis in, 21; cosmopolitan elite view of, 73–74; French colonialism and, 56; Konaré hybridity narrative and, 58–59, 64–67; martyrdom theme in, 61–62; state support for, 139–40
Kratz, Corinne A., 5, 10, 26
Kurukan Fuga, 45

Laing, Alexander Gordon, 62
Lambek, Michael, 25
Larkin, Brian, 9
Library of Djenné's Manuscripts, 143
Libya, 50, 117, 137
Liebmann, Matthew, 58
lieux de mémoire (sites of memory), 11
Louis Archinard Statue. See Archinard, Louis (statue)
Ly, Hassimiyou, 35

Maas, Pierre, 104
Mage, Eugène, 62
Mahmoud, Cheick Sidi, 118–19, 125, 166n32
Maison du Patrimoine, 115, 163n44
Male, Salia, 82
Malinké, 15
Mali Nouveau monument, 59
Maliweb, 124
Mande ethnic political hegemony, 15–16

Mann, Gregory, 156n15
Mara, Moussa, 140
Marchand, Trevor H. J., 162n42
Mariko, Oumar, 46–49
Marka, 108
mausoleums. *See* Sufi saints' mausoleums
Maussen, Marcel, 100
Mawlud national holiday, 122–24, 147, 164n17, 164nn21–22
MC (Le Mouvement citoyen), 40–41, 154n20
memory: collective/social, 11–12, 65; counter-, 11, 27, 46–50, 155n28; destruction of sites of, 71–72; emotionality of, 50; failed heritagization, 14–15; forgetting, 13, 151n21; heritage and, 13–15; Konaré-era and, 36, 50–51; *milieux de mémoire*, 11, 55, 70; narrative, 25; political, 12–13; popular, 3, 11, 14, 152n2, 155n28; rationalist critique of, 20, 25–27, 45, 49; repressed/silenced, 21, 55, 70–72, 73; social practices and, 55; state, 11, 21, 49, 58, 70–75; trauma/loss and, 3–4, 30, 49–51, 58, 65, 155n30, 156n13. *See also* heritage; museums
Ministry of Culture, 5–6, 16, 18, 23, 40, 129, 133, 140–41, 143–44, 168n16
MNLA (Mouvement national de Libération de l'Azawad), 125
modernity: democratic modernist discourse, 25–26, 110; hybridity narrative and, 65–66, 156n14; memorialization and, 11, 13–14; modern power and, 2, 5–8; Muso Kunda progress narrative, 82–83; parallel modernities, 9; postcolonial memory and, 21; rationalist-modernist state, 20, 25–27, 45, 49; renovation of national culture, 51
Modibo Keita Memorial, *34–35*; conflicts over, 38–40; inadequate support for, 129, 139–40, 143; inauguration of, 35–36; public reception of, 14–15, 38, 142. *See also* Keita, Modibo
Monument aux Martyrs, 49, 61
Monument de l'Indépendance, 82
Mopti mosque, 100
Morton, Pat, 99
Moya, Alpha, 119, 125
MUJAO (Movement for Unity and Jihad in West Africa), 125
multiparty democracy: counterheritage projects and, 26; democracy of consensus and, 41–45, 138–39; elections and, 149n1; heritagization strategies, 25–26; memory discourse and, 35, 154n15; multipartism in, 1, 142, 152n2; precolonial traditions and, 45–46. *See also* democracy; governmentality; Konaré era; nation-state; opposition; Touré era
museums: cities as, 103, 136; cultural patrimony and, 143–44, 169n24; governmentality and, 5; as heritage institutions, 135–36; modern power and, 2, 5, 34, 88–89, 103, 135; role in nation building, 2–3; students as visitors to, 91–93. *See also* Djenné Museum; heritage; memory; Muso Kunda; National Museum of Mali
Muso Kunda (women's museum): ethnographic and fashion exhibits at, 84–88, 91–92, 94, 158–59nn17–22; founding of, 22, 78; inadequate support for, 76–77, *77*, 157n1, 157n3, 157n6; mission and operation of, 79–82, 88–93; as paradigmatic heterotopia, 136; privatization and, 21, 77–78, 139–40; progress narrative and, 82–83; student views of, 19; women's empowerment and, 78–80, 93. *See also* women
Mustafa, Hudita Nura, 85–86

Nagy, Rosemary, 50–51
Nahdi, Fuad, 124
National Museum of Mali, 102
National Park of Mali, 102, 140, 154n21
nation-state: anthropology of the state, 2–8, 95–97, 149n1, 149n5, 150n8; classification work and, 6; cultural loss narrative, 74; as guarantor of diversity, 23, 41–42, 110–11, 133, 141, 144; heritage role in, 2–3; homogeneity of the state critique of, 137; Mawlud nationalization, 122–24, 147, 164n17, 164nn21–22; production of statehood, 55–56; rational-critical model, 20, 25–27, 45, 49, 51, 139; religious sphere intervention, 132; secular statehood, 113–14, 123–24, 130; state memory, 11, 21, 49, 58, 70–75; top-down state power, 10, 40, 67, 154n17. *See also* democracy; governmentality; multiparty democracy
neofeminism, 89–90
neoliberal/neoliberalism, 1; budget cuts, 32, 137–38; democratic governance and, 1, 25–26, 31, 52, 56, 138; deregulation/decentralization, 16–18, 96, 121; Djenné heritagization and, 96, 102, 114; economic independence initiatives and, 2,

*Index* 199

50, 52, 137–38; economy, 7, 32, 50, 150n14; heritage budget cuts, 16, 129, 140–41; of Konaré reforms, 31–32, 137–38; Mali era of, 2, 7, 9–10, 18, 20, 25, 37, 117, 120, 137, 140, 154n16; power relations and, 4–5; public culture and, 9; SAPs and, 7–8, 150–51nn14–15; Timbuktu tourism and, 116, 121. *See also* governmentality; private heritage

Netherlands, 95, 103–5, 109

NGOs (nongovernment organizations), 7

Nora, Pierre, 11, 55

North Korea, 137

O'Dell, Emily Jane, 126, 128

opposition: countermemory project, 27, 46–47; disputed 1997 election, 38, 152n4; Keita era, 28; Konaré era, 142; oppositional organizations, 8; party splits, 32–33, 153n6; single-party system and, 32–33; Traoré era, 21, 27–30, 46, 152n4. *See also* multiparty democracy

ORTM (Office de Radiodiffusion-Télévision du Mali), 131

Ousmane, Sembène, 66

Palace of Aguibou Tall, 98

Palace of Ahmadou, 98

pan-Africanism, 34–35, 37, 46–47

patrimony: Djenné city, 102–7; Mali democracy and, 5–6; private heritage and, 4; religious, 121; secular, 23, 96–97, 112–14; Ségou city, 72–73

Pedrocco, Sebastiano, 110

Peul, 82, 123

Pivin, Jean Loup, 33

Place des Cités et Villes Martyres, La, 61–62, 61

Place des Explorateurs, La, 60, 62, 63

Place des Martyrs de Thiaroye, La, 66

Ponty, William, 100, 112

postcolonial period: architecture of, 22; Djenné heritagization and, 101–2; France-Mali relationship, 65–66; Islamic religious authority and, 112–14; transnational media and, 9; women's organizations, 83

postmodernism, 11, 58

power: *griot* mystical, 33–34; Koulouba monument complex and, 59; modern, 2, 5, 7–8, 13, 23, 34, 51, 59, 103, 111, 114, 115, 135, 145; multisitedness of, 8; museums as facilitators of, 89, 135; neoliberal governance and, 4–5; women's esoteric, 81–82

precolonial era (pre-1880): Keita heritagization of, 15, 56–57, 151n27; Konaré critical reading of, 26, 139; Touré heritagization of, 46; Traoré heritagization of, 57

private heritage: Biennale art groups, 17; cultural patrimony and, 143–44, 169n24; Diarra family, 71–73; Djenné Patrimoine initiatives, 10, 95, 106–8, 111–15, 136, 161n22, 162n35; festival initiatives and, 17, 140–41, 143, 150n12, 168n16; international appeal of, 18, 169n24; Konaré-era privatization, 164n14; Muso Kunda as, 21, 77–78, 139–40; private Keita commemoration, 38; representation and, 3–4; Timbuktu manuscripts and, 6, 121–22, 127, 143, 164n14, 167n50; Touré-era privatization and, 32

Prussin, Labelle, 97–99, 101

PSP, new (Parti pour la solidarité et le progress), 44

PSP, old (Le Parti soudanais progressiste), 36, 43–44, 153n8

public culture, 8–9, 70; counterheritage projects and, 26; decentralization and, 17–18; nongovernmental structures, 10; political autonomy of, 10–11; reclaimed heritage and, 56, 70; religious heritage and, 111. *See also* democracy

public sphere: democracy and, 9, 20, 26, 74, 88, 97, 149n7, 168n9, 168n17; Djenné heritagization and, 96–97, 111, 114–15; Habermas and Fraser on, 149–50n7; heritagization strategies and, 26, 88; Konaré era democratization and, 74; neoliberal governance and, 3; public culture and, 9; transnational, 97

Pyramide du souvenir, 48

Radical Middle Way, 124

Ranger, Terence, 158n16

Rassool, Ciraj, 7, 26, 97

reconciliation initiatives, 27, 40, 42–44, 49–51

revolution of 1991, 30–31, 41, 46–48, 49, 52, 57–58, 61

Ronen, Yehudit, 123

Rosaldo, Renato, 161–62n30

Rovine, Victoria L., 86

Rowlands, Michael, 3, 14, 65, 70, 97, 102–3, 105

Saad, Elias N., 116
SADI (La Solidarité africaine pour la démocratie et l'indépendance), 46–49, 51–52
saho (youth house), 23, 108–11
Saint-Lary, Maud, 130
saints' mausoleums. *See* Sufi saints' mausoleums
Sakoiba, 27–28
Sakoi-Fulala, 27–28
Salafism, 126, 147
Sankoré Mosque, 118–20
SAPs (structural adjustment programs), 7–8, 150–51nn14–15
Schulz, Dorothea E., 34, 57, 114
Ségou: Archinard statue relocation, 21, 53–55, *54*, 67–75, 142; Diarra family heritage, 71–73; Festival sur le Niger, 17, 53, 140–41, 169n27; heritage budget cuts, 141; opposition to ADEMA, 21, 67, 73; Palace of Ahmadou, 98; resistance to state heritage, 56; violence of 1958–60, 27–28; *wulafèbarokèyòrò* as city patrimony, 72–73
Semaine nationale de la jeunesse, 15–16, 57
Semaine nationale des arts et de la culture, 152n32
Semaine nationale du patrimoine culturel, 18, 152n34
Senegal, 57, 85–86, 156n2
Sharma, Aradhana, 8, 55
Shaw, Rosalind, 12–13
Sidi Yahya Mosque, 118–20
Sissoko, Cheick Oumar, 47, 50, 139
Sissoko, Fily Dabo, 28, 36, 91, 153n8
Sissoko, Sada, 57
Soares, Benjamin F., 112, 119, 123, 131–33, 147
socialism, 26, 37, 46–49, 59
Songhai ancient empire, 15
Soudan (French Soudan). *See* French Sudan colonial era
South Africa, 7, 10, 50, 97, 137–38
Sow, Alioune, 30
Statue of Ciwaras (Koulouba), *60*
Statue of Literacy (Koulouba), *60*
Steiner, Christopher B., 112
Stoller, Paul, 12
structural adjustment programs, 7–8, 150–51nn14–15
students: Archinard statue relocation protest, 67–69, 73; Malian youth crisis and, 89; as museum visitors, 91–93; as oppositional entity, 21, 29–32, 34; role in 1991 coup, 47–48, 68. *See also* education
Sufi saints' mausoleums, 8, 23, 116–18, 125–33, *126*, *132*, 164n9, 166n31
Sufism, 118–19, 123–24, 131, 147–48, 162n1, 164n9
supranational bodies, 7. *See also* UNESCO
survivor narratives, 21, 25, 47–52, 61–62, 66. *See also* hero narratives

Tall, al-Hajj Oumar, 62, 71–72
Tamanrasset Accords, 30
Tamba-Tamba, Cheick Mahmoud, 119
Thiam, Thierno Hadi, 132
Timbuktu: as Islamic site, 116–21; manuscripts, 6, 121–22, 127, 143, 164n14, 167n50; neoliberal heritagization and, 116, 121, 143; summit in, 124; Western fascination for, 62. *See also* Sufi saints' mausoleums
Timbuktu Declaration, 124
Tomb of Askia in Gao, 128
top-down state power, 10, 40, 67, 154n17
Touré, Almami Samori, 62
Touré, Amadou Toumani: hero narrative and, 43–44; neoliberal transformation of, 10; revolution of 1991 and, 30–31, 41, 46–48; survivor narrative and, 48, 52. *See also* Touré era
Touré, Boureima, 112–14
Touré era (2002–12): absence of opposition in, 21, 27–30, 46, 142; coup of 2012, 1, 52, 117, 153n11; cultural narratives of, 20–21, 140; democracy of consensus approach, 41–45, 138–39; fiftieth anniversary celebration, 44, 45, 139; *griots* embraced in, 33–34, 45, 155n27; Islamic policy, 112–14, 121–23, 140; laissez-faire governance, 76, 139–40, 157n3; monuments of, 140, 154n21; privatization initiatives, 32, 157n3; reconciliation initiatives, 27, 40, 42–44, 49, 51–52; SADI critique of, 46–47; socialist historical narrative and, 26, 37; state commemorations during, 42, 49; Timbuktu heritage and, 121–23; women's issues and, 157n7. *See also* multiparty democracy; Touré, Amadou Toumani
tourism: Archinard statue relocation and, *54*, 70; classificatory work and, 6; Djenné residents and, 96, 105, 115, 160n2; heritage association with, 14; local economy and, 115, 162n43; public heritage and, 111; Tim-

buktu heritage and, 116–17, 120; tourists as museum visitors, 22; Western tourists in Mali, 53
transnationality: aid organizations, 8; audiences and, 78, 89, 93; Djenné Patrimoine and, 95, 111, 115, 137; fashion/dress and, 85, 87; governmentality and, 5, 7–8, 11, 96; heritage work and, 3, 10, 19, 95–96, 114; neoliberal governance and, 3, 96; public sphere, 97; Touré reconciliation and, 27; tourists as transnational actors, 89; translocal Islam, 114; women's organizations, 78. *See also* Western culture
Traoré, Lobo, 45–46
Traoré, Moussa, 29, 30, 47, 61, 68, 156n13. *See also* Traoré era (1968–91)
Traoré, Tiramakan, 45
Traoré era (1968–91): Biennale modifications, 16, 152n32; as a contested past, 20, 48–49, 155n30; coup of 1968, 16, 28, 40, 153n6; cultural politics in, 16, 57; historical treatment of, 20, 49; Islamic politics, 148; political opposition in, 21, 27–30, 36, 46, 152n4; revolution of 1991 and, 30–31, 41, 46–48; state violence in, 20–21, 27, 29–30, 37, 61; student protests in, 29–30, 46–47; UNFM role in, 28, 83. *See also* Traoré, Moussa
Triaud, Jean-Louis, 6, 162n37
Tuareg: defined, 148; ethnographic representation of, 85–86; Mande ethnic political hegemony and, 15; organizations, 8; revolts of early 1960s, 28; Tamanrasset Accords, 30; Traoré-era rebellions, 16
Tuareg-Islamist 2012 occupation, 153–54n11; reassessment of democratic governance, 1–2; responses to, 127–33, 166n36; Sufi saints' mausoleums destruction, 8, 23, 116–17, 125–33, *126*, *132*, 166n31; Sufi veneration of saints and, 120–21; Timbuktu manuscripts and, 121–22, 127, 143, 164n14, 167n50

UDPM (L'Union démocratique du peuple malien), 29
UDS party (L'Union démocratique ségouvienne), 27–28, 36–37, 153n6
UM-RDA (L'Union malienne du rassemblement démocratique african/faso jigi), 43, 153n6
UNEEM (L'Union nationale des élèves et étudiants du Mali), 29

UNESCO (United Nations Educational, Scientific and Cultural Organization), 3, 5–6, 127–29, 143, 161–62n30
UNESCO World Heritage Sites: Djenné heritage, 22, 95, 97, 101–2, 115; Konaré support for, 17; and management of living spaces, 103–7, 114–15; as national policy influence, 76–77; Sufi saints' mausoleums, 8, 23, 116–18, 125–33, *126*, *132*, 164n9, 166n31
UNFM (L'Union nationale des femmes du Mali), 28, 82
US-RDA party (Union soudanaise–Rassemblement démocratique africain): Archinard statue relocation and, 70, 142; economic independence and, 50, 52; history of, 153n6, 153n8; ideological integrity of, 46–47; Aoua Keita role in, 83; Konaré-era status of, 37–38; post-independence violence, 27; private Keita commemoration, 38; socialist vision of, 37–38, 43–44, 46–47; Touré-era reunification of, 42–44

van de Walle, Nicolas, 8
Villalon, Leonardo A., 30, 32
Villesuzanne, Marie-Laure, 106–7

Wahhabiyya, 90, 148, 165n22
Wertsch, James V., 11
Western culture: confrontational style of democracy in, 41; feminism in, 89–90; private heritage and, 18, 169n24; and production of Mali heritage, 6; resistance to, 55; transnational media and, 9; Tuareg-Islamist 2012 occupation response, 127–29. *See also* transnationality
witchcraft, 13, 81–82
women: class difference in groups, 80; commemoration of, 61, 156n10; development agenda, 22, 77, 80–81, 89–90, 93–94; distance vs. feminism in Mali, 90; as educators, 80; fashion as class status, 84–88, 91–92, 94; history of political participation, 157n7; male sexism and, 92, 159n28; neofeminism, 89–90; postcolonial transformation and, 28, 83; Touré-era family code, 76, 83, 130; traditional work of, 82–83, 93; Tuareg-Islamist 2012 occupation and, 127. *See also* Muso Kunda
women's movement, international, 84
World Bank, 31, 150n14
world wars monuments, 57, 66
Wright, Gwendolyn, 100

**ROSA DE JORIO** is an associate professor of anthropology at the University of North Florida.

## Interpretations of Culture in the New Millennium

Peruvian Street Lives: Culture, Power, and Economy among Market Women of Cuzco   *Linda J. Seligmann*

The Napo Runa of Amazonian Ecuador   *Michael Uzendoski*

Made-from-Bone: Trickster Myths, Music, and History from the Amazon   *Jonathan D. Hill*

Ritual Encounters: Otavalan Modern and Mythic Community   *Michelle Wibbelsman*

Finding Cholita   *Billie Jean Isbell*

East African Hip Hop: Youth Culture and Globalization   *Mwenda Ntarangwi*

Sarajevo: A Bosnian Kaleidoscope   *Fran Markowitz*

Becoming Mapuche: Person and Ritual in Indigenous Chile   *Magnus Course*

Kings for Three Days: The Play of Race and Gender in an Afro-Ecuadorian Festival   *Jean Muteba Rahier*

Maya Market Women: Power and Tradition in San Juan Chamelco, Guatemala   *S. Ashley Kistler*

Victims and Warriors: Violence, History, and Memory in Amazonia   *Casey High*

Embodied Protests: Emotions and Women's Health in Bolivia   *Maria Tapias*

Street Life under a Roof: Youth Homelessness in South Africa   *Emily Margaretten*

Reinventing Chinese Tradition: The Cultural Politics of Late Socialism   *Ka-ming Wu*

Cape Verde, Let's Go: Creole Rappers and Citizenship in Portugal   *Derek Pardue*

The Street Is My Pulpit: Hip Hop and Christianity in Kenya   *Mwenda Ntarangwi*

Cultural Heritage in Mali in the Neoliberal Era   *Rosa De Jorio*

The University of Illinois Press
is a founding member of the
Association of American University Presses.

---

Composed in 10.5/13 Minion Pro
with Chaparral and Nueva display
by Jim Proefrock
at the University of Illinois Press
Manufactured by Sheridan Books, Inc.

University of Illinois Press
1325 South Oak Street
Champaign, IL 61820-6903
www.press.uillinois.edu